Demystifying Academic Writing

Informative, insightful, and accessible, this book is designed to enhance the capacity of graduate and undergraduate students, as well as early career scholars, to write for academic purposes. Fang describes key genres of academic writing, common rhetorical moves associated with each genre, essential skills needed to write the genres, and linguistic resources and strategies that are functional and effective for performing these moves and skills.

Fang's functional linguistic approach to academic writing enables readers to do so much more than write grammatically well-formed sentences. It leverages writing as a process of designing meaning to position language choices as the central focus, illuminating how language is a creative resource for presenting information, developing argument, embedding perspectives, engaging audience, and structuring text across genres and disciplines. Covering reading responses, book reviews, literature reviews, argumentative essays, empirical research articles, grant proposals, and more, this text is an all-in-one resource for building a successful career in academic writing and scholarly publishing.

Each chapter features crafts for effective communication, authentic writing examples, practical applications, and reflective questions. Fang complements these features with self-assessment tools for writers and tips for empowering writers. Assuming no technical knowledge, this text is ideal for both non-native and native English speakers, and suitable for courses in academic writing, rhetoric and composition, and language/literacy education.

Zhihui Fang is the Irving and Rose Fien Endowed Professor of Education in the School of Teaching and Learning at the University of Florida, USA.

Demystifying Academic Writing

Genres, Moves, Skills, and Strategies

Zhihui Fang

Routledge
Taylor & Francis Group

NEW YORK AND LONDON

First published 2021
by Routledge
52 Vanderbilt Avenue, New York, NY 10017

and by Routledge
2 Park Square, Milton Park, Abingdon, Oxon, OX14 4RN

Routledge is an imprint of the Taylor & Francis Group, an informa business

Library of Congress Cataloging-in-Publication Data
Names: Fang, Zhihui, author.
Title: Demystifying academic writing: genres, moves,
skills, and strategies / Zhihui Fang.
Description: New York: Routledge, 2021. |
Includes bibliographical references.
Identifiers: LCCN 2020047512 (print) |
LCCN 2020047513 (ebook) | ISBN 9780367675080 (hardback) |
ISBN 9780367653545 (paperback) | ISBN 9781003131618 (ebook)
Subjects: LCSH: Academic writing.
Classification: LCC LB2369 .F344 2021 (print) |
LCC LB2369 (ebook) | DDC 808.02—dc23
LC record available at https://lccn.loc.gov/2020047512
LC ebook record available at https://lccn.loc.gov/2020047513

ISBN: 978-0-367-67508-0 (hbk)
ISBN: 978-0-367-65354-5 (pbk)
ISBN: 978-1-003-13161-8 (ebk)

Typeset in Goudy
by codeMantra

Access the Support Material: routledge.com/9780367653545

Printed in the United Kingdom
by Henry Ling Limited

Contents (Brief)

Contents (Detailed)

Author Biography

Zhihui Fang (Ph.D., Purdue University) is the Irving & Rose Fien Endowed Professor of Education at the University of Florida, Gainesville, FL, USA. He has published widely in the areas of language and literacy education, English teacher education, and functional linguistics in education. His latest book, *Using Functional Grammar in English Literacy Teaching and Learning*, was published in 2020 by Foreign Language Teaching and Research Press (Beijing, China). He can be reached at <zfang@coe.ufl.edu>.

Preface

This book is designed to enhance the capacity of graduate and undergraduate students, as well as early career scholars, to write for academic purposes. It describes key academic genres (or text types) you are expected to write in college and beyond, common rhetorical moves associated with each genre, essential skills needed to write these genres, and linguistic resources and strategies for instantiating these moves and skills. It also presents evidence-based guidelines and tips for building a successful career in academic writing and scholarly publishing.

The underlying assumption of the book is that much of the writing difficulty experienced by students and scholars, especially those for whom English is an additional (e.g., second or foreign) language, stems from their struggle with language. In this book, language is conceived of not as a set of prescriptive rules and grammatical conventions to be followed but as an interlocking system of lexical and grammatical options for making meaning. Thus, one salient feature of this book is a functional focus on how language is used as a creative resource for presenting information, developing argument, infusing points of view, engaging readers, incorporating other people's ideas and voices, organizing discourse, and addressing audience needs in genre-specific ways. As such, the book is more about how to make language choices that are functional, appropriate, and effective for the particular writing task at hand than about how to write grammatically well-formed sentences.

Another feature of the book is that it uses many authentic writing samples to illustrate the rhetorical moves and linguistic features of different academic genres and the skills, resources, and strategies needed for writing these genres. These samples are drawn from a wide range of disciplines in colleges such as liberal arts and sciences, engineering, law, education, business, design and construction, journalism and communications, medicine, health sciences, and fine arts. The book also suggests activities in each chapter that encourage readers to reflect on and apply the key points and insights discussed in relation to their own individual needs and disciplinary contexts. With a focus on genre-specific writing crafts (e.g., moves, skills, resources, and strategies) that are generalizable across disciplines, the book is relevant and useful to students and scholars from all academic backgrounds.

The discussion of writing necessitates the use of a metalanguage—a language for talking about language and text—in the same way that discussion about geometry requires the use of specialist terms such as *vertex*, *diameter*, and *rhombus*. Using a metalanguage promotes more effective explanation of crafts in writing. I drew primarily on the traditional grammar terminology (e.g., *noun*, *verb*, *preposition*, *clause*) for the metalanguage so as to facilitate access. While these metalinguistic terms are used throughout the book, the presumably less familiar ones (e.g., *appositive*, *non-finite clause*, *nominalization*) are defined and exemplified at the outset of the book (see Tables 2.2 and 2.3), where they are first mentioned. They are further explained and exemplified in places where they become relevant again later in the book.

The book combines focused discussion of common academic genres with detailed description of essential skills, resources, and strategies for academic writing through careful selection and insightful analysis of model samples. It consists of 12 chapters (divided into three sections) and 2 appendices. Section I includes four chapters (Chapters 1–4) that unpack academic writing. Chapter 1 defines and exemplifies academic writing, suggesting that there are as many different kinds of academic writing as there are tasks for different academic purposes. Chapter 2 discusses and exemplifies some of the key linguistic features of academic writing that make it at once academic and challenging. It suggests that academic writing exists on a stylistic continuum along the dimensions of generality, density, technicality, abstraction, explicitness, authoritativeness, conventionality, formality, connectivity, precision, tentativeness, rigor, and responsibility.

Chapters 3 and 4 describe the essential skills needed to write for academic purposes and the linguistic resources and strategies that are functional and effective for performing these skills. These skills include how to situate what you want to say within the broader context of the field; how to paraphrase, summarize, synthesize, evaluate, quote, and source what other people have said on the same topic in an angle that fits your purposes and needs; how to agree or disagree with what others have said in a substantive but considerate way; how to explain a phenomenon or articulate a rationale for an action; how to describe a thing or a process; how to define a concept briefly or in an expanded way; how to incorporate examples to support claims, clarify explanation, or enrich description; how to evaluate claims, knowledge, or evidence; how to classify and categorize things; how to compare and contrast different but related things; how to integrate the visuals (e.g., diagrams, tables, graphs, pictures) and the linguistic prose in a seamless fashion; how to acknowledge and respond to opposing or alternative viewpoints in a way that bolsters your argument; how to make recommendations in a measured and non-hortatory style; and how to construct a cohesive text where sentences and paragraphs are tightly woven.

Section II consists of six chapters (Chapters 5–10) that describe common rhetorical moves, as well as effective linguistic resources and strategies, for writing key academic genres that are often assigned and highly valued in the academic community. These genres include reading responses, book reviews, literature reviews, argumentative essays, empirical research articles, and grant proposals. They can be considered the staples of academic writing. Each chapter also provides and annotates model writing samples to illustrate the key points made in the chapter.

Section III encompasses two chapters (Chapters 11 and 12). Chapter 11 presents ideas and strategies for building capacity and sustaining success in academic writing. The last chapter (Chapter 12) provides a brief overview of the publication process and manuscript review criteria. It also shares a handful of tips for beating the odds and increasing the chances of getting published.

As a whole, the book offers students and scholars in higher education and other settings an informative, insightful, and accessible volume that prepares them to successfully undertake the writing tasks commonly found in academic and disciplinary contexts. Most of the materials presented in the book have been piloted in an academic writing course that I designed and taught for the past decade at my own institution, an American university with an exceptionally diverse student/scholar body and an extraordinarily broad range of academic disciplines. The course has attracted native and non-native speakers of English from a variety of academic disciplines across the campus. I hope you, too, will find this book relevant, accessible, and helpful.

I am grateful to the graduate and undergraduate students, as well as the international visiting scholars, with whom I have had the privilege of working over the past two decades. They are the inspiration for this book. I am especially indebted to the students and scholars who have given me permission to use their writing as examples in this book. I also acknowledge, with gratitude, the support from the University of Florida, which awarded me a sabbatical year (2019–2020) that enabled the completion of this book. Finally, I thank Karen Adler of Routledge for her insights and guidance during the conception and writing of this book and for her professionalism in shepherding the book through the publication process.

Section I
Unpacking Academic Writing

1
What Is Academic Writing?

Importance of Academic Writing

Academic writing is ubiquitous in school and beyond. It is a means of producing, codifying, transmitting, evaluating, renovating, teaching, and learning knowledge and ideology in academic disciplines. Being able to write academically is widely recognized as essential to disciplinary learning and critical for academic success. Control over academic writing gives students and scholars capital, power, and agency in knowledge building, disciplinary practices, identity formation, social positioning, and career advancement.

Given the high stakes nature of academic writing, it is no wonder that students and aspiring scholars like you may have misconceptions about it. In fact, many inexperienced writers think that academic writing involves saying smart things in a convoluted, rigid way. They believe that academic writing presents an unnecessary barrier to academic learning and disciplinary socialization. They resign themselves to the notion that academic writing can only be done by people with sharp intelligence. They both revere and fear academic writing. Their veneration likely stems from the observation that academic writing is usually done by disciplinary experts and often required in the process of school learning and disciplinary practices. Their trepidation probably comes from the challenges they experience in striving to write in a style that is consistent with academic expectations but often sounds unfamiliar and feels alienating.

Defining Academic Writing

What is academic writing then? Simply put, academic writing is the writing done for academic purposes. It is entering into a conversation with others (Graff & Birkenstein, 2018). However, the way this conversation is constructed is different from how conversation in your everyday life is constructed. In other words, writing for academic purposes is different from writing for the purpose of everyday social interactions with friends and family members. Yes, academic writing involves expressing your ideas, but those ideas need to be presented as a response to some other person or group, and they also need to be carefully elaborated, well supported, logically sequenced, rigorously reasoned, and tightly woven together.

Moreover, academic writing is not monolithic, meaning that there is more than one kind, or genre, of academic writing. In academic settings, we write for many different purposes. We write letters, memorandums, reading responses, argumentative essays, technical reports, research articles, literature reviews, lab reports, grant proposals, conference abstracts, policy briefs, PowerPoint presentations, commentaries, book reviews, editorials, blogs, emails, and many other text types. Each of these kinds of academic writing has its own purpose, organizational structure, and linguistic features. Consider, for example, the following seven samples of academic writing from various sources (see Table 1.1).

Table 1.1 Academic Writing Samples

Text 1-1: Abstract of an Article in an Engineering Research Journal	Rebuilding and maintaining the nation's highway infrastructure will require very large capital outlays for many years to come. While the expenditures involved in the maintenance and construction of highway facilities are large, current methods of pavement design used in common engineering practice do not routinely take advantage of design optimization methodologies. This paper presents an optimization formulation for mechanistic-empirical pavement design that minimizes life-cycle costs associated with the construction and maintenance of flexible pavements. Sensitivity analysis is performed on the model to understand how the optimal design changes with respect to variations in the critical design inputs. Using typical values for the costs associated with the construction of each pavement layer and the reconstruction of failed pavement sections, it is determined that extended-life flexible pavements may provide significant life-cycle cost savings despite their higher initial construction cost. However, perpetual pavements that control critical strains to levels near the fatigue and endurance limits for the hot mix asphalt (HMA) and subgrade soil should be designed only when traffic levels are sufficiently high to warrant them or when sufficient uncertainty exists in the mean values of design input probability distributions. Optimization studies performed under uncertainty have showed that designs for extended-life pavements are robust with respect to physical variability in material properties, but are significantly impacted by a lack of knowledge of probability distributions. (McDonald & Madanat, 2012, p. 706)

Text 1-2: Excerpt from a College Finance Textbook	Total interest expense is the sum of cash and non-cash interest expense, most notably the amortization of deferred financing fees, which is linked from an assumptions page (see Exhibit 5.54). The amortization of deferred financing fees, while technically not interest expense, is included in total interest expense as it is a financial charge. In a capital structure with a PIK instrument, the non-cash interest portion would also be included in total interest expense and added back to cash flow from operating activities on the cash flow statement. As shown in Exhibit 5.30, ValueCo has non-cash deferred financing fees of \$12 million in 2013E. These fees are added to the 2013E cash interest expense of \$246.6 million to sum to \$258.6 million of total interest expense. (Rosenbaum & Pearl, 2013, pp. 265–266)
Text 1-3: Excerpt from a Legal Contract in a Call for Grant Proposals	Dispute Resolution. 12.1 At the option of the parties, they shall attempt in good faith to resolve any dispute arising out of or relating to this Agreement by negotiation between executives who have authority to settle the controversy and who are at a higher level of management than the persons with direct responsibility for administration of this Agreement. All offers, promises, conduct and statements, whether oral or written, made in the course of the negotiation by any of the parties, their agents, employees, experts and attorneys are confidential, privileged and inadmissible for any purpose, including impeachment, in arbitration or other proceeding involving the parties, provided evidence that is otherwise admissible or discoverable shall not be rendered inadmissible. (Delaware Department of Education, 2020, p. 48)
Text 1-4: Excerpt from an Edited Scholarly Yearbook	My empirical work around this topic has emerged from the designed experiments of which I have been a part. These designed spaces, what I term social design experiments (Gutierrez, 2005; Gutierrez & Vossoughi, 2010), are distinguished by sociocultural and proleptic views of learning in which learning is understood as the "organization for possible futures" (Gutierrez, 2008, p. 154). In these spaces, we design worlds that engage youth in expansive forms of learning that connect learning across relevant ecologies, principally peer and youth cultures, and academic and home communities "in ways that enable student to become designers of their own social futures" (Gutierrez, 2008, p. 156). A central component of this design has been the development of syncretic forms of expansive learning that leverage both everyday knowledge and school-based practices, including academic text structures, conventions, dispositions, and engagement with a range of texts fundamental to college-going, community-based and work-related literacies. (Gutierrez, 2014, p. 48)

(Continued)

Text 1-5: Excerpt from an Academic Journal in Music	As we can see it in Example 1, the first two notes in the right hand are Db and Bb, whereas those in the left hand are E and G, together forming the diminished seventh chord of E-G-Bb-Db. Similarly, if we combine the following two notes in the right hand (F#-Eb) with those in the left hand (A-C), we get another diminished seventh chord (A-C-Eb-F#). The combination of the two chords results in the octatonic collection of A-Bb-C-Db-Eb-E-F#-G. The rest of the descending passage is just a repetition of this same collection. At the same time, the lines unfold the minor seventh tetrachords (right hand: Db-Bb-F#-Eb and G-E-C-A; left hand: E-G-A-C and Bb-Db-Eb-F#) in each hand. (Tooth, 2016, p. 155)
Text 1-6: A Campus Email Memo to Undergraduate Students	March 19, 2019

Dear Emory Students,

In light of the challenges and uncertainties posed by the coronavirus disease (COVID-19), Emory University has reached the difficult decision to indefinitely suspend all university-sponsored international travel including Summer 2020 study abroad programs.

I know that you must be very disappointed and frustrated. As so many aspects of our lives change, I know this is likely just one of the ways your academic plans have been disrupted. We hope that by making the decision now to cancel Summer 2020 study abroad programs, you will have more time to reassess your academic plan.

Our decision to cancel Summer 2020 study abroad programs means that no student will lose the $350 deposit, and all students will be refunded the $75 application fee. Your study abroad advisor will work with you individually should you have any questions about this process.

We know that your course planning may be impacted by this decision. We encourage you to look for suitable alternate plans through Emory online courses this summer. You may review the 2020 Summer course offerings in the Course Atlas or OPUS. Additional sections of online courses may be added to accommodate the capacity in high demand courses. Be sure to add yourself to the waitlist if an online course is currently full. Questions regarding online course offerings or enrollment may be directed to summerprograms@emory.edu. In addition, the Office of Undergraduate Education (OUE) advisors are aware of this situation and available to support you with your academic planning. |

	If you have any questions for the study abroad office, please reach out to your summer study abroad advisor. We wish you the best as you determine the next steps for your academic plan.
	Sincerely,
	xxx
	Associate Dean, Office of International and Summer Programs
Text 1-7: One Graduate Student's Reading Response to Course Readings	This week's articles tied in well with some of the discussions we had last week about the needs of struggling learners, because struggling learners are often from non-mainstream backgrounds, whether it's due to ethnic, socioeconomic, or cultural differences. As our country becomes more culturally diverse (or more accepting/accommodating of cultural differences that have existed for centuries) and academic standards become more standardized and rigorous, it is becoming more and more essential for educators to figure out how teach to a diverse community of students with varying abilities and needs. The first article seemed congruent with the books I have read on literacy learning for non-mainstream learners (and, you could argue, for all learners), that contextualizing literacy and giving students ownership of their literate life create more interested, empowered students. I enjoyed reading about Alfredo in the second article, it reminded me of some of the work that Dr. Coats has done with non-native speaking Mexican American children. She gave a talk in a course I took last semester and she emphasized that getting to know the family, their social practices, their lifestyles, etc. should drive pedagogy for "linguistically diverse learners". I was honestly thrilled to read John Baugh's article about the African American Vernacular. I am so sick of people treating those who speak AAVE and the language in general as less educated or inferior in some way. AAVE makes just as much sense as Standard American English, and many African Americans display amazingly creative language skills. If more educators were not only mindful but appreciative of the linguistic perspective that diverse students bring into the classroom, the classroom environment would be more inclusive and could foster relevant dialogue about literacy and language. I also enjoyed reading about syntax, particularly because it is so controversial. I remember discussing syntax in an Introduction to Linguistics course that I took in undergrad and feeling challenged to explain why one structure is "better" than another, even though I implicitly knew which structure was more appropriate.

(Continued)

> I feel like I would most effectively teach syntax through exposure to literature and modeling. I am not sure I feel 100% confident in my ability to teach syntax after reading the chapter, but I do feel like I would possibly be better at identifying underlying issues in a student's writing and developing instructional strategies to help students understand the decision making process behind syntactic structure. Also, I am not sure I agree with the statement, "Clearly we do not learn to produce sentences by imitation or memorization because most of what we say is novel." I feel like one could argue that all our language practices are learned by modeling, mirroring, or whatever you want to call it. Can someone else perhaps shed light on what that sentence means?

These writing samples differ not just in social purpose but also in the ways text is structured and language is used to achieve that purpose. They illustrate that academic writing exists on a stylistic continuum with many different varieties. The forms of academic writing vary across tasks, genres, disciplines, and contexts. Each of these forms has a specific purpose, is structured differently, and uses a distinct set of linguistic and other semiotic (e.g., symbol, diagram, picture) resources. As junior members of the academic community, you are expected to be able to read and write the kinds of texts, such as those presented in Table 1.1, that are integral to the social practices of disciplinary experts and inalienable from academic life.

Envoi

Academic writing is an important tool for academic learning and disciplinary practices. Yet, many undergraduate and graduate students, as well as early career scholars, struggle with comprehending and composing academic and disciplinary texts. One major source of this struggle is language. In other words, it is unfamiliarity with the language patterns of academic genres, above and beyond a lack of deep understanding of the topics to be written about, that contributes principally to the difficulties that students and scholars like you experience in writing for academic purposes. In the next chapter, we will examine some of the key linguistic features that make academic writing at once academic and challenging.

Reflection/Application Activities

1 Complete the survey in Appendix A to determine what your needs are for academic writing.

2 How would you define academic writing? Why is academic writing needed in academic learning or disciplinary practices? Do you think everyday writing is capable of fulfilling the same functions performed by academic writing in your discipline?

3 Select a sample of academic writing and a sample of everyday writing that address the same topic. Compare and contrast how language is used to present the topic across the two samples.

4 Reread the seven texts in Table 1.1. What linguistic features stand out in each text? To what degree do these features reflect disciplinary differences? In what ways do they reflect the different purposes of the texts?

5 Collect five to seven pieces of writing you encounter in your academic life. Examine their language patterns (words, sentences, text structure, visuals) and discuss with your peers the similarities and differences in the ways language is used in these samples. Can you provide a rationale for any similarity or difference in language use across these samples?

References

Delaware Department of Education (2020). *Request for proposals for professional services.* Dove, DE: Author.

Graff, G., & Birkenstein, C. (2018). *They say I say: The moves that matter in academic writing* (4th ed.). New York: Norton.

Gutierrez, K. (2014). Syncretic approaches to literacy learning: Leveraging horizontal knowledge and expertise. In P. Dunston, S. Fullerton, M. Cole, D. Herro, J. Malloy, P. Wilder, & K. Headley (Eds.), *63rd Yearbook of the Literacy Research Association* (pp. 48–60). Altamonte Spring, FL: Literacy Research Association.

McDonald, M., & Madanat, S. (2012). Life-cycle cost minimization and sensitivity analysis for mechanistic-empirical pavement design. *Journal of Transportation Engineering, 138*(6), 706–713.

Rosenbaum, J., & Pearl, J. (2013). *Investment banking: Valuation, leveraged buyouts, and mergers & acquisitions* (2nd ed.). New York: Wiley.

Tooth, P. (2016). Symmetrical pitch constructions in Liszt's piano music. *International Journal of Musicology, 2,* 149–164.

2

Linguistic Features of Academic Writing*

Introduction

What is it about academic writing that makes it sound academic and at the same time presents challenges for novice writers? To answer this question, let's compare the two informational texts in Table 2.1.

Text 2-1 is an excerpt from an American middle school textbook (Horton et al., 2000, p. 579) and presumably written by a science expert. Text 2-2 is written by an American high school student whose first language is English in response to an explicit request to assume the role of a scientist author and write authoritatively about a familiar animal of personal interest. Both texts belong to the genre commonly recognized as report, presenting factual information about fish or alligators.

One major difference between the two pieces of writing has to do with the way information is structured. Text 2-1, where sentences are numbered for ease of reference, starts with a general statement that classifies fish as ectotherms (first sentence). This is then followed by a series of statements that clearly describe different body parts of fish (e.g., *gills*, *fins*, *scales*) and how they work. Each sentence in the text is linked to the other in some logical way. For example, sentence #2 begins with and says something about *gills*, a concept that is introduced in sentence #1. Sentences #3–5 continue the discussion of blood flow, a concept that is first mentioned in sentence #2. Similarly, sentence #7 (second paragraph) begins with and says something about *fins*, a concept introduced in sentence #6. Sentences #8–10 provide more information about how fins work. The third paragraph (sentences #11–13) says something about *scales*, with sentence #11 introducing the concept, sentence #12 defining the concept, and sentence #13 distilling what is presented in sentence #12 into *these protective plates* and then saying some more about it. This way of structuring information,

* Note: Portions of this chapter were reproduced in Fang (2020).

Table 2.1 Two Sample Informational Texts

Text 2-1	[1] Fish are ectotherms that live in water and use gills to get oxygen. [2] Gills are fleshy filaments that are filled with tiny blood vessels. [3] The heart of the fish pumps blood to the gills. [4] As blood passes through the gills, it picks up oxygen from water that is passing over the gills. [5] Carbon dioxide is released from blood into the water. [6] Most fish have fins. [7] Fins are fanlike structures used for steering, balancing, and moving. [8] Usually, they are paired. [9] Those on the top and bottom stabilize the fish. [10] Those on the side steer and move the fish. [11] Scales are another common characteristic of fish, although not all fish have scales. [12] Scales are hard, thin, overlapping plates that cover the skin. [13] These protective plates are made of a bony material.
Text 2-2	Alligators are almost like a really big lizard. I have been observing these incredible species for a couple months now. You have no idea how fascinating alligators and crocodiles are. I have some incredible pictures showing some information about alligators. Alligators are amphibious, they live on both land and water. They like to swim a lot, and usually stick just their head out. You could mistake their head for a log or tree if you didn't look hard. Alligators have lots and lots of teeth. A lot of their teeth hang out of their mouths like fangs. Their body is covered in scales, like a pattern almost. Alligators have webbed feet, from my research, I think that they have webbed feet to help them swim better. Alligators eat things like fish and other critters in the water and outside of the water. They are fierce creatures and can attack humans. I have heard stories of alligators drowning humans and biting them. If you ever turn from an alligator they are very fast so you need to run in zig-zags and confuse them. After all my months of research, I have learned so much about this awesome animal. What I have written is just a little of what I have learned. Alligators are so cool to research, I would recommend you researching them. There is still so much more I need to learn about alligators, they are such a mystery.

illustrated more visually in Figure 2.1, facilitates presentation and elaboration of content, contributing to a tightly knit structure.

By some contrast, the information in Text 2-2 is presented in a much less tightly knit structure. Although the text consists of five paragraphs, with the first paragraph serving as an introduction to the topic and the last paragraph

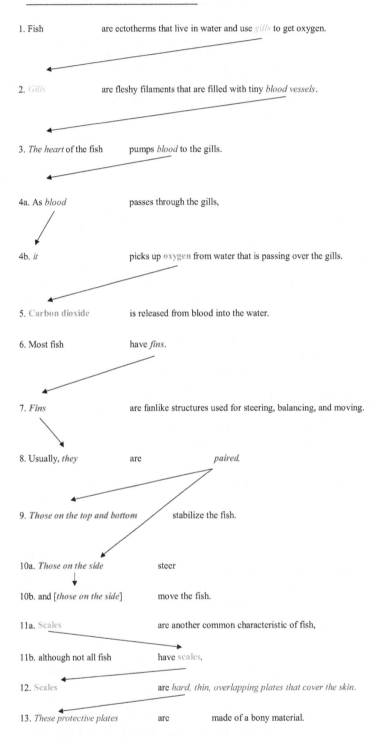

1. Fish   are ectotherms that live in water and use *gills* to get oxygen.

2. *Gills*   are fleshy filaments that are filled with tiny *blood vessels*.

3. *The heart* of the fish   pumps *blood* to the gills.

4a. As *blood*   passes through the gills,

4b. *it*   picks up *oxygen* from water that is passing over the gills.

5. *Carbon dioxide*   is released from blood into the water.

6. Most fish   have *fins*.

7. *Fins*   are fanlike structures used for steering, balancing, and moving.

8. Usually, *they*   are   *paired.*

9. *Those on the top and bottom* stabilize the fish.

10a. *Those on the side*   steer

10b. and [*those on the side*] move the fish.

11a. *Scales*   are another common characteristic of fish,

11b. although not all fish   have *scales.*

12. *Scales*   are *hard, thin, overlapping plates that cover the skin.*

13. *These protective plates* are   made of a bony material.

Figure 2.1 Information Structuring in Text 2-1

intended as a conclusion, the ideas in the middle three paragraphs (i.e., alligators are amphibious, alligators have lots of teeth, alligators eat fish and other things) are presented somewhat haphazardly. They lack elaboration and do not seem to follow any particular order of a conceptual kind.

Another salient difference between the two texts lies in the way they use language to convey information. Text 2-1 draws almost exclusively on the lexical (vocabulary) and grammatical resources that sound academic. These academic language features include:

- technical vocabulary that denotes discipline-specific concepts, such as *ectotherms, gills, oxygen, filaments, carbon dioxide, fins, vessels,* and *scales.*
- general academic vocabulary that can be used across multiple disciplines, such as *release, steer, stabilize, characteristic,* and *protective.*
- long noun phrases with multiple layers of embedding and modification to pack dense information, such as *ectotherms that live in water and use gills to get oxygen; fanlike structures used for steering, balancing, and moving; water that is passing over the gills;* and *hard, thin, overlapping plates that cover the skin.*
- cautious language to temper knowledge claims and ensure precision of information, such as *usually* and *not all.*
- passive voice (e.g., *is released*) that foregrounds the concept and buries the actor performing the action.

Text 2-2, on the other hand, draws heavily on the lexical and grammatical resources of everyday spontaneous conversation. These everyday language features include:

- colloquial expressions (e.g., *almost like, really big, a lot, a lot of, lots and lots of, like a pattern almost, so much, still so much more, awesome, just a little of, so cool, such a mystery*),
- first or second personal pronouns (e.g., *you, I*),
- reference to writer's mental process (e.g., *I think*),
- ambiguous or inconsistent references (e.g., *If you ever turn from <u>an</u> alligator <u>they</u> are very fast.*), and
- run-on sentence (e.g., *If you ever turn from an alligator they are very fast so you need to run zig-zag and confuse them.*)

Although the text also uses some academic language features such as specialized terminology (e.g., *species, amphibious, scales*), general academic vocabulary (e.g., *observing, recommend*), long noun phrases (e.g., *incredible pictures showing some information about alligators, stories of alligators drowning humans and biting them*), and cautious language (e.g., *usually, can*), its heavy reliance on the interpersonal and interactive resources of everyday language makes it sounds less academic and more colloquial as a whole.

The two texts above illustrate some of the key differences between a more academic way of writing and a more everyday way of writing. The difference between academic writing and everyday writing is not dichotomous, however. Rather, it is best conceived of as a continuum where the degree of density, abstraction, formality, conventionality, technicality, generalization, connectivity, caution, precision, organization, explicitness, authoritativeness, and responsibility increases as writers move from writing for more mundane purposes to writing for more academic purposes, as Figure 2.2 demonstrates.

l<--->l

More Everyday	**More Academic**
concrete	abstract
lexically sparse/light	lexically dense/heavy
informal	formal
commonsensical	specialized
loosely strung together	tightly knit
liquid like that of a running river	solid like that of a diamond formed under pressure
dynamic/flowing	crystalline/stasis
fuzzy/imprecise	clear/precise
interactive/dialogic	monologic
personally involved	personally detached
rarely sourced or referenced	well sourced or referenced
grammatically intricate	grammatically simple
casual/unplanned/spontaneous	cautious/planned/deliberate
unreliable	authoritative
unconventional	conventional
dependent on physical context of interaction	independent of physical context of interaction
crude/unpolished	refined/polished
random/haphazard	rigorous/logical

Figure 2.2 Stylistic Continuum in Academic Writing

Compared to everyday writing, that is, writing done for ordinary, out-of-school purposes, academic writing is generally considered more formal, dense, abstract, objective, rigorous, and tightly knit. These features—formality, density, abstraction, objectivity, rigor, and structure—are interconnected in that a text that has a high degree of, for example, formality also tends to have a high degree of abstraction and density. They manifest in different ways across different genres, disciplines, and social contexts, as can be seen in Text 1-1 through Text 1-7 in Chapter 1. In the rest of this chapter, we spotlight these six key features of academic writing, drawing on Text 2-3 below to illustrate each feature. Text 2-3 is the introduction section in an article that reports on an empirical study of noun phrase complexity in school children's informational writing (Fang, Gresser, Cao, & Zheng, 2021). For ease of reference, all sentences in the text are numbered.

Text 2-3

[1] Informational writing is a type of nonfiction whose primary purpose is to present factual information on a topic (Duke, 2014). [2] It is a macrogenre that is emphasized in the U.S. Common Core State Standards (NGA & CCSSO, 2010) and has received a considerable amount of attention in literacy education (e.g., Donovan & Smolkin, 2011; Maloch & Bomer, 2013). [3] This interest was stimulated in part by the growing recognition that experience with and competence in informational writing are vital to both academic success and career readiness. [4] Despite this interest, we still know very little about how children's competence in informational writing develops in the K-12 context, for much of this research was descriptive in nature and focused on a single grade level at a time (e.g., Avalos, Zisselsberger, Gort, & Secada, 2017; Seah, Clarke, & Hart, 2015; Wollman-Bonilla, 2000). [5] Moreover, while this body of work has examined the lexical and grammatical resources that children used to instantiate the genre, few focused specifically on nominal expressions—i.e., nouns and noun phrases, arguably the most powerful grammatical resource for making meaning in academic and disciplinary contexts (Biber & Gray, 2016; Fang, Schleppegrell, & Cox, 2006; Halliday & Martin, 1993). [6] Our cross-sectional study was designed to fill these gaps by investigating the use of nominal expressions in school children's informational writing across four grade levels. [7] Specifically, we examined the nominal resources used by third, fifth, seventh, and ninth grade students in their informational writing. [8] An understanding of how nominal complexity develops in school children's informational writing can inform future efforts to promote language learning and support academic writing development among students in disciplinary contexts.

Structure

Everyday writing features a linear, or horizontal, structure. Its sentences are often strung together casually, in much the same the way sentences in spontaneous speech are structured. In this type of writing, you are essentially writing the way you speak, with minimal preplanning or fine-tuning. As a result, the writing shows little evidence of rhetorical crafting or rigorous conceptual organization, and tends to read like natural speech written down. By contrast, academic writing presents information and develops arguments in a logical, hierarchically structured way. An idea or argument is presented and then restated, clarified, explained, or exemplified. Each paragraph in the text starts with a topic sentence, which is subsequently elaborated or supported with evidence or examples. The examples or evidence provided are expected to be both relevant and credible. The logical connection between the thesis/claim and supporting evidence is expected to be clear and coherent. As a whole, the linkage between paragraphs and among the sentences within each paragraph is expected to be so tight that a discursive flow is created.

In Text 2-3, for example, sentences are closely stitched together; each sentence is informed in some way by the sentence before it and at the same time foreshadows what is to come in the next sentence. For example, the first sentence of the excerpt defines the key concept "*informational writing*". This concept is then referred to as *it* in the subject position of the second sentence. Sentence #3 begins with *this interest*, a concept that distills the information presented in sentence #2. A prepositional phrase (*despite this interest*) in sentence #4 enables the author to link back to sentence #3 and then move on to identify a knowledge gap in research. The conjunction *moreover* in sentence #5 signals that an additional knowledge gap is presented. The next sentence (#6) addresses these knowledge gaps by stating the purpose of the study. This purpose is then elaborated in sentence #7, as indicated by an adverb (*specifically*). The last sentence (#8) describes the potential contributions of the study.

Taken together, the eight sentences in Text 2-3 contribute in an organic way to the overall goal of an introduction to an empirical research article (see also Chapter 9), which is to describe the significance and purpose of the proposed research. This goal is accomplished by providing relevant background information, identifying existing knowledge gaps, stating how these gaps will be filled, and explaining why the gaps are worth filling.

Formality

An obvious feature of academic writing is that it sounds more formal than everyday writing. According to Hyland and Jiang (2017, p. 48), formality is likely "an underlying constant" of academic writing because it is necessary for construing precision and informativity and for avoiding ambiguity and misinterpretation. Formality is achieved in part through strict adherence to conventions in grammar, spelling, and punctuation. More importantly, it is achieved through the deployment of a constellation of lexical and grammatical choices that scholars (e.g., Biber & Gray, 2016; Hyland, 2004; Schleppegrell, 2004) have identified as "academic". Samples of these academic language features, or formality markers, are provided in Table 2.2. These markers may be found sporadically in everyday writing, but they tend to appear with higher frequency and heavier concentration in the writing done for academic purposes, as can be seen in Text 2-3, which uses specialized terminology, expanded noun phrase, nominalization, passive voice, appositive phrase, participial phrase, and epistemic hedge.

Table 2.2 Sample Academic Language Features

Academic Language Feature	Explanation	Example
Specialized Terminology	Words, phrases, or acronyms that denote discipline-specific meanings and encapsulate key disciplinary concepts	*CCSS, systemic functional linguistics, photon, Boston Massacre, monotonicity*
General Academic Vocabulary	Words that frequently appear across academic disciplines, including the widely cited Academic Word List compiled by Averil Coxhead (2000)	*estimate, territory, classify, suggest, evidence, contribute*
Nominalization	Abstract nouns derived from adjectives, verbs, adverbs, or clauses	*similarities* (similar), *movement* (move), *tendency* (likely), *the phenomenon* (A plant's stem may bend toward the light to allow as much as possible light to reach the maximum number of food-making cells.)
Non-restrictive Relative Clause	Clause introduced, after a comma, by a relative pronoun such as *which, when, who,* or *where*	*She will carry them in her mouth to the water, <u>where they will be safer under her watch</u>.* *The monsoon, <u>on which all agriculture depends</u>, is erratic.*
Nonfinite Clause (also called Participial Phrase or Participle Clause)	Clause introduced by a verb (usually in *-ing* or *-ed* form) that does not show tense	*The young frogs leave the water, <u>switching from a plant diet to one of insects</u>.* *<u>Once settled in the West</u>, farmers realized that the Appalachians barred trade with the East.*

(Continued)

Academic Language Feature	Explanation	Example
Logical Metaphor	Use of nouns, verbs, prepositions, or clauses—instead of conjunctions—to realize logical-semantic links	*Overuse of antibiotics by doctors* <u>*contributed to*</u> *a serious rise in the incidence of some infectious diseases,* <u>*with*</u> *a 2000 study by Wenzel and Edward suggesting that half of all antibiotics are prescribed unnecessarily.* [contribute to indicates causation, *with*=for example] <u>*Alarmed by the fire,*</u> *people in Ohio began a massive campaign to clean up the Cuyahoga.* [first clause denotes cause]
Expanded Noun Phrase	Noun phrase with multiple layers of embedding and modification through the use of premodifiers (e.g., adjective, noun) and/or postmodifiers (e.g., embedded clause, prepositional phrase, participial phrase, adverb, and the infinitive)	*many* <u>*children who have been making steady reading progress during the primary years of schooling*</u> *the only plains* <u>*animal*</u> <u>*left in sizable herds to roam outside Africa*</u>
Appositive Phrase	Noun or noun phrase that renames or explains another noun or noun phrase right next to (before or after) it	<u>*A 17.6-mile crossing of lower Chesapeake Bay,*</u> *the Chesapeake Bay Bridge-Tunnel is the only direct link between Virginia's Eastern Shore and Virginia Beach.* *The solution,* <u>*a tunnel through the mountains,*</u> *was first proposed in 1819.*
Impersonal Use of Passive Voice	Passive voice used without mention of the actor doing the action	*Remains* <u>*have been found*</u> *of carved masks of alligators.* *Laws* <u>*were passed*</u> *protecting the saigas.*

Academic Language Feature	Explanation	Example
Thematic Prominence	The positioning of a grammatical structure that is not usually the subject (or beginning) of a sentence at the beginning of the sentence in order to give it prominence	*For the discovery of nuclear fission, Meitner was awarded the 1944 Nobel Prize in chemistry.* *Scattered across a hillside and its surrounding flats were hundreds of large, round fossilized dinosaur eggs.*
Interruption Construction	A group of words that are strategically inserted between the subject and the main verb of a sentence or clause to qualify the information presented	*This, some paleontologists believe, gives them about 200,000,000 years of hunting genetics to rely on.* *Curled inside one of the eggs lay a tiny embryo—a baby dinosaur that, if it had lived, would have grown up to be one of the giants of the planets.*
Epistemic Hedge	Words or phrases indicating the degree of commitment to (or certainty about) a particular claim or showing deference to experts/authority	*The analysis indicated that barium appeared to be a result of neutron bombardment of uranium.* *These investors may be more comfortable holding only senior debt instruments in relatively safe emerging market investments.*

At the same time, formality can also be achieved by minimizing or avoiding the use of a range of everyday language features, such as those identified in Table 2.3. It is worth noting that there has been an increase in the use of some of these informality markers—such as first/second personal pronouns (e.g., *we, I, you*), interrogative sentences (e.g., *What are the ramifications of such indifference to his markings?*), sentence initial conjunctions and conjunctive adverbs (e.g., *because, and, but, also, still*), contractions (e.g., *isn't, we'll*), and colloquial expressions (e.g., *of course, too, in fact, look at*)—in academic writing over the past 50 years, due perhaps to a growing willingness on the part of the author to establish "a more direct and egalitarian relationship" with readers in order to engage and persuade them (Hyland & Jiang, 2017, p. 49). Two cases in point are Text 2-4 and Text 2-5, where informality markers (underlined) are used.

Table 2.3 Sample Everyday Language Features

Everyday Language Feature	Explanation	Example
Interrogative Sentence	Sentence that asks reader a question	*Have you ever watched a tree swaying in the breeze and wondered where wind comes from?* *Why do musicians today ignore these markings from Mozart's own hand?*
Imperative Sentence	Sentence that gives a direct command to reader	*Be aware of the activities you do that release greenhouse gases, such as driving and using electricity.*
First or Second Personal Pronoun	Personal pronouns (e.g., *I, we, you*) and their possessive forms (*my, our, your*)	*As you may have learned, plants remove carbon dioxide from the atmosphere.* *We address the following two research questions in our study.*
Discourse Filler	Continuity adjuncts (e.g., *like, so, you know, well, because*) that have no substantive meaning in the text and only serve as a linguistic mechanism to keep the discourse going without disrupting its flow and rhythm	*Alligators are also incredibly old, like, you know, back to the cretaceous period old.*
Reference to Writer's Mental Process	Use of thinking or feeling verbs (e.g., *think, feel, want*) to indicate writer's beliefs, preferences, or opinions	*I think that they have webbed feet to help them swim better.* *The achievement disparity between the two groups is, we surmise, a reflection of their motivational differences.*
Run-on Sentence	Three or more clauses chained together using coordinating conjunctions such as *and* or *but*	*Also they are amphibian but they like the water better compared to the pictures I took and if they aren't in water they are in swampy areas.*
Ambiguous Pronoun	Pronoun whose referent is unclear or inconsistent	*If one was to start chasing you, run in a zig zag because they are very fast running straight.*

Everyday Language Feature	Explanation	Example
Colloquial Expression	Casual or imprecise word/ phrase (e.g., *kid, stuff*), slang (e.g., *lyte* for *light, grass* for *marijuana*), multiword verb (e.g., *run into* for *encounter, put off* for *postpone, look at* for *examine*), or listing expression (e.g., use of *and so on, etc,* or *and so forth* when ending a list)	*This amphibian is highly dangerous but <u>very cool</u> to study.* *The event was <u>put off</u> for various reasons, including budget cut, lack of interest, traffic congestion, <u>and so on</u>.*
Contraction	Shortened version of a word or word group, created by omission of internal letters	*The plant <u>can't</u> survive without water or light.*
Sentence Initial Conjunction or Conjunctive Adverb	Sentence that begins with a conjunction (e.g., *and, because, but, plus*) or conjunctive adverb (e.g., *also, still, actually*)	*<u>Because</u> the nature of a Ponzi scheme is to operate in a state of prolonged insolvency, the collapse of a Ponzi scheme frequently results in bankruptcy proceedings.* *<u>Still</u>, should we accept the account of political trust in responsive terms?*
Sentence Final Preposition	Ending a sentence with a preposition	*The mudslide destroyed the house they used to live <u>in</u>.*
Amplificatory Noun Phrase Tag	Noun phrase at the end of a clause used to refer to the pronoun in the subject position of the clause	*They are really precious, <u>those alligators</u>.*
Recapitulatory Pronoun	Pronoun used to refer to the noun or noun phrase immediately preceding it	*Alligators <u>they</u> are very popular in Florida.*

Text 2-4 is a short excerpt from an essay published in a top scholarly journal in the field of literacy education (Fisher, 2018, p. 240), and Text 2-5 is an excerpt from an undergraduate sociology textbook (Henslin, 2007, p. 117).

Text 2-4

<u>Of course</u>, the five concerns that <u>I</u> raised can be disputed, and readers of this article can almost certainly point to a favorite disciplinary literacy text that explicitly pushes against one or more of these general tendencies. <u>Also</u>, <u>of course</u>, readers can likely raise many partial explanations for these tendencies; [...].

Text 2-5

For most of <u>us</u>, <u>it's</u> difficult to accept the reality of another's behavioral system. <u>And, of course</u>, none of <u>us</u> will ever become fully knowledgeable of the importance of every nonverbal signal. <u>But</u> as long as each of <u>us</u> realizes the power of these signals, the society's diversity can be a source of great strength rather than a further—and subtly powerful—source of division.

The increase in informality markers is, however, unremarkable and slow. In fact, academic writing has remained largely formal over the past few decades, with small increases in markers of formality such as nominalizations and expanded noun phrases with multiple pre- and post-modifications. According to corpus linguists Biber and Gray (2010), "[t]his preference for nominal/phrasal structures influences academic written texts at the most basic level, while occasional direct acknowledgements of the author/reader are much less common and do not counteract the preference for nominal/phrasal structures when they do occur" (p. 18). In other words, academic writing has stayed largely formal because of its extensive use of phrasal resources such as noun phrases, adverbial phrases, and prepositional phrases, despite the occasional use of informality markers.

Density

Unlike everyday writing that typically focuses on people and their actions and feelings, academic writing typically focuses on concepts/ideas and their relationships. As such, it is generally loaded with information, meaning that it has higher informational density than does everyday writing. In academic writing, sentences are heavily nominalized, meaning that they contain expanded noun phrases linked by verbs. These long noun phrases enable more information to be packed into the sentence. Compare, for example, the following two brief texts (Text 2-6a & Text 2-6b) provided by Derewianka (1999, p. 24) to illustrate how academic texts differ from spoken texts:

Text 2-6a

<u>We</u> **need** <u>our</u> **forest** // because **plants** can **turn** <u>carbon dioxide</u> into <u>oxygen</u> // and if <u>we</u> didn't have <u>oxygen</u> // <u>we</u> would **die**. // <u>People</u> are **worried** // that if <u>the</u> **rainforest** in **Brazil** is **cut** down // <u>the</u> **earth** will not have enough <u>oxygen</u> to **keep** <u>humans</u> and <u>animals</u> alive.

Text 2-6b

<u>Our</u> **reliance** on **forest vegetation** for its **life-sustaining capacity** to **generate oxygen** through **photosynthesis** had led to **concern** that the **destruction** of **Brazilian rainforest** will **result** in **depleted supplies** of oxygen.

In Text 2-6a, there are seven clauses, demarcated by //. (A clause is a grammatical unit consisting of one subject and one main verb.) Each clause contains simple nouns (underlined), such as *we, our forest, plants, people,* and *the rainforest.* A total of 20 content words (bolded) —i.e., words such as nouns, adjectives, and verbs that carry substantial ideational information—are sprinkled across the seven clauses, meaning there are less than three content words per clause. The remaining 26 words in the sentence are called grammatical words. These are articles (*the*), pronouns (e.g., *we, our*), modal verbs (*can, would*), linking verbs (*have, is*), prepositions (e.g., *to, in, into*), and conjunctions (e.g., *if, and*). They carry little ideational information, and their primary function is to indicate grammatical relationships in the sentence.

By contrast, Text 2-6b consists of only one clause and has 18 content words (bolded). These content words are packed into two long noun phrases (underlined) linked by the verb phrase *has led to.* The informational density of Text 2-6b is significantly higher than that of Text 2-6a.

As can be seen through the above comparison, the density of a text is achieved primarily through the use of long/expanded noun phrases. A long noun phrase, such as *those fifty delicious chicken hamburgers from the McDonald's that were purchased on Peach Street yesterday to feed the homeless people during the COVID-19 pandemic,* results when a head noun, such as *hamburgers,* is expanded through the addition of a series of pre- and postmodifiers. Premodifiers can be the article (e.g., *a, the*), the demonstrative (e.g., *this, those*), the numeral or ordinal (e.g., *five, fifth*), the adjective (e.g., *delicious, urgent*), and the noun (e.g., *chicken*). Postmodifiers can include the prepositional phrase (e.g., *from the McDonald's, on Peach Street, during the COVID-19 pandemic*), the embedded (also called restrictive relative) clause (e.g., *that were purchased*), the adverb (*yesterday*), and the infinitive (e.g., *to feed the homeless people*). An anatomy of the long noun phrase follows:

those	*fifty*	*delicious*	*chicken*	**hamburgers**
[demonstrative]	[numeral]	[adjective]	[noun]	[head]

from the McDonald's	*that were purchased on Peach Street*	*yesterday*
[prepositional phrase]	[embedded clause] [prepositional phrase]	[adverb]

to feed the homeless people	*during the COVID-19 pandemic*
[infinitive]	[prepositional phrase]

Text 2-3 is replete with long noun phrases. It is the use of these grammatical resources, sampled below, that contributes principally to the informational density of the text and, hence, its compact style of writing. Note that an appositive phrase, such as *arguably the most powerful grammatical resource for making meaning in academic and disciplinary contexts* in the fifth example below, can also be considered a nominal modifier.

- a type of nonfiction whose primary purpose is to present factual information on a topic
- a macrogenre that is emphasized in the U.S. Common Core State Standards
- the growing recognition that experience with and competence in informational writing are vital to both academic success and career readiness
- the lexical and grammatical resources that children used to instantiate the genre
- nominal expressions—i.e., nouns and noun phrases, arguably the most powerful grammatical resource for making meaning in academic and disciplinary contexts
- the use of nominal expressions in school children's informational writing across four grade levels
- the nominal resources used by third, fifth, seventh, and ninth grade students in their informational writing
- an understanding of how nominal complexity develops in school children's informational writing
- future efforts to promote language learning and support academic writing development among students in disciplinary contexts

As the above examples show, information can be compacted into a clause or sentence through multiple layers of phrasal (e.g., nominal, prepositional, adverbial) embedding and modification. According to Biber and Gray (2010), academic writing has historically developed "a unique style, characterized especially by the reliance on nominal/phrasal rather than clausal structures" (p. 18). Another case in point is the following sentence from a book on how a group of paleontologists made the discovery of dinosaur embryos in Argentina (Dingus & Chiappe, 1999): *We traced the layers that contained the eggs across the rugged ridges and ravines of the badlands back to the area around the flats where we had measured the stratigraphic section.* The sentence contains a noun phrase with an embedded clause (*the layers that contained the eggs*), followed by one preposition phrase (*across the rugged ridges and ravines of the badlands*), which is then followed by an adverbial phrase (*back to the area around the flats*), which is further modified by an adverbial clause (*where we had measured the stratigraphic section*). This way of compacting information, characteristic of academic and disciplinary writing, results in a highly dense sentence.

Abstraction

Another feature of academic writing is that it tends to be more abstract than everyday writing. One main reason for abstraction is that academic writing often deals with concepts, ideas, and generalizations. Three kinds of abstraction are relevant here. One is generic abstraction, which results from the use of nouns that refer to groups of people (e.g., *educators, workers, Southerners*), classes of things (e.g., *reptiles, factories, white-collar crimes*), or other entities without specific perceptual correlates (e.g., *interest rate, engineering research*). These nouns are abstract in the sense that they do not refer to concrete individuals or things in the physical world, and it is difficult for us to wrap our minds around them.

The second is technical abstraction, which results from the use of specialist terminology with discipline-specific meanings and often has to be linguistically defined. These terms construe uncommensense knowledge, representing more theorized—hence more abstract—interpretation of the human experience with the environment. For example, an academic text on weather likely uses technical terms such as *precipitation* and *asperatus*, whereas an everyday text on the same topic may use vernacular terms such as *rain* and *cloud*. *Precipitation* and *asperatus* are both conceptually more abstract than *rain* and *cloud*.

The third, and more significant, kind of abstraction is metaphoric abstraction, which results from the use of nominalizations. As indicated in Table 2.2, nominalizations are nouns that derive from verbs, adjectives, adverbs, conjunctions, or clauses. Words like *flexibility, frequency, adoption, reason*, and *the situation* are considered nominalizations because they derive from, respectively, *flexible* (adjective), *frequently* (adverb), *adopt* (verb), *because* (conjunction), and *The traffic in the city's Central Artery came to a standstill* (clause). They are a kind of what linguists (e.g., Halliday & Matthiessen, 2014) called "grammatical metaphor". Grammatical metaphor realizes meaning in ways that are incongruent with how we humans typically interpret our everyday experience. In congruent realizations, things are presented in nouns (*stars, car*), processes in verbs (*run, manufacture*), qualities in adjective (*agile, nocturnal*), circumstances (when, where, how, to what extent) in adverbs (*yesterday, quickly, reluctantly, completely*) or prepositional phrases (*in 1985, over the counter*), and logical-semantic relations in conjunctions (*because, if*). In incongruent realizations, processes, qualities, circumstances, and logical-semantic relations can all be presented in nouns. This results in greater abstraction of text. Compare the following two sentences:

(a) Mr. Hansen did not attend the board meeting yesterday because his child was ill.
(b) The reason for Mr. Hansen's absence from the board meeting yesterday was the illness of his child.

Sentence #a presents information in a way that is typical of how we would normally use language in our daily life. It consists of two clauses—a main clause

(*Mr. Hansen did not attend the board meeting yesterday*) and a subordinate clause (*because his child was ill*). The main clause states the action/inaction (*did not attend*) of a grammatical participant (*Mr. Hansen*), which serves as the subject of the sentence. The subordinate clause states the reason for his absence from the board meeting using a causal conjunction *because*.

In sentence #b, on the other hand, information is presented in a way that is atypical of how we would normally use language in our everyday living. Cause-effect is presented here within one clause, instead of between two clauses (main clause + subordinate clause), as is the case with sentence #a. In other words, logical reasoning is now made within one clause, rather than between two clauses. This transformation is enabled with the use of nominalizations. The conjunction *because* now becomes *the reason*, the main clause *Mr. Hansen did not attend the board meeting yesterday* now becomes an abstract noun phrase *Mr. Hansen's absence from the board meeting yesterday*, and the subordinate clause *his child was ill* now becomes another abstract noun phrase *the illness of his child*. These kinds of grammatical shifts are what makes academic writing more abstract than everyday writing because they take away the immediacy and vitality of action and transform it into a stasis that is detached from the concrete happenings.

In academic writing, nominalizations are often embedded within long noun phrases to create a densely abstract textual world that students find alienating to read and challenging to process. Text 2-3, for example, contains numerous nominalizations (e.g., *attention, interest, recognition, success, competence, understanding, complexity, development*), many nested in long noun phrases.

Nominalization not only makes a text more abstract, it also has consequences for text organization. By synthesizing or condensing prior discourse into a noun or noun phrase that then functions as a grammatical participant in a new sentence, nominalization increases the informational load, or density, of the sentence. At the same time, it also helps create a cohesive text that flows. For example, as noted earlier in Text 2-3, *this interest* in sentence #3 distills the idea presented in a previous sentence (sentence #2) and becomes the point of departure for continuing discussion on the idea. This, in effect, creates discursive flow that makes a text tightly woven together.

Highly nominalized discourse, such as academic writing, is often difficult to comprehend and critique. With every nominalization, the agency is buried, concrete referential information is eliminated, and readers are taken further away from the actual happenings of everyday life. This has the effect of naturalizing something that is fuzzy and opaque, making it sound technical, precise, stable, and authoritative. It also masks power relationships by downplaying individual responsibility for an action or completely removing people or other agents from the happenings. Because nominalization tends to obscure many of the semantic relations that are otherwise transparent in the clause structure, it reduces readers' sense of what is truly involved in a social interaction. As such, nominalization is an instrument of manipulation often exploited by experts in many disciplines. Understanding how nominalization works is, therefore, key to encoding and decoding hidden meanings in academic writing and to developing as critical writers and readers.

Objectivity

Academic writing prefers to foreground ideas and arguments and background the author who presents the ideas and makes the arguments. What readers are interested in is not so much what you (the author) think or believe, but what information, idea, or evidence you have presented to help build up your argument or reach your conclusion (Gillett, Hammond, & Martala, 2009). This means that any reference to the writer's mental process (*I think*, *We believe*, *In my opinion*) should be minimized in academic writing. Thus, instead of saying *I think that arson is the cause of last week's forest fire.*, a more academic way of writing would be *Arson is likely the cause of last week's forest fire*, or *Arson is believed to be the likely cause of last week's forest fire.*

Similarly, rather than saying *In my humble opinion, how tumors become resistant to treatment is poorly understood*, it suffices to simply say *How tumors become resistant to treatment is poorly understood* because the statement is presumed to come from you (the author), unless, of course, a reference is provided at the end of the statement, as in *How tumors become resistant to treatment is poorly understood (Rubin & Sage, 2019)*. By the same token, when you write *Derivatives are a blessing, not a curse*, it is presumed to be what you (the author) believe, think, or take to be true. There is no need to put *I think* or *we believe* at the beginning of the sentence.

It is worth noting, however, that when the first-person plural pronoun "we" refers not to the writers themselves but to the broader discourse community that is being addressed, it is appropriate and, in fact, quite common for authors to use the phrase "we know" to indicate the current state of knowledge in the field, as can be seen in Text 2-3 (i.e., … *we still know very little about how children's competence in informational writing develops…*). So, it is important to differentiate the inclusive "we" (referring to the author[s] and the audience) from the exclusive "we" (referring only to the authors themselves) in reading/writing because writers often use "we" in different senses within the same article (e.g., *we know* vs. *we surmise or our study*).

Another way to background your thinking and feeling is through the use of passive voice. Passive voice enables you to elide agency when the actor doing the action is unknown or need not be foregrounded. For example, when you do not want or need to mention yourself as the one who believes or thinks, you can simply say *It is believed that […]* or *Something is thought to be […]*. Thus, instead of saying *I believe that trade imbalance is detrimental to a nation's economic health*, you can say *It is believed that trade imbalance is detrimental to a nation's economic health*, *Trade imbalance is believed to be detrimental to a nation's economic health*, or simply, *Trade imbalance is detrimental to a nation's economic health*. In so doing, you position your readers to focus on the concept (*trade imbalance*) you are discussing rather than on the agent (you or someone else) who holds the belief.

As noted earlier, the first person pronouns (*I/we*), and even the second person pronoun (*you*), have become more common nowadays in academic writing. This is especially true with persuasive essays and research articles that embrace a qualitative paradigm. A case in point is Text 2-7, an excerpt from an article (Festenstein, 2020, pp. 451–452) published in a leading international journal titled *Political Studies*. The excerpt contains not only the first and second person pronouns (*I/my, we/us, you/your*), but also other informality markers such as the interrogative sentence (*Still, should we accept the account of […]?*) and sentence initial conjunctive adverbs (e.g., *Still, So*).

Text 2-7

Still, should we accept the account of political trust in responsive terms, embodied 'by an attitude of optimism with respect to the competence and will of other citizens and officials'? (Lenard, 2012: 18–19; Murphy, 2010: 77). One important line of scepticism about this was developed by Hardin, for whom the specific barriers to political trust are epistemological and motivational. You cannot know the motives of politicians and officials so it would not be sensible to assume that these encapsulate your interests. The cognitive opacity of politicians and officials means that the epistemic demands of trust are impossible to satisfy when it comes to ascertaining whether or not to trust them. To say I trust you is to say that I expect you to act for your reasons in a way that tracks my reasons in some matter. Your interest encapsulates my interest. It is not possible to have cognitive trust in officials and citizens on the whole, because of the size and complexity of modern societies: we do not have the ongoing cooperative relationships or thick personal knowledge of one another that helps to overcome, or at least address the problems of opacity and conflict of interests (Hardin, 1999: 28). Furthermore, we cannot view government as cooperating with us, since we are generally subject to its immense power. This means I cannot trust it 'because my power dependence undermines any hope I might have to get you to reciprocally cooperate with me' (Hardin, 2006: 152; cf. Farrell, 2004). So there is generally nothing we can do to make governmental agents entirely trustworthy.

Even though both the first person and the third person are widely accepted in academic writing, it is important to remember that the decision regarding which grammatical person to use has consequences for not only voice (e.g., subjective/personal vs. objective/impersonal) but also text organization and discursive flow, as the two examples below illustrate. Text 2-8a is a conference presentation published in a top archeology journal (Schmidt, 2017, p. 397), and Text 2-8b is a rewrite of Text 2-8a using the third person.

Text 2-8a

I now examine the third theme set out earlier—Archaeologies of Listening—that privilege[s] local voices, not to the exclusion of professional views, but accepting the idea that we have much to learn from those who are closest to the cultures we are studying. Alice Kehoe, Innocent Pikirayi, and I chaired a session at WAC 8 Kyoto devoted to discussions of how we may discard our tin-ears and open our minds to the wisdom of elders schooled in millennia of cultural knowledge. I want to share several examples from my research in Africa as the most approachable way to communicate this message.

Text 2-8b

The third theme that was set out earlier is now examined. The theme—Archaeologists of Listening—privileges local voices, but not to the exclusion of professional voices. It accepts the idea that there is much to be learned from those who are closest to the cultures being studied. A session at WAC 8 Kyoto, chaired by Alice Kehoe, Innocent Pikirayi, and Peter Schmidt, discussed how researchers may discard their own tin-ears and open their minds to the wisdom of elders schooled in millennia of cultural knowledge. This message is best illustrated below with several examples from Schmidt's own research conducted in Africa.

An additional aspect of objectivity is that you do not want to sound biased. Instead, you need to reason through evidence in order to put forth a claim or arrive at a conclusion. Like any other type of writing, academic writing is done by people. As human beings, we all have emotions, pet perspectives, and biases. As scholars, we may be invested in a particular idea, technique, approach, perspective, theory, or ideology. Thus, every piece of academic writing has, admittedly, some affective elements in it. However, in academic writing, such emotions are often minimized and conveyed subtly. In other words, you need to avoid sounding impassioned, for arguments in academic writing are built through logical reasoning and supporting evidence, not emotional appeals. This means that you should, as Alvermann and Reinking (2006) cautioned, manage your emotions, biases, and interpretive preferences carefully in your writing.

One way to do this is to acknowledge that there are other perspectives on the issue that you care deeply about and that these perspectives could just be as valid as yours. Another way is to be careful when making knowledge claims or when critiquing others' work. Compare, for example, the following two excerpts, where the authorial emotion is managed differently. In Text 2-9a, the author sounds assertive and hortatory in his argument against the prevalent instructional practices and in favor of a more language-focused, discipline-specific approach to literacy instruction (e.g., *should, ought to, absolutely no need, must*). In Text 2-9b, excerpted from Fang, Schleppegrell, and Moore (2014, p. 316), the emotion is much more carefully managed, such that the argument comes across as more reasoned and less emotive. Instead of tearing down the currently popular approaches, as Text 2-9a seems to be doing, Text 2-9b suggests a different approach (i.e., a linguistic approach) that builds on and enhances the existing approaches. Its tone is also more humble and tentative, as the proposal is presented as a recommendation, rather than a command, through the use of the modal verb *can*. This makes the argument sound more objective and hence less susceptible to rejection by readers.

Text 2-9a

In order to effectively read, write, and talk about disciplinary texts, students should develop language skills and literacy strategies that are more embedded in each discipline. To meet this need, literacy instruction within the disciplines ought to move beyond the prevalent practices of teaching cognitive and metacognitive strategies such as predicting, inferring, thinking-aloud, and visualizing. Students typically have acquired these generic strategies by the time they enter school and use them effectively in their daily speaking-listening practices (Hirsch, 2006). While some initial teaching of these strategies can be helpful in making students aware that reading/writing, like speaking/listening, is an active meaning-making process, there is absolutely no need to teach them year after year from kindergarten all the way through high school. Students must have knowledge of both disciplinary language and disciplinary content in order to effectively apply the cognitive and metacognitive strategies they already possess to help them make sense of the texts they read.

Text 2-9b

A functional focus on language can be incorporated into other approaches that have been found effective in helping students develop advanced literacy. For example, research with adolescent learners has emphasized the need to teach cognitive and metacognitive strategies for reading comprehension and written composition, and to apprentice students into the epistemological processes of disciplinary experts (e.g., Conley, 2008; Nokes & Dole, 2004; Schumaker & Deshler, 2006). The scaffolds offered through cognitive approaches can be elaborated and enhanced through attention to the language choices that are functional for working with the scaffolds. [...]

Other work on adolescent literacy has foregrounded the need to value students' out-of-school literacies and use their everyday knowledge and discursive practices as both a bridge to and a resource for promoting the development of academic literacy and critical literacy (e.g., Gutierrez & Rogoff, 2003; Lee, 2001; Moje et al., 2004). Comparison of the language used to accomplish the out-of-school and in-school work can illuminate for students the different kinds of language choices available to them. Incorporating a functional focus on language into discussions about reading and writing offers greater potential to accomplish what Moje (2008) has suggested should be the goal of discipline learning: to build both knowledge about the disciplines and an understanding of how knowledge is produced in the disciplines. Attention to the cognitive, social, cultural, and linguistic aspects of literacy are all necessary for engaging students in ways that build on what they bring to school and apprentice them into new ways of speaking, reading, and writing across subject areas.

In Text 2-10 below, the author expresses her disappointment with and frustration at the state of language-content integration in science teaching through the use of highly charged words such as *sadly, painful, disappointingly poor, fruitless,* and *abject failure.* This sort of language choices can be counter-productive, as it is likely to offend the people whose work is being cited or critiqued, making it more difficult for the reader to buy into her argument. The author's emotion could be better managed through eliminating or toning down the emotive words and using hedges (e.g., *can, may, perhaps*) to temper claims.

Text 2-10

Sadly, Bruna, Vann, and Escudero's (2007) case study highlights a painful reality that many science teachers have a disappointingly poor understanding of the language of science. And yet, as Patrick (2009) reported, efforts to develop science teachers' expertise in teaching the language of science are often rendered fruitless by factors such as teachers' beliefs (e.g., language is an "English thing" and it's the language arts teacher's job to teach it), prior experience (e.g., a lack of basic knowledge of English grammar), time (e.g., I am too busy covering curriculum content and have no time for the language stuff), resources (e.g., lack of appropriate reading materials outside textbooks), and school culture (e.g., little incentive for cross-discipline collaboration). This explains why the recent push toward the integration of language and content in science classrooms has been an abject failure.

It is worth noting that while the use of explicitly biased or emotive terms is generally discouraged in academic writing, they are not unheard of, especially in genres such as reading responses (see Chapter 5) and argumentative essays (see Chapter 8). A case in point is this sentence from an article (Robbins,

2016, p. 78) in the *International Journal of Musicology*, where an adverb (underlined) expressing subjective bias is employed: <u>*Unfortunately*</u>, *the performances of Mozart's music in the competition are but typical examples of how it is commonly represented, or rather misrepresented, by most musicians today*. Other language choices that explicitly convey authorial attitudes include *surprisingly, amazingly, clearly, sadly, interestingly, certainly, importantly, luckily, unexpectedly, as expected, occasionally*, and *coincidentally*. The point here is that occasional, judicious use of explicitly biased terms is not unacceptable in academic writing, as it can sometimes help writers achieve the kind of effect they desire, thereby enhancing the power of their argument.

Rigor

Academic writing is highly scrutinized and thus generally more rigorous than everyday writing. As Alvermann and Reinking (2006) pointed out, writing for academic purposes "needs to be distinctly intense and meticulously slow in attending to every word, phrase, and sentence" (p. 77). The rigor manifests not only in word choices but also in logic of argument. When you write for academic purposes, you need to make word choices that are clear, accurate, and precise. Depending on who your audience is, you will use words with varying degrees of technicality. For example, when you write about birds of prey for specialists, you may use specialized terms from technical taxonomies such as *acciptridae, pandionidae,* and *sagittarlidae*; whereas for a more general education audience, you may use more vernacular taxonomic terms such as *hawks, ospreys,* and *secretarybirds*.

You will also use terms that are more accurate and precise in their meaning. For example, in discussing topics on economics and finance, terms such as *fund, cash, capital,* and *currency* are often used instead of the more commonplace generic term *money*. In linguistics, you will use terms such as *phoneme, allophone, vowel, consonant, diphthong, schwa, onset, rime,* and *syllable* in the discussion of the all-encompassing concept *sound*, which is a term commonly used in everyday writing.

Likewise, you can increase accuracy and precision by minimizing the use of fuzzy terms with vague meanings, such as *thing, stuff, a lot, some, many,* and *most*. You will need to specify what that *thing* or *stuff* is or approximately how many is meant by *a lot, some, many,* or *most*. When, for example, you are writing a qualitative research article, instead of saying *few, some, many,* or *most* of your 20 participants believe in creationism, it is better to specify, to the degree possible, the exact number of participants who hold this belief (e.g., 3 out of 20, 8 out of 20, 13 out of 20, 18 out of 20).

Another way to be accurate and precise is to use, as Text 2-3 does, grammatical resources such as hedges (e.g., *in part, can, arguably, generally, tend to, may, relatively*) and modifying devices (e.g., determiner, embedded clause, nonfinite clause, comparative clause, prepositional phrase, appositive phrase, interruption construction) to restrict, modify, or elaborate on the meaning of the term or idea being discussed. This results in compact structures that make the meaning of the concept or idea well defined. For example, in the sentence, *Places that are particularly sacred or whose use is restricted to certain types of ceremonies are closed to visitors and photography is prohibited*, two embedded clauses (i.e., *that are particularly sacred, whose use is restricted to certain types of ceremonies*) are used to convey the meaning that only specific areas, but not all places, are closed to visitors and prohibit photography.

Similarly, the sentence—*Companies with stable and predictable cash flow, as well as substantial assets, generally represent attractive LBO candidates due to their ability to support larger quantities of debt*—contains a prepositional phrase (*with stable and predictable cash flow*) and a conjunctive phrase (*as well as substantial assets*) to identify precisely the sort of companies that are attractive LBO candidates. It also uses a hedging device (*generally*) to suggest that there may be exceptions to the idea presented in the sentence; that is, on rare occasions, these same companies may not be attractive LBO candidates.

In the sentence—*The correlation of the OPIs across modalities was strong, albeit not perfect, with some neurons appearing to predict outcome differently for olfactory and auditory decisions*—the interruption construction, *albeit not perfect*, qualifies the preceding statement by suggesting that the correlation of the OPI across modalities was not perfect (even though it is strong). The prepositional phrase that follows (i.e., *with some neurons...*) exemplifies this kind of strong but imperfect correlation, with the use of two devices (a determiner *some* and a hedging device *appearing to*) further adding accuracy and precision to the discussion.

In yet another example—*Our Patagonian eggs are round and relatively large, about the size of a softball. The eggshell, however, is rather thin, roughly a tenth of an inch thick. This may seem thick in relation to a chicken's egg, but it's much thinner than other dinosaur eggshells*—the appositive phrase (e.g., *about the size of a softball, roughly a tenth of an inch thick*), the comparative clause (*in relation to a chicken's egg, much thinner than other dinosaur eggshells*), and hedging devices (*relatively, rather, roughly, may seem*) elaborate on, and add accuracy and precision to, meaning, thereby contributing to the rigor of writing.

To be rigorous in your writing, you also need to exercise caution when making claims and arguments. You are, in many cases, writing for experts within your field, and so you need to be deferential to their expertise by avoiding making categorical assertions without qualification in the absence of overwhelming evidence or making blunt critique that may be construed as naïve, disrespectful, or arrogant. This is why exercising caution is vitally important when presenting claims or arguments. For example, instead of saying *This is a topic that has never been explored* or *No one has ever studied the topic before*, you can say *This is a topic that has rarely/seldom been explored* or *Few researchers have explored this topic*. The point here is that you need to mince your words, instead of making categorical assertions without evidence.

A further, albeit often overlooked, aspect of rigor is to be sure that sources for your ideas are properly credited. As noted in Chapter 1, in academic writing, you present your ideas as a response to what others have said about the topic/ issue at hand. Your ideas are often built on what others have presented. Therefore, it is important that you acknowledge, as Text 2-3 does, those whose work has informed your thinking. The acknowledgment is typically done through a system of giving credits called referencing and quoting, which are described in more detail in Chapter 3.

Conclusion

Academic writing differs from everyday writing in many ways. In general, academic writing is more formal, dense, abstract, objective, tightly knit, and rigorous. These features are what makes a text more or less academic. They enable experts to engage in the advanced literacy practices of generalization, abstraction, definition, distillation, interpretation, and argumentation. As such, they are highly valued by the academic communities, and students and scholars are expected to demonstrate proficiency in understanding and using them in their writing.

Reflection/Application Activities

1   Identify three to five writing samples from different disciplines/genres or two to three writing samples on the same topic but written for different audiences (e.g., specialist vs layperson, adults vs children). Compare and contrast their language choices along the dimensions of structure, formality, density, abstraction, objectivity, and rigor. Discuss the reasons for the similarities and differences.

2   Select an article written by an expert in your field and a paper you wrote on the same topic. Discuss the similarities and differences in the ways language is used in these two texts. In what ways do these similarities and differences impact the effectiveness of the texts?

3 Select an article from a journal and a podcast of the article by the same author. Compare the ways language is used in the published article versus the podcast along the dimensions of structure, formality, abstraction, objectivity, density, and rigor.

4 Find a paper you wrote before and try to rewrite it in a different grammatical person (e.g., first or third person). Discuss the impact of this change in grammatical person on language choice, discursive flow, and rhetorical style.

References

Alvermann, D., & Reinking, D. (2006). Writing for research journals. In S. Wepner & L. Gambrell (Eds.), *Beating the odds: Getting published in the field of literacy* (pp. 72–84). Newark, DE: International Reading Association.

Biber, D., & Gray, B. (2010). Challenging stereotypes about academic writing: Complexity, elaboration, and explicitness. *Journal of English for Academic Purposes, 9,* 2–20.

Biber, D., & Gray, B. (2016). *Grammatical complexity in academic English: Linguistic change in writing.* Cambridge: Cambridge University Press.

Coxhead, A. (2000). A new academic word list. *TESOL Quarterly, 34*(2), 213–238.

Derewianka, B. (1999). An editorial footnote. *Australian Journal of Language and Literacy, 22*(1), 22–25.

Dingus, L., & Chiappe, L. (1999). *The tiniest giants: Discovering dinosaur eggs.* New York: Random House.

Fang, Z. (2020). *Using functional grammar in English literacy teaching and learning.* Beijing: Foreign Language Teaching and Research Press.

Fang, Z., Gresser, V., Cao, P., & Zheng, J. (2021). Nominal complexities in school children's informational writing. *Journal of English for Academic Purposes.* https://doi.org/10.1016/j.jeap.2021.100958

Fang, Z., Schleppegrell, M., & Moore, J. (2014). The linguistic challenges of learning across academic disciplines. In C. A. Stone, E. R. Silliman, B. J. Ehren, & G. P. Wallach (Eds.), *Handbook of language and literacy: Development and disorders* (2nd ed., pp. 302–322). New York: Guilford.

Festenstein, M. (2020). Political trust, commitment and responsiveness. *Political Studies, 68*(2), 446–462.

Fisher, R. (2018). Reconciling disciplinary literacy perspectives with genre-oriented activity theory: Toward a fuller synthesis of traditions. *Reading Research Quarterly, 54*(2), 237–251.

Gillett, A., Hammond, A., & Martala, M. (2009). *Inside track: Successful academic writing.* London: Longman.

Halliday, M., & Matthiessen, C. (2014). *An introduction to functional grammar* (4th ed.). London: Routledge.

Henslin, J. (2007). *Down to earth sociology: Introductory readings* (14th ed.). New York: Free Press.

Horton, P., Werwa, E., Ezrailson, C., Mccarthy, T., Feather, R., Burns, J., Snyder, S., Daniel, L., Ortleb, E., Biggs, A., & National Geographic Society (2000). *Science voyages: Exploring the life, earth, and physical sciences*. Columbus, OH: Glenco/McGraw-Hill.

Hyland, K. (2004). *Disciplinary discourses: Social interactions in academic writing*. Ann Arbor: University of Michigan Press.

Hyland, K., & Jiang, F. (2017). Is academic writing becoming more informal? *English for Specific Purposes, 45*, 40–51.

Robbins, M. (2016). Mozart: The elephant in today's classroom. *International Journal of Musicology, 2*, 77–121.

Schmidt, P. (2017). Decolonizing archaeological practice: Gazing into the past to transform the future. *Archaeologies: Journal of the World Archeological Congress, 13*(3), 392–411.

Schleppegrell, M. (2004). *The language of schooling: A functional linguistics perspective*. Mahwah, NJ: Erlbaum.

3
Skills and Strategies for Academic Writing: Part One

Introduction

Academic writing communicates complex ideas in clear, logical, reasoned, and evidence-based ways. It is an advanced literacy task that requires a host of demanding skills. Learning to write for academic purposes involves learning, for example, how to contextualize your ideas and arguments in the existing scholarship of the field; how to synthesize, summarize, paraphrase, quote, source, and evaluate others' work; how to define and explain concepts; how to describe things or processes; how to classify/categorize and compare/contrast things; how to agree or disagree with others' points of view; how to present examples and offer explanations; how to engage with opposing views; how to integrate visual images with the linguistic prose; how to acknowledge limitations and make recommendations; and how to connect sentences and link paragraphs.

These skills, together with the linguistic resources and strategies for instantiating them, are described in this chapter and the next chapter. For this chapter, we focus on contextualizing, summarizing, quoting, sourcing, agreeing/disagreeing, and evaluating—skills that are more heavily dependent on the writer's reading proficiency. In the next chapter, we focus on other equally important skills for writing, such as defining, exemplifying, explaining, describing, comparing/contrasting, classifying/categorizing, referencing visuals, entertaining opposition, recommending, and connecting.

For each skill, many templates are provided so that you have choices when it is your turn to write. Templates, also called "sentence skeletons" (Thomson & Kamler, 2016), are extracted from the existing literature. They are essentially the bones, or structures, of sentences from texts written by experts. In these structures, the meat has been removed, revealing the skeleton of rhetorical moves and thus allowing students to imitate. According to Graff and Birkenstein (2018), templates have a "generative quality" in that they can prompt students to "make moves in their writing that they might not otherwise make or even know they should make" (p. xvii). As you will likely realize later in this book, academic writing requires a considerable amount of repetition through rephrasing, elaborating, explaining, exemplifying, recapitulating, and reminding. This means that you will need to say your key points multiple times throughout your writing. Having a rich array of templates at your disposal can help you repeat your points in varied and interesting ways.

Contextualizing

Academic writing is a process of engaging in an intellectual exchange with members of the scholarly community. You write because you have something worthy or interesting to say, but you do not say it in a vacuum. In other words, what you want to say always builds on, responds to, and extends in some way what others before you have said. Moreover, when you write, you also have an audience for your message. This audience could be those "others" whose message(s) you are responding to and/or those who are simply interested or have a stake in what you want to say. Therefore, every time you write for academic purposes, you are in fact engaging in a conversation with others who have written about the same topic/issue or who are potentially interested in what you have to say. This process of making connections with others in the field is called contextualizing.

Contextualizing involves three inter-related moves. The first is to establish a territory for inquiry. This is done by introducing the broader field in which your work is situated. It shows that your work is relevant to what is out there and can potentially make an important contribution to the existing literature. As the territory of inquiry is being established, you also need to identify areas in the existing literature that deserve further examination or exploration. Once these knowledge gaps or trends have been identified, you must then address them, partially or wholly, by stating what you want to do in light of the gap(s) or trends (i.e., purpose statement) and how your work makes new contributions to the field (i.e., significance statement). Ultimately, contextualizing should help you make the case for your work, enabling your readers to see the relevance and significance of what you are attempting to say/do in light of what others in the field have said/done.

Consider, for example, Text 3-1, which is a slightly modified version of the introduction from an article (Fang, Sun, Chiu, & Trutschel, 2014, pp. 55–56) reporting on a qualitative study of classroom teachers' perception of "functional language analysis", a new approach to teaching reading in secondary (middle/ high school) content areas. The sentences in the excerpt are numbered for ease of reference in analysis and discussion. The authors contextualize their research in the existing scholarship on content area reading. They do so by first stating that content area reading has become a hot topic of discussion on adolescent literacy (sentence #1). They then identify a prominent theme in this discussion as approaches to teaching content area reading (sentences #2 & 3). Next, they introduce "functional language analysis" as one of the new approaches to content area reading instruction that deserves to be studied (sentences #4 & 5). Beginning with the second paragraph, the authors identify a research gap (sentence #6), which is then filled through a purpose statement (sentence #7). The paragraph concludes by highlighting the potential contribution their study makes to the field (sentences #8 & 9). In this way, the authors enable their readers to see how "functional language analysis" relates to the existing scholarship on content area reading and why it matters. Making this connection transparent to readers is a crucial contextualizing task in academic writing.

Text 3-1

[1] With the recent spotlight on adolescent literacy in the United States (CCAAL, 2010; Heller & Greenleaf, 2007; Jetton & Shanahan, 2012), content area reading has once again become a hot topic of discussion. [2] A prominent theme in this discussion is that reading instruction in content areas should move away from the traditional emphasis on applying generic strategies and skills to a focus on building "an understanding of how knowledge is produced in the disciplines" (Moje, 2008, p. 97). [3] A key to building this understanding is to develop insights into how disciplinary experts use language to present information, develop arguments, infuse perspective, and create specialized texts (Fang, 2012a). [4] One approach for developing such insights was recently described by Schleppegrell and her colleagues (Fang & Schleppegrell, 2008, 2010; Schleppegrell, Achugar, & Oteiza, 2004). [5] The approach, called functional language analysis (FLA), provides teachers with a set of practical tools for engaging students in systematically analyzing the language patterns and discussing the meanings of these patterns in content area texts.

[6] As a relatively new approach to the K-12 education context in the United States, FLA has received little attention within the literacy research community. [7] The purpose of our study is to explore teachers' perception of this language-based approach to content area reading. [8] The study is important because it can generate information that will help us better understand how FLA is received by teachers, who are typically used to the more traditional approach to content area reading that focuses on the development of basic skills and generic literacy strategies. [9] Understanding teachers' perspectives on FLA is also key to gauging its potential for success in promoting content area reading.

There are many linguistic devices, or templates, that you can use to help you contextualize your work in an academic manner. Some of these templates are listed below:

- It is well established that understanding [...] can provide important insights for [...]. While there has been a great deal of research about [...], much less is known about [...]. But focusing specifically on [...] can be especially useful with respect to [...]. It can provide insight into [...]. In this paper, we investigate [...]. The contributions of this study are two-fold: First, [...]. Second, [...].
- In the last two decades, there has been a tremendous growth in [...] research on [...]. Research in this area has examined [...], including [...], [...], and [...]. Other research has focused on [...], [...], and [...]. Still other research has investigated [...], including [...] and [...]. Several researchers have noted that one area that has received comparatively little attention is [...]. In particular, more research is needed on [...]. The purpose of this article is to address this need.
- Researchers have claimed for decades that [...]. In addition, researchers have claimed that [...]. That is, [...]. A few early studies present a different perspective, arguing [...]. For example, [...]. However, despite these earlier studies, the strong perception that [...] persists up to the present time. Our central goal in the present study is to challenge these stereotypes, based on the results of [...].
- [...] is a topic that has received much attention in the [...] community over the past decade. Although there is now considerable research evidence suggesting that [...], much less is known about [...]. Particularly lacking is the research on [...]. Drawing on the theoretical perspective of [...] and using analytical tools provided by [...], the present study addresses this gap by examining [...]. More specifically, it explores [...]. This research is important in that [...].
- Research shows that [...]. Mounting evidence suggests that [...]. Of current interest to [...] is [...]. This issue/question is of particular importance because [...]. The study reported here contributes to this line of work by discussing [...].
- [...] is a major problem in modern society, as it accounts for [...]. Its proper handling is one of the most pressing issue in [...]. To date, no paper has, to our knowledge, been published in [...]. To fill this gap, we analyze [...].
- Numerous researchers have recognized [...]. Among them are [...]. [...] asserted that [...]. Similarly, [...] proposed that [...]. Given the importance of [...], there is a need to understand [...]. This study sets out to understand [...].
- [...] is now indisputably [...] and is increasingly becoming also [...]. For example, [...]. For these reasons, the [...], and particularly [...], is an ever-expanding need. Given this need, it is important that [...]. In this introductory review, I will set out a range of issues in play as far as [...] is concerned, but with a special focus on [...].
- [...] has increasingly become a topic of interest in [...] because of its contribution to [...]. It has become commonplace to argue that [...]. Moreover, [...] is being

increasingly understood in the field as a malleable factor that can [...]. In fact, one of the central shifts in [...] calls for [...]. Paradoxically, though, [...]. In response to various researchers' calls for [...], this study examines [...]. To be clear, we do not focus on [...]. Instead, we focus on [...].

- The new [...] has turned the spotlight on a number of issues surrounding [...]. Nowhere is this more evident than in [...], where questions such as [...] have arisen. These questions are critical to [...]. The paper reports on a small-scale study to [...]. We are interested in [...]. Throughout, our intention is to contribute to discussions around [...].

Templates for instantiating each of the three moves in the contextualizing task are next presented. With respect to establishing a territory for inquiry, you can say

- It has been argued by many that [...].
- During the past several decades, researchers have endeavored to identify [...].
- In recent years, [...] has gained broad acceptance among [...].
- There is currently an upsurge of interest in [...].
- The concept of [...] is becoming increasingly essential in the field of [...].
- [...] has become an increasingly important aspect of [...] in today's rapidly globalized society.
- Developing [...] is a complex task. One aspect of the current endeavor to prepare [...] for this task in Australia is addressing [...]. This has involved [...].
- [...] has been the topic of policy, research, and philosophy for many decades. [...], a more specific concern, has become an interest of [...] in just the past 20 years.
- A considerable amount of ink has been spilled on the subject of [...]. In this debate, some have emphasized the importance of [...]. Others have noted the value of [...]. Most of these authors and others have focused on [...].
- In the last several years, there has been a renewed interest in [...].
- In the past two decades, we have witnessed [...].
- In the past 15 years, the concept of [...] has been the focus of a wave of studies in a number of fields concerned with [...].
- An important question that often arises in the context of [...] is this: [...].
- [...] has become a key issue in [...], and a large body of literature addresses [...].
- [...] has attracted significant research interest in recent years. In particular, [...].
- The field of [...] research has traditionally [...], focusing primarily on [...]. However, recent theoretical developments in areas such as [...] cast doubt on [...], proposing instead [...].
- A recent poll conducted in the United States showed that [...]. What might be the source of this erroneous belief among American youth?
- [...] research has a long and rich history. There is much that we can say about [...]. Most of what we know has been learned since [...]. Why have we been able to make so much progress so fast?

- Researchers have long been concerned about the quality of [...]. For example, [...]. For these scholars, the heart of the problem was [...].
- [...] is a growing focus in studies of [...], especially in [...] research. As [...] suggested, [...]. Over the past 30 years, [...]. As the range of this scholarship suggests, [...] is a complex concept, and its importance is clear in [...] from [...] to [...].
- It is widely acknowledged that [...]. While there has historically been tension between [...] and [...], [...] warns of the misrepresentation and marginalization of [...] in an approach that [...].
- A growing body of literature highlights the importance of [...] in the development of [...] that involve [...].

Once a research territory has been established, you can then move on to identify knowledge gaps or research needs in the existing literature, using templates such as:

- A great deal of research has been designed to study [...], but fewer studies address [...].
- Although many studies have been published on [...], these studies have not been directly related to [...].
- Although the literature shows a great number of [...], there has been a surprising lack of research into [...].
- It is well documented in the literature that [...] are important for [...], regardless of [...]. Most studies on [...] have focused on [...], however, rather than on [...].
- Despite the increasing use of [...], limited attention has been given to the use of [...].
- Amid the seeming certainty that [...], there is much that we do not yet understand about [...].
- In recent years, studies of [...] in [...] has been keeping pace with those of [...]. Many of these draw on [...]. In contrast, there have been few studies of [...] in [...], and even fewer studies of [...] in [...]. There are likewise few [...] studies of [...] that examine [...]
- Evidence also is available indicating that [...]. However, little evidence exists indicating that [...], that is, [...].
- Research on [...] is emerging; however, we know little about [...].
- One limitation of most of these studies and research syntheses for our purposes is that [...].
- One important consideration, however, has been relatively neglected in research in [...], and that is the [...].
- Although the research literature has identified [...], the existing models tend to focus on [...], with the consequence that [...].
- While research on [...] has been relatively plentiful, much less research has focused on [...].

- The intrigue of this subject lies in the fact that, in spite of agreement on the importance of [...], it is not an area that has been extensively investigated in [...] research.
- Amidst the enthusiasm over [...], however, few studies have [...].
- Despite its remarkable success in practice, the model ignores [...], which has been frequently cited as one of its major limitations.
- The research on [...] is still in its infancy. There exist a number of gaps in [...].
- Earlier studies indicated that [...]. To the author's knowledge, however, very few experimental data exist on [...].
- They claim that [...], but they tell us nothing about [...].
- There has been a considerable amount of research on [...]. Much of this research, however, focuses on [...].
- The impact of [...] has been well documented. Less is known about [...]. Consequently, there remains a need to [...].
- These studies have made a persuasive case for [...], though they have not necessarily suggested [...]. The question persists: [...].
- Although extensive research has been carried out on [...] in general and [...] in particular, there has been no detailed investigation of [...].
- Preliminary indications are that [...]. However, nothing definitive is known.
- Such efforts, though important, fail to address [...].
- Although [...], an explicit examination of [...] has not yet been offered.
- Most of this literature, however, does not attempt to fully articulate [...].
- Previous studies of [...] have focused on [...], but few studies have considered [...].
- Recent research has presented an incomplete picture about [...].

The final step in contextualizing involves a statement of purpose for your work. In this statement, you indicate your intent to fill some or all of the gap(s) or need(s) identified earlier. Sometimes, the purpose statement is followed by a statement of significance highlighting the proposed study's potential contribution, as Text 3-1 does. Some of the templates for specifying your purpose follow:

- The central purpose of this study is to examine [...].
- The purpose of this study was to evaluate [...].
- This study aims to investigate [...].
- The aim of this paper is to [...].
- This paper sets out to develop and test [...].
- This paper describes/presents/provides/discusses/documents/reviews [...].
- In this study, we explore [...]. More specifically, we seek to answer two questions: [...].
- Therefore, the broad objective of this review is to [...]. The specific objectives are to [...].
- In this paper, we demonstrate/describe/explore/focus on [...].

- In this review, we will analyze [...]. For this purpose, we will focus mostly on [...]. First, we will [...]. Then, we will [...]. Finally, we will [...].
- A major goal of the present study was to investigate [...].
- My aim/goal in this article is to [...].
- Our intention in this article is to [...].
- The intention of this paper is to address [...].
- Our group was interested in [...].
- This investigation fills the gap by examining [...].
- The foregoing discussion provides motivation for the current research, which has two specific objectives. [...]
- We designed this research study to address [...].
- The present article takes up the issue of [...]. Our goal is to [...].
- The main interest of this paper is in [...]. The aim is to [...].
- Here we seek to [...]. We aim to [...].
- The investigation described in this article represents an initial attempt to [...].

Summarizing

Summary is an essential part of academic writing. In contextualizing your work within the relevant literature of the field, you will need to summarize the work of others. You do this by not only giving a brief statement of their main point that is most relevant to the focus of your writing but also making explicit connections between this main point and your thesis. Your summary must represent what others said accurately and fairly. It must also connect with the point you want to communicate in your writing. In other words, you need to summarize others' work objectively; and at the same time, your summary also needs to interpret what you have read in a way that connects with and bolsters your point of argument, as the summary is only a component of a larger text.

Writing such a summary presents a challenge for many novice writers, as they tend to make a list of the author's various points without carefully thinking about which of these points is most pertinent to their writing and how it can be used to advance their argument. A case in point is the following summary (Text 3-2) by a doctoral student, who attempts to argue, through a review of relevant research literature, that language is central to the reading comprehension process and that knowledge about language should thus be part of the professional knowledge base for every reading teacher.

Text 3-2

The reading comprehension process entails a wide range of elements, including background knowledge, linguistic knowledge, (meta-)cognitive strategies, motivation, and relevant cultural experience (e.g., Lewis,

Walpole, & McKenna, 2014; Turner and Paris, 1995). Among the many elements of the reading process, Fang (2008) pointed out "three pillars of comprehension" (p. 478) that readers must possess. These are: (1) language knowledge (e.g., words, sentences, discourse structure); (2) relevant background knowledge; (3) a repertoire of self-regulating strategies (e.g., monitoring, inferring, visualizing, questioning, clarifying). He argued that the reading process takes place within interaction among the three pillars, where the reader's understanding of language and knowledge about the text functions as a catalyst for the effective use of skills and strategies in reading. Similarly, Spiro, Bruce, and Brewer (2017) asserted that reading involves a "multilevel interactive process" (p. 3) between text-based and knowledge-based processes, and that the interaction is essential to reading comprehension so that reading must be an inferential, constructive process to evaluate what the text is about.

In this summary, the student summarizes the work of several scholars (e.g., Lewis, Walpole & McKenna; Turn & Paris; Fang; and Spiro, Bruce & Brewer) who have written about the topic of reading comprehension. The summary, however, simply regurgitates some of the key points in these scholars' work, without discriminating which point made by the scholars is the most relevant to the point she tries to argue and discussing how she can use the point to enhance her argument. Nor is there an explanation or interpretation of others' ideas, a move that is critical to establishing the link between the work of others and her proposed work.

In a separate essay that similarly argues for the need to develop an explicit knowledge about language among middle and high school literacy teachers, the author is more selective in his summary, presenting only points from prior research that are most germane to his argument and at the same time explaining and interpreting these points in an angle that connects with and supports his argument. As a result, the summary is much more focused, relevant, and effective.

Text 3-3

Reading research over the past few decades has shown that the extent to which a reader comprehends a text is influenced by three key factors (Fang 2008; Pearson, Palincsar, Biancarosa, & Berman, 2020). The first is the reader's prior knowledge about the topic of the text. Familiarity with the text topic contributes to constructing a meaningful situation model of what the text is about. The second is the reader's proficiency with the language of the text. Without this proficiency, the reader would have trouble accessing prior knowledge, much less text content. The third is cognitive strategies, which facilitate integration of text information with the reader's background knowledge. Effective use of these strategies, however, hinges upon the extent to which the reader understands the text language and is familiar with the text topic (Kintsch 2004). One reason students are able to use cognitive strategies proficiently in everyday listening comprehension is that the topic of conversation is usually familiar and its language commonsensical. With disciplinary texts, however, the topic is typically unfamiliar and the language is often challenging; and to learn the unfamiliar content, students must first of all be able to process the challenging language in which this content is codified and transmitted. This means that a focus on language is of paramount importance in secondary literacy instruction. After all, content is made prototypically of language and presented to students primarily through language in textbooks and other written media. Students who struggle with reading and learning often exhibit a range of language problems, including difficulties in vocabulary, grammar, and text-level processing abilities (Stone, Silliman, Ehren, and Wallach 2013). This is particularly true in middle and high schools, where the texts students are expected to engage with become more specialized and complex. Students need support when interacting with these texts in disciplinary learning. To provide such support, teachers need to develop knowledge about the language that constructs these texts. Research (e.g., Love, 2010; Myhill, Jones, & Watson, 2013) has suggested that teachers who have an explicit understanding of the structures of language are better able to scaffold language learning and more effective in promoting academic literacy development.

Text 3-4, also written by a doctoral student, is another example where the summary does not match the point he tries to establish, which is that writing is important to science and should therefore be taught in school science classrooms. In this summary, the author simply inventories the ideas presented by scholars who have conducted research on science writing. The problem is that it is not clear how all these ideas connect with one another or with the point he tries to make. In other words, his summary lacks focus, or spin, as well as interpretation, that would have enabled him to establish the link to his work in a way that supports his argument and justifies the need for his study.

Text 3-4

In the early to mid-1990s, researchers started to recognize that science writing could serve as more than a simple "knowledge-telling model," that was utilized to evaluate student's memorization of facts (Yore, Bisanz & Hand, 2003). An increasingly constructivist view of science education asserted that writing could and should be an epistemic (way of knowing) process, a tool that increased communication, and enabled the construction and transformation of knowledge. Writing is recursive in nature; it helps to clarify existing ideas and to spark new ones. Glynn and Muth (1994) contended that the writing in science evolves and becomes epistemic: "The goal of epistemic writing about science is to reflect on and increase one's knowledge of science topics" (cited in Yore et al., 2003). Researchers in science writing trace a progression from the novice to the expert. Where novices use writing to "tell knowledge," the expert uses writing, "to construct, to build, or to transform knowledge" (Florence & Yore, 2004).

Explicit instruction in, and utilization of, science writing is the very tool that can transform the novice writer to an expert writer in science.

In the late elementary grades, middle school, and beyond, students are expected to read and write more technical and abstract texts, which typify the kind of advanced knowledge experienced in the later years of secondary and post-secondary schooling. As challenging as these new demands in reading and writing are for all upper elementary and middle school students, they are often even more challenging for ELLs, who are dealing with unfamiliar topics in their nonnative language. The "unfamiliar technical language as well as the genres characteristic of school science present unique challenges to upper elementary students" (de Oliveira, & Lan, 2014). Besides the technical terms and the different genres, science becomes less relevant to students (Yager, 2004), and attitudes toward the subject worsen. Science becomes an exercise in memorization and regurgitation of decontextualized facts.

In his discussion of the connections between language arts and science, Yore (2004) argues that "writing-to-learn science needs to move away from knowledge-telling approaches and toward knowledge-building approaches" (89). Yore sees science writing optimally as "an interactive-construction process in which students address a specific conceptual problem with written discourse," paralleling science debating and science reading. This approach is evident in the studies that follow, particularly those by Chen, Hand, and McDowell (2013) and Kohnen (2013).

A revised summary, presented in Text 3-5, is much more focused. This time, he is selective in presenting what others have said about the importance of writing to science, explicitly tying what others have said to the point he tries to make. As a result, the summary contributes to the development of his argument.

Text 3-5

Science is widely recognized as a discipline that involves the empirical work of observing, manipulating, and experimenting with the material world (Yore, Bisanz & Hand, 2003). At the same time, however, it is also a form of discourse involving argument (Kuhn, 2010; Osborne, 2010). Scientists use language and other semiotic resources such as graphs, charts, pictures, diagrams, and sonograms to record, describe, classify, explain, model, and theorize the natural phenomena. They use evidence gathered from their reading, observation, and experiment to make their case for new ideas or alternative interpretations. These ideas or interpretations are in turn subjected to scrutiny and critique by the scientific community and the public. For example, a study by Yore, Hand, and Florence (2004) found that scientists engage in many different types of writing in their daily work, including journal articles, grant proposals, manuscript reviews, seminars, reports, essays, emails, lab notes, field notes, and lecture notes.

Given the centrality of writing to the conception of science and to the social practices of scientists, it is not surprising that the science education community has long embraced the view that writing should be an integral part of the K-12 science curriculum. In fact, writing is seen as not only an indispensable tool for doing science but also a powerful vehicle for learning science (Yore, 2004). It has been shown to enhance content understanding, promote conceptual change and inquiry, improve retention and learning, and cultivate scientific habits of mind (e.g., Chen, Hand, & McDowell, 2013; Key, Hand, Prain, & Collins, 1999; Rivard & Straw, 2000). The National Research Council (2012, p. 42), in developing a framework for K-12 science education, identified eight science and engineering practices that are important for K-12 students to learn: asking questions and defining problems, developing and using models, planning and carrying out investigations, analyzing and interpreting data, using mathematics and computational thinking, constructing explanation and designing solution, engaging in argument from evidence, and obtaining/evaluating/communicating information. These practices are "language intensive" (Lee, Quinn, & Valdes, 2013, p. 2), requiring students to write and visually represent—along with other activities such as speaking, listening, reading, and viewing—as they develop models, present ideas, offer explanations, and engage in evidence-based reasoning and argumentation. Thus, if students are to develop as scientifically literate individuals, they must simultaneously develop facility in writing.

It must be noted that the same text can be summarized in different ways depending on your purpose for writing. You can foreground/highlight or background/ignore certain information in your summary so as to make it fit your purpose. That is to say, you can be selective in what you include and how you include the chosen information in your writing based on the focus of your writing. This does not mean, however, that you can misinterpret or distort the information or message in the source text in order to make it fit the focus of your writing. For example, in relation to Text 3-6 (Hasan, 1996, p. 398) below, if the purpose of your writing is to argue that reading and writing are important to the teaching and learning of history as a school subject, you can summarize it this way to support your thesis: *According to Hasan (1996), knowing a discipline like history is synonymous with being able to read and write the texts in that discipline.* If, on the other hand, the focus of your writing is on the importance of literacy to achieving educational equality for all students, you can summarize the excerpt this way: *According to Hasan (1996), developing the ability to read/write disciplinary texts is essential to building knowledge across disciplines and ensuring academic success for all students.*

Text 3-6

[T]urning to the schooling context, so long as we hold the ideal of egalitarian education, there will be a need to teach literacy in the sense of developing pupils' discursive abilities in relation to educational registers, since this is a necessary condition for 'having education', for getting to know knowledge! In fact, it would be difficult to draw a distinction between pupils' knowledge of an academic discipline and their discursive ability to listen/read, speak/write the discourses of that discipline. Academic disciplines are, after all, largely a constellation of certain types of discourse, and, in the end, what counts as knowing a discipline is the ability to participate successfully in the discourses of that discipline.

Two other points about summarizing are worth mentioning here. One has to do with how long each summary should be. You have undoubtedly noticed in the articles or books you have read that some summaries are longer than others. The general rule is that the length of each summary should be proportionate to the degree of relevance or importance the source text has to the thesis of your work. The more important or closely related a source text is to your work, the longer your summary of the text should usually be. This means that some articles can be summarized in 1–2 sentences, whereas others require summaries of one paragraph or longer. For example, in Text 3-5 above, a document produced by the National Research Council is summarized in more than half of a paragraph because it is a landmark publication that reinforces the author's argument that writing is central to science learning in school. On the other hand, the work of *Yore, Hand, and Florence (2004)* was summarized in one sentence. Regardless of their length, each of these summaries connects with and bolsters the point Text 3-5 tries to make. In short, depending on your purpose for summarizing a particular piece of work, you need to think about what to highlight or foreground and what to ignore or background so that your summary meets your discursive needs without distorting the work being summarized.

Another aspect of summary that deserves attention is that you need to be precise with the verbs you use to report what others have said (Gillett, Hammond, & Martala, 2009; Graff & Birkenstein, 2018; Swales & Feak, 2018). Authors do not just *say, note, offer,* or *state,* they *explain, describe, suggest, admit, acknowledge, concur, maintain, affirm, endorse, support, confirm, corroborate, plead, demand, encourage, urge, implore, extol, prioritize, argue, assert, claim, complain, lament, question, warn, caution, contend, challenge, emphasize, declare, deny, refute, contradict, object, reject, deplore, renounce, repudiate,* or *conclude* when they present their ideas or points of view. This means it is important that you use vivid and precise signal verbs when reporting other scholars' ideas and arguments in your summary. This is essential for two reasons. First, it ensures that you capture the true intention of the scholar(s) whose work you are summarizing. Second, it enhances the aesthetics of your writing. Imagine if every time you summarize an article or a book, you keep saying "this author said" and "that author said". That would indeed make your writing monotonous and boring to read. On the other hand, if you vary the use of reporting verbs in a way that is consistent with the source text author's voice and intent, you can make your writing more accurate and interesting. In an article by Fisher (2018), for example, the author used a variety of reporting verbs in his summaries of others' work:

- Carter (2007) <u>suggested</u> that the field of writing composition [...].
- Russell (1997) <u>described</u> four major components [...].
- Goatley, Raphael, and Brock (2014) <u>hoped</u> that [...].
- Both Moje (2007) and Russell (1997) <u>emphasized</u> the unique function of language [...].
- Bazerman (1997) <u>argued</u> that [...].
- Prior (2008) <u>took the view</u> that [...].
- Fang and Coatoam (2013) <u>explained</u> that disciplinary literacy is [...].
- Shanahan and Shanahan (2008) <u>privileged</u> [...].
- As Shanhan and Shanahan (2008) <u>acknowledged</u>, disciplines are [...].
- Bawarshi and Reif (2010) <u>contrasted</u> [...] against [...].
- Bawarshi and Reif (2010) <u>cautioned</u> that [...].
- De La Paz et al. (2017) <u>claimed</u> to apply [...].
- Van den Broeck (1977) <u>focuses</u> on [...].
- Schwartz (1983) <u>contends</u> that [...].
- As Kenny (2002) <u>elucidates</u>, [...].
- Clandinin and Rosiek (2007) <u>indicate</u> that [...].
- Bista (2011) <u>found</u> that [...].
- As Wellington and Osborne (2001) <u>affirmed</u>, [...].

Writing a summary regularly requires paraphrasing the words, phrases, and sentences that others use. In paraphrasing, inexperienced writers tend to engage in "patchwriting" (Howard, Serviss, & Rodrigue, 2010), which involves copying from a source text, replacing some words, and moving a few words around. This practice potentially indicates a lack of source text comprehension and/or language proficiency, and runs the risk of inadvertent plagiarism. To avoid lifting words, phrases, or sentences directly from the source text(s) you are summarizing, you can follow the process Gillett, Hammond, and Martala (2009) described for writing summaries of others' work. The first step in summarizing is to carefully read the source text you want to summarize and make sure you truly understand what the author says. As you read, think about the purpose of the text you are summarizing in relation to your own purpose for writing, asking yourself questions such as (a) what is this author's purpose in writing this text? (b) why am I drawing on this text for my writing? and (c) am I summarizing it to support my argument or to critique it before I introduce my argument? You can use the Cornell Notes, the Frayer model, or another kind of note-taking system you find suitable when taking notes. These tools help you organize the information you have gleaned from the text and at the same time note its source (e.g., author, page number), write personal reactions to it, and indicate

Source (author, year, page number)	Quote	My Interpretation or Reflection	Possible Use

Figure 3.1 A Multi-Column Note Sheet

how it relates to your current work and how you might use it in your writing. Figure 3.1 shows a multi-column note sheet that can be used for note taking.

Once you know what you want the summary to do for you, you can then select relevant information from the source text based on your purpose. After you have identified the relevant information in the text to be summarized, you should reread the portion of the text to gain a clear understanding of its gist, including key concepts/ideas and their relationships. During rereading, you will want to distinguish between main ideas and subsidiary information. Main ideas can often be found in the topic sentence/paragraph or the concluding sentence/paragraph. In most cases, you can delete details, examples, anecdotes, data, or illustrations from the source text. In cases where a lengthier summary is needed, you can also include key statistics or details that would bolster your argument.

Once the main ideas have been identified in the source text, you need to paraphrase them. You can do this by changing the structure of the selected excerpt and replacing some of its words or phrases, with the exception of specialized terminology. This involves identifying meaning relationships between ideas (e.g.

cause/effect, generalization, elaboration, contrast, condition, concession) and then expressing these relationships in a different way. Often, there are signal words or phrases in the excerpt that provide cues to the logical-semantic links among the ideas. You can change the grammar of the excerpt by rearranging words and sentences, such as changing nouns to verbs, breaking up long sentences, or combining short sentences. For example, this topic sentence from a legal text—*The Constitution establishes that the states may not deprive any person of life, liberty, or property without due process*—can be restructured and reworded as *According to the Constitution, due process is required in any move by the states to take away people's life, liberty, or property*. As another example, compare the following two texts: Text 3-7a is a concluding statement from an empirical research article investigating the phrasal complexity of students' writing (Ansarifar, Shahriari, & Pishghadam, 2018, p. 69), and Text 3-7b is a paraphrase of this statement.

Text 3-7a

While our findings suggest a tendency towards greater use of phrasal constructions by more experienced writers, the exact predicted sequence of development hypothesized by Biber et al (2011) could not be traced in our data and in some instances (e.g., -ed participles and -ing participles), a re-consideration of features among these stages is advised.

Text 3-7b

Ansarifar, Shahriari, and Pishghadam (2018) concluded that their data did not support the developmental sequence of phrasal complexity that Biber et al. (2011) hypothesized, even though they showed that more experienced writers tended to use more phrasal constructions than did less experienced writers. The researchers further suggested that in light of their findings, some features (e.g., -ed/-ing participles) within Biber et al.'s developmental stages may need to be realigned.

The next step is to combine paraphrased sentences into a piece of continuous writing, using conjunctions, adverbs, or other devices to show the connections among ideas (see Chapter 4 for crafts of making connections). Once the summary is complete, you need to double check to make sure that (a) your purpose is clear, (b) the strength of the original claims is maintained, (c) the meaning is the same, and (d) the source is credited.

Sometimes, you need to write a summary based on more than one source. This kind of summary, called synthesis, can be more challenging to write because it requires you to analyze and use information from two or more source texts that may overlap, slightly differ, or sharply contradict one another (see Chapter 7 for more on writing an integrated literature review that involves synthesizing). When working with multiple sources, you often need to infer and make explicit the relationships among them. Like writing a summary, writing a synthesis requires that you read and understand the sources, identify relevant ideas in each source, detect the meaning relationships among ideas, organize the information from different sources in some meaningful way, note similarities and differences among these sources, paraphrase the needed information, and stitch together what you have paraphrased into a coherent whole that connects with and supports the point you want to make in your own writing. Once the synthesis is written, you need to check it against the source texts for accuracy and relevance.

Quoting

In summarizing, you will sometimes want to quote directly from the source text. Quoting someone else's words gives credibility to your summary. It means that you have read the original source of the ideas that you are summarizing, instead of relying on secondary or tertiary sources, which can be unreliable at times. In quoting, you need to make sure that the quote you use is connected in some way with what you want to say in your writing. In other words, you should not present a quote for the sake of having a quote or as if the quote could speak for itself (see Text 3-4 for instances of this type of quotes). Rather, you need to have a sense of what the quote can do for your writing. This could be to reinforce, elaborate on, or distill your point. You will also need to be willing to discard quotes or search for new quotes as the focus of your writing changes during multiple rounds of revision (Graff & Birkenstein, 2018). Sometimes a quote fits perfectly with your first draft; however, after several rounds of revision, the quote may no longer be relevant or most appropriate because the focus of your writing has shifted. In this situation, you should not hesitate to delete the quote and, if necessary, search for a new quote.

In Text 3-8 below, the student writer uses a quote that does not seem to support the point she was arguing for in the two preceding sentences—that is, content area teachers (e.g., history or mathematics teachers) are also literacy (reading/language arts) teachers. Instead, the quote seems better suited for a text that emphasizes the importance of teaching students to act and think like content experts in their disciplinary learning.

Text 3-8

Content area teachers must realize they are also literacy teachers. These teachers have the responsibility to help their students develop literacy skills in the content areas they are studying. In other words, to borrow from Woolsey and Lapp (2017), "every student can better comprehend the fascinating world we inhabit by looking at it from the perspectives of experts who know their parts of the world well" (p. 4).

It is important not to overquote in your writing. The answer to the question of how much quoting is overquoting will vary depending on your field of study and the type of publication you are targeting. Ideally, each double-spaced page of your writing should generally contain no more than two quotes, with the total amount of quotes not exceeding 20% of the total words on the page. Shorter quotes (<40 words) are usually integrated into your text with quotation marks, but longer quotes (40 words or more) are typically made into blocks without quotation marks. You would use a quote when you cannot say the same thing better than the quote itself. Too much quoting gives your readers the impression that either you do not understand what you have read or you are too lazy or inept to paraphrase. Writers with a superficial understanding of what they have read or limited language proficiency tend to rely on extensive quoting when summarizing others' work. This should be avoided.

Furthermore, you should do more than just lifting a quote from the source text to your writing; that is, you should avoid what Graff and Birkenstein (2018) referred to as "dangling" or "hit-and-run" quotes. You need to introduce the quote to your text and then explain how the quote is related to your writing. A good analogy here is this: If you want to bring your college roommate home for dinner on a Saturday night, you will first need to prepare your parents for her arrival by saying something to the effect that "Hey, mom/dad, my roommate Liz would like to come over to our house for dinner tomorrow." Once your roommate arrives at your parents' house, you would then need to explain to your parents by saying something to the effect that "This is my roommate, Liz. She's my best friend. She is tired of eating out." It makes little sense to bring your roommate to your parents' dinner table one evening without some kind of introduction and explanation to your parents.

Graff and Birkenstein (2018) proposed the use of "quotation sandwich" to properly blend the quote with your own writing. The top slice of the sandwich introduces the quote; the middle part, or meat, of the sandwich is the quote itself; and the bottom slice explains what the quote means and how it relates to your point in the text. In the following excerpt (Text 3-9) from Fang and Chapman (2020, p. 2), the phrase *As Christie and Maton (2011, p. 5) explained* introduces a quote. The quote is explained in subsequent sentences beginning with *In other words.*

Text 3-9

Academic disciplines are highly specialized fields of inquiry where people with shared norms and habits of mind engage in similar professional practices. Each discipline is a distinct discourse community with its own ways of creating, structuring, communicating, critiquing, teaching, and learning knowledge (Hyland, 2020). [...] As Christie and Maton (2011, p. 5) explained,

Membership in a disciplinary community offers shared, intersubjective bases for determining ends and means, approaches and procedures, ways to judge disciplinary findings, the bases on which to agree or disagree, and problems apprehended (if not always solved, since many require hard work and are at time intractable), as well as providing shared pleasures in intellectual pursuits and the excitements of possible new understandings emerging from jointly constructed knowledge of many kinds.

In other words, each community of experts establishes and maintains its own set of concepts, principles, processes, standards, and genres for inquiries and debates in knowledge building. These discipline-legitimated conventions shape—and evolve in response to—new developments in the discipline. They reflect the unique epistemology, methodology, and goals that characterize each discipline. [...].

Sometimes, explicit linguistic markers, such as *in other words* or *that is to say*, may not be present when quotes are explained. For example, in the following excerpt (Text 3-10) from an article published in *Harvard Law Review* (Anonymous, 2020, p. 2123), the second sentence explains the quote at the end of the first sentence without indicating explicitly the logical-semantic relationship between the two sentences. The omission of such explicit linguistic markers benefits disciplinary insiders who are well-versed in the topic but can disadvantage disciplinary outsiders who may not have the necessary background knowledge to infer logico-semantic relations between sentences (see also Chapter 11); on the other hand, too many signaling devices can make the text sound unnatural, a point to be further discussed in Chapter 4.

Text 3-10

This hope for a return to health of the judging practice touching on restitution is eloquently reflected in Karl Llewellyn's "Grand Style of the Common Law": "[T]he better and best law is to be built on and out of what the past can offer; the quest consists in a constant re-examination and reworking of a heritage." The vision is not one in which the standards are "immune from criticism," but one in which development is organic and preserves the basic structures of the practice.

Some useful templates for introducing quotes are provided below:

- According to Catts (2009), "[...]".
- As Halliday (2016) observed, "[...]".
- Gee (1999) highlighted this need, arguing, "[...]".
- Swales writes, "[...]".
- They conclude their article by stating that "[...]".
- Leander and Boldt (2013) state, "[...]".
- This progression is summarized by Macken-Horarik (1996) as follows: "[...]".

- The significance was recently addressed by Chen (1994): "[...]".
- As Coffin (1996) pointed out, "[...]".
- Martin (1993) provided the following example: "[...]".
- As Lemke (1990) argues, "[...]".
- Wells (1986) argues a similar thesis: "[...]".
- Martin (2012) defines a genre as "[...]".
- As Wellington (2004) puts it, "[...]".
- The CCSS (2010) explicitly notes that it is "[...]".
- Villalva (2006) has described functional approaches as those that "[...]".

Some useful templates for the bottom slice of the quote include:

- In other words, the author encouraged teachers to [...].
- Essentially, Smith rejected the notion of collectivism as [...].
- Here, Pearson was arguing that [...].
- Snow's point is that [...].
- That is to say, [...].
- To paraphrase Cummins, [...]
- From Wiggin's perspective, then, [...]
- In essence, Dupree was calling for [...]

As you will undoubtedly discover in the research literature you have read, not all quotes need to have a sandwich structure. Sometimes, a quote is used to summarize, or distill, what has previously been discussed in some detail. In this case, the quote does not need to have the bottom slice. Other times, a quote is woven into the text without the introductory slice in order to preserve the particular wording used or foreground a particular point made by the scholar(s) being quoted. In this instance, the quote still needs to be explained and linked to the point it is intended to support. Take Text 3-11 from Fang and Wei (2010, p. 262) as an example. The first quote is inserted into the first sentence without an introduction because it is succinctly said by Halliday. The quote is then explained in the next five sentences. At the end of the paragraph, another quote is used to summarize, or distill, the preceding explanations. Had the quote been unpacked again, then we would be engaging in a never-ending circular discussion, which is unnecessary because it sounds repetitive.

Text 3-11

Science is a discipline that involves "both *material* and *semiotic* practices" (Halliday, 1998, p. 228). On one hand, science is an organized human activity that seeks knowledge about the natural world in a systematic way. It requires the use of scientific methods for observing, identifying, describing, and experimentally investigating the natural phenomenon. On the other hand, science is also a form of discourse that involves the use of language, particularly written language. Scientists use language in conducting scientific inquiries and in constructing theoretical explanations of the natural phenomenon. They also use language to communicate scientific knowledge, principles, procedures, and reasoning to others. For these reasons, science has been characterized as "a unique mix of inquiry and argument" (Yore et al., 2004, p. 347).

Sourcing

Academic writing is well supported with evidence, example, or elaboration. This often necessitates the use of sources. As a writer, you are responsible for not only faithfully summarizing these sources but also acknowledging them. Sources can be incorporated into text in many different ways. You can position sources in the beginning, middle, or end of a sentence using different wordings. The variety in the way sources are acknowledged enhances both the aesthetics and the flow of your writing. It would indeed be boring to always begin each sentence with author and date, such as *Barone (2006)*, when crediting sources. Diversifying the way sources are cited enables you to foreground or background certain information and craft discursive flow in a way that facilitates the presentation of information and the development of argument. It is worth noting here that in some disciplines (e.g., law, medicine), sources are incorporated into the text through an enumeration system, with each number expounded in a footnote or an endnote. In these disciplines, linguistic means of source incorporation may not command as much emphasis in academic writing. To facilitate citation of sources, you can also use reference management software programs such as Refworks, Zotero, Mendeley, Endnote, or Citations.

Listed below are some ways of incorporating sources into your writing:

- Stefancic and Tsemberis (2007) found that [...].
- Barone (2006) pointed out that [...].
- As Greene (1993) wrote, [...].
- What we have attempted to do in this article is to offer [...] in which people are treated as "things"—to use Freire's (1994, p. 255) terminology—and at the same time announces [...].
- Curriculum reformers ask, as Schon (1987) asked of professions more generally, "[...]?".
- We defined [...] as "[...]" (Clandinin & Connelly, 2005, p. 7).
- Previous studies in human and non-human animals have identified [...] (Fleming and Dolan, 2012; Hanks and Summerfield, 2017).
- A final issue that we wish to reflect on is the theories that are specifically rooted in what Brookfield (2003) calls "[...]".

- This view of knowledge has, in common with Dewey (1938), the idea that [...].
- This augurs the need to challenge what Fisher (2018) referred to as [...].
- According to Nelson (1995), a counterstory is "[...]".
- Emphasis on the importance of prior experiences [...] was clearly evident in the work of Spalding et al. (2007) and Adams et al. (2005).
- As underlined by Lesaux and Gamez (2012), the amount of teacher talk influences [...].
- In Bauer's (2005) view, teachers must embrace and utilize technology to [...].
- We take seriously Lensmire's (1998) charge that "[...]".

Occasionally, you may have to resort to citing what is called "secondary sources" because you do not have access to the original source. In this case, you should provide references for both the original and the secondary sources, as the following two excerpts show.

- What bothers critics, she suggests, is "the insertion of personal stories into what we have been taught to think of as the analysis of impersonal social facts" (Bahar, 1996, p. 13, as cited in Romm, 2010, p. 299).
- According to Jaffe (2009, cited in De Costa, 2011), language ideologies may refer to a number of phenomena [...].

In the first example, Bahar is the original source and Romm is the secondary source from which the writer obtained the Bahar quote. In the second example, Jaffe is the original source, and De Costa is the secondary source. It is best to minimize the use of secondary sources in your writing. That is, you should try your best to locate the original source when citing or quoting, as sometimes secondary sources may have misinterpreted the original source or have interpreted the original source in an angle that does not match your needs. Moreover, reading the original source can yield additional insights or information that you may find valuable and helpful in your writing.

Agreeing or Disagreeing

As stated earlier, academic writing entails not only presenting but also responding to others' work. In your response, you will need to express your agreement or disagreement with what others have said. Your point of view can be expressed explicitly by using such phrases as *I think*, *in our opinion*, and *my view is*, although such expressions are typically minimized in academic writing, as discussed in Chapter 2. More often, you would convey your stance implicitly by using expressions such as *It can thus be argued that [...]*, *The foregoing analysis shows that [...]*, and *It is clear that [...]*. You can also express your position through the reporting verbs you choose to summarize or quote others' work. For example, when you write *Stevenson (2014) claimed [...]*, it means you believe what Stevenson said lacks evidence or is at least debatable, as the word *claim* has negative connotations. When you write *Stevenson (1994) asserted [...]*, you are implying that Stevenson stated his point forcefully and with confidence, regardless of evidence base. When you write *Stevenson (2014) insisted that [...]*, you are implying that Stevenson was urging, albeit politely, his readers to accept his claim regardless of evidence base. Novice writers sometimes use reporting verbs like these indiscriminately, without a deep understanding of the nuances associated with these words and the true intention of the author(s) whose work is being cited.

In agreeing or disagreeing, it is important to do more than merely echoing or dissenting a particular view that others have presented. You need to provide details to substantiate your agreement or disagreement. In other words, you need to present your rationale for why you support or reject a particular view. The rationale can be given in the form of elaboration, evidence, or example. If you are worried about not being able to meet the length requirements of your course assignments because you think that you have said everything you wanted to say, then discussing why and how you agree or disagree with the cited work is one way of extending the length of your writing to meet the assignment requirements. More importantly, it makes your points clearer, stronger, and easier to understand.

Specifically, when you agree with someone, you need to add something new or different that the author of the cited work has not mentioned in order to reinforce the view you are embracing. Graff and Birkenstein (2018) recommended that you do so by

- pointing out some unnoticed evidence or line of reasoning that supports the view,
- citing a personal experience or an additional set of data that corroborates with the view,
- paraphrasing the way the view was presented by the author to make it more accessible to the reader, or
- pointing out unnoticed implications of the view.

Text 3-12 below is an excerpt from an article in Fox Business (Garber, 2020) that discusses the Trump administration's proposed ban of Chinese social media app WeChat. The author cites and agrees with Ker Gibbs, but does more than just echoing Gibbs' view that the ban endangers US businesses in China. Instead, he provides two specific examples in the last two sentences to illustrate the potential impact of the proposed ban.

Text 3-12

A U.S. ban on WeChat "would be simply devastating," Ker Gibbs, president of the American Chamber of Commerce in Shanghai, told Fox Business. "It's hard to see how some of these American companies could survive in this market without being able to use WeChat payments."

The immediate impact would be lost sales for companies like Nike as customers who couldn't use their preferred payment method would respond by taking their business to rivals such as Adidas, based in Germany. But there is also the possibility that a ban from the Trump administration would cause companies domiciled outside the U.S. whose applications ride on the WeChat system to stop using the app in fear of secondary sanctions.

When you disagree with someone, you can state your disagreement in frank but considerate ways without tearing him/her down. You can do so by saying, for example, that the author failed to take relevant factors into consideration, used flawed logic, or overlooked the real issue; you can also say that the author's conclusion is based on incomplete evidence, the author's argument rests on questionable assumptions, or the author is self-contradictory in argument (Graff & Birkenstein, 2018).

In Text 3-13, an excerpt from Schleppegrell (2007, p. 121), which argues about the role of grammar in literacy teaching, the author disagrees with the "purportedly research-driven notion" that grammar is just a set of prescriptive rules and has little to do with writing development (first sentence). She counters this argument in the second and third sentences by presenting examples of how teachers are already intuitively teaching grammar as a way to improve student writing. In so doing, she shows that grammar is a powerful resource for making meaning and that grammar instruction is in fact useful to writing improvement.

Text 3-13

But when it comes to discussion of language, many researchers and teachers still promote the purportedly research-driven notions that grammar is no more than a set of rules for accuracy in language use and that grammar plays no role in writing development. Yet writing instructors regularly engage in activities such as suggesting alternative wording when students' phrasing is awkward, proposing different organizational strategies when students' texts do not flow easily, and recommending that students think about the audience they are addressing and how their wording choices will be received by that audience. Writers choose both form and content, and it is through the rhetorical and syntactic forms they choose that the content is constructed and evaluated.

Evaluating

In academic writing, it is often necessary to make clear your attitude toward the topic you are writing about and toward other people's work that you are summarizing or quoting. Your attitude can be softened or strengthened, depending on the degree of your commitment or hesitancy. Compare, for example, the three sentences below:

- <u>It may be said/It appears that</u> Trump's commitment to these social issues is not as strong as Biden's.
- Trump's commitment to these social issues is not as strong as Biden's.
- <u>It is clear that/Of course</u> Trump's commitment to these social issues is not as strong as Biden's.

The second sentence presents a claim that is not qualified in any way. The first sentence softens this claim by using *it may be said that* or *it appears that*. The third sentence strengthens the claim by adding *it is clear that* or *of course*.

As can be seen from these examples, there are two ways to indicate the strength of your stance on a particular subject. They are called hedging and boosting. Hedging is the expression of tentativeness and possibility (Hyland, 2004). In hedging, you use cautious, or deliberately vague, language (e.g., *somewhat, sort of, perhaps, tend to, may, seems, likely*) to delimit claims, temper critiques, increase precision, show deference to authority, or reduce the risk of potential opposition from the reader. This lack of certainty does not necessarily undermine your credibility; instead, it shows that you are knowledgeable and sophisticated, but not arrogant or all-knowing. This stance helps you build writer-reader relationships, making it more effective to persuade your readers and gain their acceptance. It also shows your respect for the author(s) whose work you are critiquing. Listed below are some of the more popular hedging devices found in academic writing:

- may, might, can, could, would, maybe, perhaps, must
- assumption, possibility, likelihood
- practically, likely, virtually, approximately, roughly, relatively, adequately, unlikely, technically, typically, usually, seemingly, admittedly, generally, essentially, presumably, until recently, mainly, normally, conceivably, ostensibly, hypothetically, supposedly, allegedly, comparatively speaking
- questionable, possible, probable
- about, around, approximately, rather, sometimes, somewhat, sort of, often
- appear, indicate, seem, tend to, suggest, assume, suppose, discern, doubt, suspect, speculate, surmise
- to our knowledge, to the best of my knowledge, in our view, to some degree, to a certain extent, in some sense, at this moment, in a way
- it might be said that, it could be the case that, it is likely that, it may be possible to, it is useful to, provided that

In boosting, you add force, focus, or strength to your claims. It increases authorial commitment or seriousness of intention but at the same time closes down discursive space for other views. The downside of boosting is that it can make you sound cocky and pompous, thus running the risk of antagonizing your readers or causing them to second-guess what you are saying (see also Chapter 2). However, if used judiciously, it can convey the right amount of confidence and certainty, making you sound authoritative and like an expert in your field. Sample devices for boosting include:

- must, have to, ought to, will
- obviously, clearly, actually, certainly, conclusively, evidently, necessarily, sharply, substantially, particularly, extremely, significantly, definitely, never, emphatically, inevitably, unquestionably, unequivocally, apparently, absolutely, always, indeed, very
- it is clear/evident/apparent/well-known that
- of course, in fact, more than, without a doubt, at least, at all
- reveal, conclude, demonstrate, show, identify, convince, determine, conclude
- doubtless, impossible, factual

In academic writing, writers hedge more than they boost. Because hedging makes the writer less susceptible to criticism, reduces the risk of reader opposition, and increases the writer's acceptability, it has become almost conventionalized in academic writing, so much so that it has in effect become an indispensable resource for conforming to an established writing style in English. According to Aull and Lancaster (2014), advanced academic writing generally privileges caution and possibilities, presenting claims that are proportionate to evidence or reasonable assumption. Less mature academic writing, by contrast, tends to use more intensifying boosters that emphasize certainty, often presenting claims that are disproportionate to evidence or reasonable assumptions (Hyland & Milton, 1997). Occasionally, you will see that authors mix hedges (underlined below) with boosters (bolded below) to create an intentionally dubious effect that gives readers a false sense of precision, as the following examples show.

- The study also **demonstrates** that it is possible to obtain relatively separate measures of implicit and explicit knowledge of L2 grammar.
- It is **very** likely that a tsunami **will** strike the coastal village again in the next decade.
- Readers of this article can almost **certainly** point to a favorite disciplinary literacy text that explicitly pushes against one or more of these general tendencies.
- Also, **of course**, readers can likely raise many partial explanations for these tendencies.
- **In fact**, we now **believe** that our eggs may represent a new species of fossil sauropod eggs.

Conclusion

This chapter describes some of the fundamental skills involved in academic writing—contextualizing, summarizing, quoting, sourcing, agreeing/disagreeing, and evaluating. Executing these skills requires a considerable amount of expertise in reading. Research has suggested that writing and reading are closely related, with improvement in one often leading to enhancement in the other (Fitzgerald & Shanahan, 2000). To be successful in academic writing, you must develop the ability to read complex academic and disciplinary texts carefully, fluently, and critically. Improvement in academic reading proficiency is thus key to improvement in academic writing performance.

Reflection/Application Activities

1 Drawing on the templates for contextualizing presented in this chapter, write an introduction to an argumentative essay or empirical research article that you are working on.
2 Select three to five samples of academic writing from your field of study and examine how the authors of these pieces contextualize their work, as well as summarize, source, quote, evaluate, and agree/disagree with others' work. Identify some templates related to these skills from the articles for potential use in your own writing.
3 Identify two to three pieces of writing you did for class assignments or other academic purposes. Discuss your strengths and weaknesses with respect to the six writing skills discussed in this chapter.
4 Identify one (or more) paragraph in a journal article or a book chapter. Try to summarize the paragraph(s) in a way that supports the point you want to argue. If two of you use the same source(s) to make different arguments, discuss how your summaries differ in ways that support either of your arguments.
5 Collect two or more articles that address the same topic. Compare/contrast the viewpoints expressed in these articles. Then synthesize these articles in a way that supports an argument you try to make about the topic.
6 Identify a controversial issue of current interest and then argue for or against a position on the issue. Try to use as many relevant linguistic resources and strategies discussed in this chapter as possible.

References

Anonymous (2020). The future of restitution and equity in the distribution of funds recovered from Ponzi Schemes and other multi-victim frauds. *Harvard Law Review, 133*(6), 2101–2123.

Ansarifar, A., Shahriari, H., & Pishghadam, R. (2018). Phrasal complexity in academic writing: A comparison of abstracts written by graduate students and expert writers in applied linguistics. *Journal of English for Academic Purposes, 31*, 58–71.

Aull, L., & Lancaster, Z. (2014). Linguistic markers of stance in early and advanced academic writing: A corpus-based comparison. *Written Communication, 21*(2), 151–183.

Fang, Z., & Chapman, S. (2020). Disciplinary literacy in mathematics: One mathematician's reading practices. *Journal of Mathematical Behavior.* https://doi.org/10.1016/j.jmathb.2020.100799

Fang, Z., Sun, Y., Chiu, C., & Trutschel, B. (2014). Inservice teachers' perception of a language-based approach to content area reading. *Australian Journal of Language and Literacy, 37*(1), 55–66.

Fang, Z., & Wei, Y. (2010). Improving middle school students' science literacy through reading infusion. *Journal of Educational Research, 103*, 262–273.

Fitzgerald, J., & Shanahan, T. (2000). Reading and writing relationships and their development. *Educational Psychologist, 35*(1), 39–50.

Garber, J. (2020). Trump's WeChat ban endangers US businesses in China. *Fox Business,* https://www.foxbusiness.com/markets/wechat-poses-looming-threat-for-us-businesses-in-china (accessed on September 12, 2020).

Gillett, A., Hammond, A., & Martala, M. (2009). *Inside track: Successful academic writing.* London: Longman.

Graff, G., & Birkenstein, C. (2018). *They say I say: The moves that matter in academic writing* (4th ed.). New York: Norton.

Hasan, R. (1996). Literacy, everyday talk and society. In R. Hasan & G. William (Eds.), *Literacy in society* (pp. 377–424). London: Longman.

Howard, R., Serviss, T., & Rodrigue, T. (2010). Writing from sources, writing from sentences. *Writing and Pedagogy, 2*(2), 177–192.

Hyland, K. (2004). *Disciplinary discourses: Social interactions in academic writing.* Ann Arbor: University of Michigan Press.

Hyland, K., & Milton, J. (1997). Qualification and certainty in L1 and L2 writing. *Journal of Second Language Writing, 6*(2), 183–205.

Schleppegrell, M. (2007). The meaning in grammar. *Research in the Teaching of English, 42*(1), 121–128.

Swales, J., & Feak, C. (2018). *Academic writing for graduate students: Essential skills and tasks* (3rd ed.). Ann Arbor: Univerrsity of Michigan Press.

Thomson, P., & Kamler, B. (2016). *Detox your writing: Strategies for doctoral researchers.* London: Routledge.

4
Skills and Strategies for Academic Writing: Part Two

This chapter continues the discussion of the skills that are essential for successful academic writing and the linguistic resources and strategies that are functional for instantiating these skills. The ten skills in focus in this chapter are defining, classifying/categorizing, describing, explaining, exemplifying, referencing visuals, comparing/contrasting, entertaining opposition, recommending, and connecting. As with Chapter 3, many templates are provided for each skill discussed so that you have at your disposal a wide range of options for executing the skill.

Defining

In academic writing, there is often a need to define concepts or terms that are key to understanding what you write but may be confusing or unfamiliar to your readers. In fact, definition is one of the most important school-based tasks, and students are required to master it. However, many learners struggle with writing formal definitions because they require the use of a different set of linguistic resources than the one commonly found in informal definitions (Schleppegrell, 2004). A formal definition is usually a concise, logical statement that identifies the characteristics of the concept being defined and reveals its relationships to other concepts in the same class. As such, definition often involves classifying/categorizing and comparing/contrasting.

In English, definition can be provided using a variety of grammatical resources, some more explicit and others less so. Samples of explicit definition follow, with resources for defining underlined.

- A bird <u>is</u> an endothermic vertebrate <u>that</u> has feathers and [...].
- The term "Ponzi scheme" <u>refers to</u> a class of frauds <u>in which</u> the fraudster [...].
- The series of changes in the female reproductive system that includes [...] and [...] <u>is known as</u> the menstrual cycle.

- Erosion <u>is</u> a process <u>during which</u> the surface of the earth is degraded by the effects of [...].
- An acrylic plastic <u>is</u> a polymer <u>which</u> can take a [...], is clear and [...], and can be shaped while [...].
- For our purposes, culture <u>is defined as</u> [...].
- A mentor may <u>be described as</u> [...].
- They <u>described</u> inclusive schools <u>as</u> [...].
- Marton (1986) <u>defines</u> phenomenography <u>as</u> "[...]".
- Academic English can <u>be viewed as</u> [...].
- The process that matches [...] and [...] on-line and in real-time <u>is</u> often <u>called</u> e-hailing, in contrast to traditional street-hailing.
- Students who experience less achievement in second language—<u>referred to as</u> dominant bilinguals—show neither [...].
- Linguistic-minority students <u>are labeled as</u> [...].
- I <u>see</u> writing <u>as</u> a way of having an extended conversation with colleagues [...].
- <u>One definition</u> of SCM <u>is offered</u> by La Monde (1998) <u>as</u> [...].
- Transfer <u>means</u> carrying over knowledge from one situation to a new situation.
- An affinity group <u>is made up of</u> people who [...].
- Encoding, in this context, <u>concerns</u> the meaningful interpretation of [...].
- ADD <u>is characterized by</u> pervasive and impairing symptoms of [...].
- The ideational meanings <u>relate to</u> what is going on in the field, <u>that is</u>, how people use language to articulate their meaning.
- Alternative schools <u>include</u> "public elementary/secondary schools that [...]".

As these examples show, an explicit definition typically consists of the target term to be defined, a linking verb, the class to which the term belongs, and an embedded clause that expands on the concept by providing further details about what it does, looks like, or is made of. Some grammatical resources that explicitly signal a formal definition include *is, is called, mean, define, refer to, is defined/viewed/seen/labeled/described/known/understood/conceptualized as, concern, is characterized by, is made up of,* and *consists of.*

Sometimes, definitions are given in more implicit or less prominent ways, as the following examples (underlined) show:

- The echidna is one of two species of monotremes, <u>or egg-laying mammals</u>, that live in Australia.
- <u>When referring specifically to</u> students who are [...], <u>we will use the term</u> emergent bilinguals.
- Average raw scores on IQ tests have been rising for years, by an estimated three IQ points per decade. This rise, <u>known as the Flynn effect</u>, has received much attention.
- Many travel forecasting models incorporate the user equilibrium route choice principle, <u>which states that</u> [...].

- One way to compile assessment results is the portfolios, <u>which is a folder that contains a variety of samples of student work related to a particular curricular area</u>.
- The layers of rock around the *puesto* were composed primarily of cemented—<u>that is, compressed and hardened</u>—sand and gravel.
- Acculturation—<u>the process of adjusting to a new or non-native culture</u>—is perhaps best illustrated by the four phases of [...].
- When 37-year-old Eero Saarinen, <u>an architect who was beginning to be recognized for his imaginative ideas</u>, heard of the contest, he decided to enter it.

The examples above present definitions in a much less explicit or noticeable way. In these instances, it is often the case that definition is not the author's emphasis or that a more explicit definition will disrupt the flow of the text. For example, the preposition *or* can introduce an appositive phrase that serves as a definition for the term preceding it. In the first example above (*The echidna is one of two species of monotremes, or egg-laying mammals, that live in Australia.*), *egg-laying mammals* can be seen as a definition for *monotremes*. Using definition this way enables the author to focus on the information presented in the main clause (i.e., *The echidna is one of two species of monotremes that live in Australia.*), without drawing too much of the reader's attention to the definition for monotremes. In other words, the definition here provides the information that is not central to the text but that the author thinks the reader may need or be interested in knowing. Had a separate sentence been used to present the definition (*Monotremes are egg-laying mammals.*), the definition will appear just as equal in importance as the other piece of information (i.e., *The echidna is one of two species of monotremes.*). This may defuse the focus of the text and disrupt the semantic flow of information, especially when your focus is on the echidna specifically, rather than on monotremes as a whole.

Similarly, in the last two examples above, the appositive phrases (i.e., *the process of adjusting to a new or non-native culture, an architect who was beginning to be recognized for his imaginative ideas*) are introduced by a dash (–) or a comma (,) and used to define a term (*acculturation*) or characterize an individual (*Eero Saarinen*). The definition or characterization is not the emphasis of either sentence. It provides ancillary information that is of less importance than the information presented in the main clause of the sentence. Had either appositive phrase been turned into an independent clause, the information presented in the main clause of the original sentence (*Acculturation is perhaps best illustrated by the four phases of [...]; Eero Saarinen heard of the contest and decided to enter it.*) will no longer be accentuated. Moreover, it may disrupt the flow from one sentence to the next.

Another interesting example is the use of the non-finite clause (also called participial phrase or participle clause elsewhere in this book) to introduce a definition. In one of the examples above, <u>*known as*</u> *the Flynn effect* indicates that the definition for the term *the Flynn effect* is provided in the preceding term (*this rise*), which in turn summarizes the information presented in the prior sentence (*Average raw scores on IQ tests have been rising for years, by an estimated three IQ points per decade*). An alternative way to define "the Flynn effect" would be to say that it refers to "the rise in average raw scores on IQ tests by an estimated three IQ points per decade". By defining the term formally in such a stand-alone sentence, you are implying that the information provided in the definition is important and that your readers should pay attention to it. The reason a formal definition like this is not used in the example above is that definition is not a focus for the author. Instead, the definition is provided in passing, so to speak, similar to what you would normally say in speech as "by the way, this rise is called the Flynn effect, in case you want to know". It is not a point you intend to emphasize in the text.

Taken together, these examples illustrate that whichever linguistic device you choose to define a term depends on not only what you want to foreground or emphasize but also the information flow of the text. Typically, what you place at the beginning of a sentence is the information you want to foreground and that connects with the preceding sentence in some way to form a cohesive chain of discourse.

Sometimes, one sentence may not suffice to define and clarify a concept because it is so central, complex, or controversial. This means that you will need to elaborate on the one-sentence definition in order to give your readers a clearer and more complete understanding of the concept. In Text 4-1 from Fang (2015, p. 105), the first sentence defines the central concept "genre" and subsequent sentences not only elaborate on what is said in the initial sentence (e.g., *social, goal-oriented, staged*) but also provide additional information that helps clarify the concept.

Text 4-1

Genre is a term used in systemic functional linguistics to refer to particular text types that "represent the system of staged, goal oriented social processes through which social subjects in a given culture live their lives" (Martin, 1997: 13). Genres are social in the sense that they are created by people in their social interaction with each other; they are goal oriented in that they exist to serve specific purposes; and they are staged because it usually takes more than one step for people to achieve their goals. Genres are also flexible and subject to manipulation in that they tend to respond to changes in people's ways of life and cultural worldviews, as well as to the immediate situational context and participants' intentions. At the same time, however, genres are predictable and recognizable because they are "recurrent configurations of meaning" in a culture (Martin, 2009: 19). Thus, while the exact shape, or textual realization, of a genre can vary from one instance to another and change across contexts and over time, each genre has a constellation of specifiable discursive conventions that derive from and encode the functions, purposes, and meanings of a particular social occasion (Kress, 1989). These conventions are what render a genre recognizable and distinctive from other genres.

Similarly, in Text 4-2 from *Harvard Law Review* (Anonymous, 2020, p. 2101), the first sentence defines the term "Ponzi scheme" and the rest of the paragraph elaborates on the concept. This creates an extended definition that gives readers a more complete understanding of the concept.

Text 4-2

The term "Ponzi scheme" refers to a class of frauds in which the fraudster promises above-market returns on investments in an investment fund or business enterprise. Unbeknownst to victims, the fraudster's fund or enterprise exists only on paper: no trades are being made, no goods are being produced or sold. Instead, the fraudster fabricates records or other evidence documenting the purported success of the fund or enterprise. Because the nature of a Ponzi scheme is to operate in a state of prolonged insolvency, the collapse of a Ponzi scheme frequently results in bankruptcy proceedings.

Classifying and Categorizing

In writing for academic purposes, you sometimes need to sort related ideas, methods, people, objects, or parts into specific groups or categories that share common characteristics. This means that academic writing may involve classification and categorization of things. When classifying or categorizing, you will need to identify the things that belong to the same group (or have the same characteristics) and then describe each of the things one by one. There are a variety of language resources that you can use to help you accomplish this task, as the following examples show:

- As shown in Table 1, <u>six basic dimensions</u> describe the cultural orientations of societies: [...].
- There are <u>two generalized expectancies</u>. <u>One of these</u> involves [...]. <u>The second kind</u> deals with [...].
- We <u>categorized</u> those <u>according to</u> political, social, cultural, and economic issues.
- <u>Three scenarios</u> were chosen to [...]. <u>Scenario A</u> corresponds to [...], and <u>scenario B</u> holds [...]. <u>Scenario C</u> is a derivation of scenario B in which [...].
- The discussion also brings to the fore <u>the following</u>: <u>(1)</u> [...]; <u>(2)</u> [...]; and <u>(3)</u> [...].
- The technicality of the expository excerpt <u>is constructed by two types of words</u>: <u>those</u> that [...] and <u>those</u> that [...].
- Historically, the shift from [...] to [...] can <u>be classified into three periods</u>.

- The references <u>are organized into several sections</u>: (1) [...]; (2) [...]; (3) [...]; and (4) [...].
- <u>Two general methods</u> can be used. <u>One method</u>, referred to as [...], is used to [...]. <u>A second, more generally used, method</u> is the so-called "block maximum" method.
- Each of these consists of <u>several subtypes</u>: [...], [...], [...], and [...].
- For the analysis, respondents <u>were split into three groups based on</u> their annual turnover.
- We <u>classified</u> our participants <u>in accordance with</u> the criteria established by the IRA.
- On the basis of their preferred walking speed, subjects <u>were classified as</u> high or low performing.
- The Finnish tests <u>were composed of five tasks</u>: <u>two</u> on [...], <u>two</u> on [...], and <u>one</u> on [...].
- <u>Of the six instances</u> of [...], <u>half</u> were [...], <u>two</u> were [...], and <u>one</u> was [...].
- A language demand <u>is categorized as</u> either [...] or an [...] <u>based on</u> whether the demand is fundamental to [...].
- The interview <u>was divided into three main sections</u>, <u>corresponding roughly to</u> the three research questions. <u>The first part</u> of the interview focused on [...]. <u>The second part</u> of the interview was concerned with [...]. <u>The third and final part</u> of the interview took [...].
- Most people with [...] <u>fall into the category of</u> [...], <u>with</u> IQs ranging between [...] and [...]. <u>Other categories</u> of intellectual disability <u>are</u> [...], [...], and [...].
- Traffic congestion and emissions are <u>two main types</u> of social cost.
- <u>Three qualifications</u> apply. <u>First,</u> [...]. <u>Second,</u> [...]. <u>Third,</u> [...].
- The VTAM <u>comprises two features</u>. <u>Firstly,</u> [...]. <u>Secondly,</u> [...].
- <u>There are two types of</u> control that have been used: [...]. <u>Some</u> focus on [...]. <u>Others</u> only address [...].
- Traffic simulations <u>can be broadly classified by</u> the type of road network and features they can stimulate. <u>The two main classes</u> for simulators are [...] and [...].
- A review of the literature in this area suggests that relevant studies <u>converge on three major issues</u>. <u>The first issue</u> is [...]. <u>The second issue</u> is [...]. <u>The third issue</u> is [...].
- Each tooth <u>has three parts</u>: the crown, the root, and the pulp cavity.
- Lavas <u>may be divided into two contrasting types</u>, acid and basic.
- It affects all the <u>three dimensions of sustainability</u>, <u>i.e.,</u> economic, environmental, and social, simultaneously.

Describing

Sometimes you will need to describe things or processes in your writing. In describing things, you present the attributes of an object, such as length, weight, position, size, shape, color, texture, structure, location, or function. Having a range of linguistic resources for describing these attributes helps you make your writing more fluent and more vivid, enabling your readers to "picture" the object. For example, when describing the length of a football field, you can say any of the following:

- The field is 53 feet long.
- The length of the field is 53 feet.
- The field is/measures 53 feet in length.
- The field has a length of 53 feet.
- Fifty-three feet is the length of the field.
- the 53-foot field
- The field, which is 53 feet long, [...].

Whichever language pattern you choose will depend on what you want to foreground (i.e., the field or its length), whether the same sentence structure has been used earlier, and how it fits within the flow of information in the text.

Many linguistic resources are useful for describing things, as they enable you to pack a large quantity of information into the sentence. These include linking verbs that connect the thing being described with its attributes (e.g., *comprise, is made of, consist of, is, have, include, show, contain, represent, range, register*) and prepositional phrases indicating location (e.g., *outside, inside, in, at, of, with, for, by, below, around, above, below*), as well as appositive phrases, expanded noun phrases, adverbs, adverbial phrases, participial phrases, and embedded clauses that serve to elaborate on the entity being described. Metaphors and similes (e.g., *The brain looks like a lump of porridge.*) are also effective in providing vivid descriptions. In these descriptions, hedging devices such as *approximately, roughly, about, usually, slightly*, and *less than* are often used to be accurate and precise. Listed below are sentences that describe various aspects of things.

- The first section consisted of a double-matrix containing 12 statements representing a sampling of youth development activities [...].
- The affected person is usually of short stature: 145–160 cm for adults, birth weight usually 10–20% below normal.
- Each tooth has three parts: [...], [...], and [...]. The crown is [...], which is outside the gum. It is covered with [...]. The ivory-colored internal part of the crown below the enamel is [...]. The root of a tooth is embedded in the jaw and covered by a [...]. The pulp cavity in the center of the tooth contains [...].
- The apparatus consisted of a large wooden box 180 cm high, 136 cm wide, and 66 cm deep.
- External examination revealed a 2-cm sutured wound on the left side of mid of the frontal area, 8.7 cm above the left eyebrow.

- Their ages ranged from 17 to 42, with most in their early 20s.
- Two teachers co-taught this class of 23 ninth-grade students on a regular basis, approximately three times per week.
- Brain growth occurs early in life: By age 6, the human brain reaches approximately 95% of its maximum size. The overall mass size of the brain peaks at age 10.5 for girls and age 14.5 for boys.
- All the schools in Beijing and Hong Kong adopted whole-class instruction, with students sitting in rows facing the teacher and the teacher leading all the activities in the classroom.
- Public transportation is provided on a network topologically congruent with the road network at a constant (usage-independent) speed of 40 km/h.
- The laboratory road network, shown in Figure 2, is defined for a circular city with a radius of 16 km.
- Because of the difference in width of the images taken from the digital and video camera, only the pixel height was equalized. This produced pairs of images with a height of 240 pixels at 72 pixels per inch.
- The 24 oblique axial slices were 3.8 mm thick with an in-plane resolution of 3.75×3.75 mm.
- Example 4 was by Fabian, a doctoral student in electric engineering who took [...].
- This bunny has a triangular body-shape with distinctive black and chocolate-brown markings on his rump and around his eyes. He had dark eyes and a nose that twitched continuously, and his long, droopy ears were eye-catching.
- The brain looks like a lump of porridge and has the consistency of blancmange. This organ, weighing an average 1,400g in an adult human, is [...]. It contains an estimated 10 to 100 billion [...] and about as many [...], which [...]. The brain contains many different types of [...] which differ in shape, size and the kinds of chemicals they produce.
- A 2.14 m (7 ft) core from a burial depth of 172.55–174.69 m (565–572 ft) below the earth's surface was obtained.

Describing processes involves noting how a method works or how a sequence unfolds. When describing a process, temporal sequence can be expressed not only through *first*, *second*, and *third*, but also through a range of other linguistic resources (e.g., *to begin with*, *next*, *also*, *a further step*, *another*, *the next step*, *first of all*, *previously*, *at the same time*, *subsequently*, *follow*, *ensue*, *later*, *prior to this*, *until*, *in the following stage*, *soon/shortly/immediately after*, *when*, *upon*, *as soon as*, *after*, *finally*, *eventually*, *over the next decade*, *during the 20th century*, *some 50 years ago*, or *concludes with*). Adverbs (e.g., *slowly*, *carefully*, *haltingly*) and prepositional phrases (e.g., *in a slow manner*, *with utmost care*, *from a distance*, *through the tunnel*) can be used to indicate the manner in which the process unfolds.

Another useful, though often misunderstood, device for describing process is passive voice. In describing how something happened, you may not need or want to mention the agent behind each happening because you either do not know or you do not think it is important for your readers to know who/what the agent is. In such cases, passive voice can be used, as it enables you to background or bury the agent behind an action (see also Chapter 2). For example, you can say *The survey was conducted online*, instead of *The researchers conducted the survey online*. The former allows you to focus on the data collection method (*the survey*), whereas in the latter, the focus becomes *the researchers*.

The issue of what you choose to foreground or emphasize in your message is also relevant when describing your purpose for a particular process. When the purpose statement (e.g., *to, in order to, so as to, so that*) is placed at the beginning of a sentence, it means that you want to emphasize the purpose of the process; on the other hand, when purpose is not an emphasis, the purpose statement is usually positioned at the end of the sentence (except when such placement results in a cumbersome expression that obscures the meaning), as the following examples illustrate:

- <u>To prevent potential order effects</u>, the questionnaire order was counterbalanced.
- The questionnaire order was counterbalanced <u>to prevent potential order effects</u>.
- <u>To create the tunnels</u>, work crews first floated their drilling equipment on barges downstream from where the dam was to be located.
- ?? Work crews first floated their drilling equipment on barges downstream from where the dam was to be located <u>to create the tunnels.</u>

Sample sentences that describe processes are presented below, with linguistic markers of description highlighted. As can be seen in these examples, passive voice is the predominant choice in process descriptions.

- <u>After</u> a pilot test with a small sample of students, adjustments were made.
- A mixed-method design was implemented. Subjects were <u>first provided</u> with a mail questionnaire, <u>followed by</u> an electronic questionnaire...
- <u>Following</u> the mode choice, <u>the next step</u> is to assign traffic to the routes.
- Children were instructed to construct a shared design. <u>After completion</u>, children could roll the marbles down the maze.
- <u>In order to</u> allow for comparability, the most syntactically succinct idea unit was entered into the table <u>first</u>, <u>and then</u> the other ideas units were mapped against this one.
- Every infant who came into the lab <u>first</u> completed the behavioral task <u>and then</u> the ERP task.
- Translation of a sensory profile <u>was completed using six steps</u>. <u>First</u>, [...]. <u>Then</u>, [...].

- A typical process of the electrophotography <u>consists of six steps</u>: <u>(i)</u>. [...], <u>(ii)</u>, [...], <u>(iii)</u>, [...].
- There were <u>two phrases</u> in the procedures of this project. <u>In the first phase</u>, [...]. <u>In the second phase</u>, [...].
- <u>First</u>, the interview transcriptions were coded. <u>Then</u> the coded segments were constantly compared [...], <u>and finally</u>, the concepts and themes were [...].
- The course of the physical impairment is progressive. <u>Initially</u>, boys with DMD appear to be [...]. <u>At ages 2 to 3</u>, slight motor impairments appear [...]. Difficulties such as [...] become increasingly apparent, and diagnosis usually occurs <u>around age 5</u>. <u>As</u> muscles continue to weaken, the boys begin to walk stiffly, [...]. <u>By age 12</u>, boys with DMD usually require a wheelchair.
- Figure 2 presents the CAT algorithm used for our ICF Activity Measure. <u>First</u>, the CAT <u>begins with</u> [...]. <u>Once</u> the initial item is presented, [...] a new person ability measure [...] is generated. [...] <u>Based on that response</u>, the person ability measure is re-calculated. <u>This process continues until</u> [...]. <u>Once</u> the stopping rule is satisfied, the respondent's final ability measure [...] is generated. <u>If</u> there are [...], <u>the next construct</u> [...] is presented. The CAT <u>finally ends when</u> the respondent [...].
- Participants [...] were instructed to read [...]. <u>After reading</u> the informed consent document, participants individually completed [...]. Participants <u>then</u> completed a surprise online recall task [...]. <u>Following</u> the recall task, participants completed another [...]. <u>After</u> completing the second questionnaire, participants were individually given [...].
- We <u>began by</u> "open coding" or going line by line to [...]. <u>Next</u>, we developed a chart of [...]. We <u>then</u> moved on to axial coding <u>in which</u> we tested the relationship [...] <u>by</u> independently [...].
- Each task <u>started with</u> instructions <u>followed by</u> a short practice block. The experimenter verified that [...] <u>before</u> they started [...]. Participants were instructed to [...] <u>as quickly and accurately as</u> they could.

Explaining

In academic writing, you will sometimes need to explain an emerging phenomenon, a unique pattern, a popular trend, or a surprising finding. You may also need to justify a particular action or claim. Thus, you should be prepared to construct cause-effect relations in your writing. In English, causal relations can be realized in many different ways (see also Chapter 2). The most familiar way is the use of conjunctions (e.g., *because, so*) or conjunctive adverbs (e.g., *thus, therefore, hence*). There are also less explicit ways of realizing causation. These include other conjunctions such as *unless, when, and, as,* and *if*, as well as adverbs (e.g., *consequently, hence, resultantly*), verbs (e.g., *ensue, engender, follow, trigger, cause, give rise to, lead to, contribute to, bring about, result in, explain, can/ could + verb*), prepositions (e.g., *with, for, from, due to, by, and, owing to, thanks to, as a result of, as a consequence, because of*), nouns (e.g., *reason, cause, result, effect, consequence*), and even clauses (e.g., the nonfinite clause). The linguistic resources (underlined) that can be used to construct cause-effect relations are demonstrated below:

- <u>By</u> building a relationship with the central office, we feel we can create a pipeline of students for [...].
- The first two strategies occur naturally and are <u>therefore</u> quite common.
- Teachers noted that their roles were altered, <u>as</u> more teaming and collaboration occurred.
- This kind of description also <u>resulted in</u> rather fragmented views, however. <u>Consequently</u>, I conducted even more detailed analysis by constructing [...].
- These shortcomings make it more difficult to [...] <u>because</u> it is unclear [...].
- Teachers' fear that [...] may also be <u>a cause of</u> reluctance to accept inclusion.
- Cummins (2001) suggests that <u>when</u> teachers affirm the identities of children in the classroom, students become engaged in their own learning.
- One problem is coral bleaching, which occurs <u>when</u> a coral becomes stressed <u>and</u> expels most of its colorful algae.
- These earlier analyses provided insight [...]. <u>Thus</u>, in this paper we chose to explore [...].
- Social class differences are prominent struggles among Latin Americans; <u>therefore</u>, it is not surprising that [...].
- The analysis further identified [...]. <u>As a result of</u> this analysis, [...].
- It is useful here to define literacy, <u>since</u> it is through literacy that academic English is advanced.
- Assessment of ELL students' academic performance has <u>resulted</u> less <u>from</u> a concern with [...] than <u>from</u> [...].
- Storm surges could <u>cause</u> saltwater intrusion and <u>result in</u> increased estuarine salinity, <u>thus affecting</u> oyster growth and production.
- <u>Given this increase</u>, it is vital for teacher education program to [...].
- <u>Given that</u> there is no behavioral evidence [...], this paper treats all the solutions equally of the same merit.
- <u>Consequently</u>, students in more developed parts of the world [...].
- Topoclimates are <u>the effects of</u> aspect, slope, relative elevation, and others [...].
- <u>Because of</u> the growing number of ELLs, all teachers need to [...].
- It was found that the addition is the dominant <u>contributor</u> in simulating flow-vegetation interaction [...].
- The above MTE scenario in Kenya is <u>a result of</u> cumulative policy omissions.
- Characteristics of crashes <u>attributed to</u> the driver having fallen asleep include [...].

- <u>Due to</u> constraints imposed by the school, the study was performed with no control group.
- Varying language in research reports more often than not <u>leads to</u> confusion.
- Both types of variation could be <u>accounted for by</u> difficulties students had in comprehending specific linguistic forms...
- The difficulty will <u>depend on</u> the particular lexical items that are used.
- Nearly 60% of the world's coral reefs <u>are threatened by</u> human activities.
- This loss of algae <u>exposes</u> the colorless coral animals [...].
- <u>Unable to grow or repair themselves</u>, the corals eventually die <u>unless</u> the stress is removed.
- More than one-fourth of the world's coral reefs have been <u>lost to</u> coastal development [...].
- <u>With</u> this amazing sensitivity, dogs can detect countless aromas [...].
- This <u>explains why</u> the biggest long-term threat [...].
- One <u>resulting</u> problem is coral bleaching.
- It absorbs some of the carbon dioxide produced mostly <u>by</u> the burning of fossil fuels.
- This <u>could raise</u> the water temperature.
- <u>Without food</u>, the coral polyps then die, <u>leaving behind a white skeleton of calcium carbonate</u>.
- Other modes are there as well. <u>As a consequence</u>, a linguistic theory cannot provide a full account of...
- <u>For these reasons</u>, it is important to analyze the impact of land use [...].
- The main <u>reason for</u> its poor performance is <u>attributed to</u> its search direction...
- <u>A possible explanation for</u> this phenomenon is that ...
- The reported high prevalence of [...] could have been <u>explained by</u> either greater persistence [...].
- <u>One reason</u> that educational aims must be researched is the concepts we use are contestable.
- At some point in their career, over 90% of music teachers will <u>incur</u> voice problems <u>as a direct result of</u> their jobs.
- Phonological working memory could be one mechanism <u>responsible for</u> differences in language proficiency...

Which linguistic device to use for causal explanation depends on what you want to emphasize (cause or effect) and on whether the resulting sentence facilitates the discursive flow. In some cases (e.g., *when, as, if*), cause and time/condition conflate. Having a range of linguistic options for constructing causal relations gives you the flexibility to vary sentence structure in your writing and the power to fashion effective explanation texts that serve your needs. In the following two excerpts, one from a history textbook (Faragher, Buhle, Czitrom, & Armitage, 2007, p. 513) and the other from a science trade book (Wilson,

2014, p. 125), the causes and effects of the Panic of 1857 and the loss of biodiversity in Mozambique's war-torn Gorongosa National Park are explained using an assortment of linguistic devices (see the underlined).

Text 4-3

Adding to the growing political tension was the short, but sharp, depression of 1857 and 1858. Technology played a part. In August 1857, the failure of an Ohio investment house—the kind of event that had formerly taken weeks to be widely known—was the subject of a news story flashed immediately over telegraph wires to Wall Street and other financial markets. A wave of panic selling ensued, leading to business failures and slowdowns that threw thousands out of work. The major cause of the panic was a sharp, but temporary, downturn in agricultural exports to Britain, and recovery was well under way by early 1859. Because it affected cotton exports less than northern exports, the Panic of 1857 was less harmful to the South than to the North.

Text 4-4

The loss of a single tree species often results in the elimination of multiple moth, beetle, and other insect species dependent on it. Similarly, the disappearance of a key pollinator can threaten multiple plant species. When honeybees recently suffered a die-off, probably from a combination of pesticides and inbreeding, some crops dependent on their services declined with them. When such symbioses are tight and highly specific, as between some tropical orchids and euglossine bees, the extinction of one partner means doom for the other.

Exemplifying

Academic writing requires that authors provide support for their ideas, claims, or arguments. One way you can do this is to include examples to make your thoughts more concrete, practical, and comprehensible to the reader. An example is a case or an instance of something. It is usually the best (and easiest) way to make your writing specific and interesting. However, examples cannot be compiled into a laundry list, as they will not be effective in substantiating your claims or generalizations. Whatever examples you give need to be artfully introduced into the text. This means that you need to select words or phrases that can help you integrate examples with the rest of the text in a way that makes your points clear and tangible and is at the same time connected with the rest of the text. A range of devices can be used for this purpose (see below). The placement of the linguistic markers of exemplification in each sentence can vary depending on the flow and emphasis of the text.

- Consider this example: 86% of students [...] identify more as a performer than a teacher.
- To illustrate this point, Bauer pointed to the results of [...].
- For example, third-year music majors often spend much more time [...].
- The system optimal problem could, for instance, be used as a benchmark to [...].
- A vivid example of tactical waiting was observed on the first day of [...].
- A case in point is the recently developed instrument called Rover.
- Much of the research within this field has examined [...]. One such study was conducted by Engelmann (2009) who [...].
- Specifically, models such as [...] are fit, where *i* indexes individuals and *j* indexes subclasses.
- Examples of these difficulties include [...].
- An example of a yielding fluid is toothpaste, which will not [...].
- Exemplifying this tendency, Settlage (2009) found that [...].
- The item behaves differently for people in different groups (e.g., culture, age, or gender).
- These beliefs include, but are not limited to, fears, stereotypes [...].
- A, B, and C are all examples of good deeds.
- To provide an example of a win-win or win-lose situation: [...].
- As an illustration, take the decision of how to allocate capital resources [...].
- Pavlenko's work, for example, captures [...].
- As an example, a system might offer [...].
- These approaches, as exemplified by naturalistic decision-making research, have [...].
- With reference to a specific example, it is shown that [...].
- To illustrate further, [...].
- Schwinge provided an example of just this [...].
- A topic like food safety is important [...].
- Advertising campaigns, including public service announcements, would help [...].
- It seems that someone always wants to know of technology making a difference. Sometimes it is a legislator [...]. Sometimes it is the college [...]. Sometimes it is the provost [...].
- Exemplars are highly typical instances. In the case of a dog, a person might compare a new animal to exemplars such as a collie, a poodle, or other typical dogs.
- The Amazon region emerged as a reserve for potential milk producers seeking to grow their operations, some of which were companies with headquarters in south Brazil.
- The proceeds from the sales will help fund our mission, namely, improving school safety.
- All mammals, excluding humans, stop drinking milk at a young age.

- Unhealthy snacks are bad for you. <u>As proof,</u> long-term use of energy bars has been found to be associated with obesity.
- The strategy will reap many benefits. <u>In particular,</u> it will increase the revenue for the company.
- Onboarding has a huge impact on retention rate. <u>Pretend/imagine</u> new employees could [...]. What impact would that have on their performance?

Comparing and Contrasting

Comparing and contrasting is regularly needed in academic writing. For example, synthesizing prior research literature often requires that you compare and/or contrast the studies being summarized. Through comparing, you are examining similarities among things (e.g., theories, models, approaches, methods, concepts, objects, findings); and to contrast, you strive to illuminate how these things are different from one another. You can compare/contrast using a point-by-point structure or a block structure (Gillett, Hammond, & Martala, 2009). For the point-by-point structure, each similarity or difference for one thing is immediately followed by that for the other thing (i.e., Point 1 for Thing A–Point 1 for Thing B, Point 2 for Thing A–Point 2 for Thing B, Point 3 for Thing A–Point 3 for Thing B, ...). For the block structure, all the information about one thing is presented and then all the information about the other thing is presented next, with comparison/contrast implied by the order of presentation (i.e., Points 1, 2, and 3 for Thing A–Points 1, 2, and 3 for Thing B).

Presented below are two sample texts, composed based on the information gleaned from several web sources, that use different methods of comparing/contrasting. In Text 4-5a, bacteria and viruses are compared and contrasted using the block structure. In Text 4-5b, the two pathogens are compared and contrasted using the point-by-point structure. Either method of organization has its own pros and cons. The block structure is easier to write but specific points of similarity/difference tend to be more difficult to discern. The point-by-point structure makes the points of similarity/difference clear but can be challenging to do, as it requires skillful management of transitions from one point of similarity/difference to the next without incurring cumbersome repetition. Whichever one you choose to employ will depend on your purpose and language proficiency.

Text 4-5a

Bacteria are single-celled, prokaryotic microorganisms that exist in abundance in both living hosts and in all areas of the planet (e.g., soil, water). Most of their bodies consist of cytoplasm, a gooey organic substance in which biochemical processes take place. They have a cell wall and all the components necessary to survive and reproduce, although some may derive energy from other sources. Most bacteria are beneficial for our good health and the health of Earth's ecosystems. Less than 1% of bacteria cause disease. Antibiotics may be used to treat some bacterial infections, but antivirals are not effective against bacteria.

Viruses are much simpler. They are small compared to bacteria. They are tiny infectious agents that replicate only inside the living cells of other organisms. They are not considered to be "living" because they require a host cell to survive long-term and to reproduce. They consist of only one piece of genetic material and a protein shell called a capsid. They survive and reproduce by "hijacking" a host cell, and using its ribosomes to make new viral proteins. Most viruses cause disease. Antibiotics do not work against viruses. Vaccination is the primary way to prevent viral infections. However, antivirals have recently been engineered that can treat some viral infections, such as Hepatitis C or HIV.

Text 4-5b

Bacteria and viruses are both microscopic microbes that contain enzymes and can cause diseases in humans, animals, and plants. They differ in their structure and in their response to medications. With respect to structure, bacteria are single-celled, prokaryotic microorganisms that exist in abundance in both living hosts and in all areas of the planet (e.g., soil, water). Most of their bodies consist of cytoplasm, a gooey organic substance in which biochemical processes take place. They have a cell wall and all the components necessary to survive and reproduce, although some may derive energy from other sources. Viruses, on the other hand, are smaller than bacteria. They are tiny infectious agents that replicate only inside the living cells of other organisms. They are not considered to be "living" because they require a host cell to survive long-term and to reproduce. They consist of only one piece of genetic material and a protein shell called a capsid. They survive and reproduce by "hijacking" a host cell, and using its ribosomes to make new viral proteins.

Because of their structural differences, the two pathogens affect us differently and are treated differently. Most bacteria are beneficial for our good health and the health of Earth's ecosystems. In fact, less than 1% of bacteria cause disease. By contrast, most viruses cause disease. Antibiotics may be used to treat some bacterial infections, but they do not work against viruses. Some severe bacterial infections may be prevented by vaccination. On the contrary, vaccination is the primary way to prevent viral infections. Antivirals have also been engineered that can treat some viral infections, such as Hepatitis C or HIV. They are, however, not effective against bacteria.

Listed below are some templates that show how comparison/contrast can be signaled linguistically:

- As with any other baby animal, the skull of our sauropod embryos was large in proportion to its body, [...]. Likewise, the eye socket in our embryos was probably slightly larger in relation to the rest of skull than the eye socket in adult sauropod.

- Racial violence was <u>relatively</u> rare. <u>In general</u>, the quality of life [...] was <u>significantly better</u> for blacks and whites in Chicago <u>than</u> it was in most Southern cities.
- <u>Whereas</u> teleological and deontological theories approach ethics by [...], a second set of theories approaches ethics from [...].
- <u>In contrast with</u> mentee selection, mentor criteria tended to be more general.
- <u>Unlike</u> the "great man" approach, which implies [...], the skills approach suggests that [...].
- <u>Like</u> all other approaches to leadership, the skills approach also has certain weaknesses.
- Results of [...] revealed that, <u>in contrast to</u> add-on programs [...], teachers stated that [...].
- Some scholars view [...] as no more than [...]; <u>rather</u>, they view [...] as intertwined with [...].
- <u>In fact</u>, there is <u>a contrast between</u> [...] <u>and</u> [...].
- Gaungxi has [...], <u>more than tripling</u> [...] in Beijing [...]. <u>However</u>, Guangxi has only [...], <u>less than half</u> of the [...] boasted by Beijing.
- The second experiment shows that [...] exhibit <u>greater</u> VDP <u>as compared to</u> [...].
- <u>Conversely</u>, the Japanese reading test results indicate [...].
- <u>Compared with</u> the GRE norm, 70% of [...] obtained <u>higher</u> scores.
- <u>On the contrary</u>, students [...] show neither positive nor negative effects [...].
- It is supported by the findings of various empirical studies (<u>cf.</u>, Pienemann, Johnston, & Brindley, 1988).
- HBCUs strive to [...], including building welcoming communities <u>as opposed to</u> communities of marginalization.
- The report text, <u>on the other hand</u>, shows a zig-zagging pattern [...].
- The most important rule [...] is that I write in large blocks of time <u>rather than</u> smaller ones.
- IRT <u>differs from</u> CCT in a number of important aspects. <u>First, while</u> CTT [...], IRT [...]. <u>Second, while</u> [...] is constant [...], the [...] under IRT varies [...]. <u>Third</u>, and probably <u>most important</u>, [...].
- The [...] model is <u>somewhat similar to</u> [...] model.
- Findings from our study <u>are consistent with</u> (or <u>contrast with</u>) prior research on [...].
- In our model, the relative efficiency of [...] decreases with [...]. This is <u>opposite to</u> the conclusion of the previous studies.
- The present study involved two programs designed to [...]. The typing program taught [...]. The keypad program <u>was similar to</u> the typing program <u>but</u> was designed to [...].
- <u>Along the same line</u>, Schmidt's study found [...].
- <u>Likewise/similarly</u>, Bauder's study confirmed [...].
- <u>Another distinction can be drawn between</u> [...] <u>and</u> [...].
- Together, these results <u>contradict</u> the idea that [...].

- <u>The opposite</u> holds true for private tolling.
- <u>Consistent with</u> the studies reviewed earlier, the <u>second-best</u> toll is <u>much lower than</u> the <u>first-best</u>.
- <u>The major difference between the two proteins</u> is that [...].
- <u>Before</u> instruction, 78% of the students [...]. <u>After</u> instruction, 97% of the students [...].

Referencing Visuals

In today's textual world, visuals (e.g., graphs, tables, photos, charts, maps, diagrams) have become an increasingly popular and even necessary meaning-making resource (Kress & van Leeuwen, 2006). Generally, diagrams, maps, pie charts, graphs, and photos are referred to as figures, and tables and word charts are referred to as tables. In academic writing, visuals supplement rather than duplicate the linguistic prose, and they are placed as close as possible to the point in the text where they are first introduced. The two resources—linguistic and visual—are expected to work in a complementary, harmonious fashion to communicate specific aspects of a message effectively.

Learning how to integrate the visuals with the linguistic prose is thus an important skill in academic writing. You are expected to learn to integrate multimedia seamlessly and to reinterpret and recontextualize the information in one modality in relation to that in other modalities. This means you need to develop the linguistic, symbolic, visual, and technological resources that will enable you to foreground or background certain information, refer back and forth between the verbal and the visual-symbolic without sounding redundant or incoherent, advance your argument, and achieve clarity in writing.

One way to integrate the visuals strategically and seamlessly into prose is to develop a repertoire of linguistic resources for referring to the visuals in the text so that readers can make easier connections between the two modalities. Some of these linguistic resources (underlined) are presented below. Whichever device you choose and where you place it in the sentence (beginning, middle, or end) will depend on how it fits into your text to create an overall flow and specific emphasis.

- <u>As shown in Figure 1</u>, transactional leaders serve to [...].
- <u>As illustrated on the left side of Figure 11.1</u>, the practice of leadership requires that [...].
- Several comprehensive models for [...] have been developed, including GERMS model (<u>see Table 3-1</u>).
- <u>This is referenced in the bottom of Table 5.1</u>, called "Variance of [...]", <u>where</u> the variance error is computed [...].

- The major themes that emerged <u>are included in Table 4</u>.
- <u>Table 2 below summarizes</u> the progress [...].
- Students also have to be able to [...], <u>as in the rectangular prism presented in Figure 1</u>.
- We called this model of bilingualism recursive, <u>as rendered in Figure 3.3</u>.
- Students then develop a visual display <u>like that in Figure 2</u>.
- <u>It is obvious from Figure 32</u> that some approximations are better [...].
- A comparison between [...] and [...], <u>displayed in Figure 13b</u>, show the extent and degree of inundation [...].
- <u>Figure 4 illustrates</u> this by showing [...].
- <u>From Table 6</u>, the link choice probabilities <u>given in Table 7</u> are obtained.
- <u>It is shown in Figure 1</u> that the growth rate [...].
- <u>In Table 1</u>, I have summarized key points relating to [...].
- <u>As noted in Table 1</u>, establishing the truth [...].
- It may help to think of each sentence [...], <u>as the figure below suggests</u>.
- <u>Figure 8.2 sketches out</u> some judgement-criteria comparisons [...].
- The themes for the three reports <u>are listed in Table 7</u>.
- <u>As can be seen in Table 1</u>, the 60-right respondents were about evenly divided [...].
- <u>Please refer to Table 1.1 for</u> an overview of key factors [...].
- Schematically, <u>this may be represented in Figure 1</u>.
- One representation of the teaching-learning cycle <u>is depicted in Figure 1</u>.
- The variables measured in this analysis <u>are described in Table 1</u>.
- <u>This figure suggests/indicates</u> that all of the propensity [...].
- The results across the six outcome variables <u>are presented in detail in Table 6</u>.
- The MPA also revealed increases in [...], <u>as shown/illustrated in Figure 5</u>.
- <u>As the above table shows</u>, vocabulary strategies such as [...].
- Lemma 1 may <u>be visualized through Figures 1 and 2</u>.
- <u>With reference to Table 1</u>, it will be clear these are serious shortcomings [...].
- <u>The graphic below is intended to convey</u> the growth of car exports [...].
- The results <u>demonstrated in Table 2</u> indicated a statistically significant difference in [...].
- <u>Figure 2</u> reports that [...].
- <u>Figure 5.7 displays/represents</u> the parameters for each item [...].
- <u>According to Figure 2.2</u>, Finland has about 6% between-school variance [...].
- <u>Table 1</u>, which summarizes these observations, <u>presents</u> land values (2010) for cropland [...].
- The upshot of this multi-scale investment process has been a precipitous decline in transportation costs, <u>as documented by Figure 1</u>. <u>This figure</u>, developed with a GIS application (see Appendix), <u>shows</u> hours of travel time [...].
- An example would be the hypothetical map of one student's concept of sports in <u>Figure 9.1</u>, <u>which illustrates</u> the relationship among the various concepts.

Entertaining Opposition

In academic writing, it is usually a good idea to acknowledge the opposition that counters your points of view. Mentioning the opposing view and addressing it directly does not undermine your credibility; instead, it shows that you are well informed and sophisticated (Graff & Birkenstein, 2018). As the old Chinese saying goes, backing up one step (i.e., making a concession) means moving two steps forward (i.e., making gains in argument). As a novice writer, you may have the wishful thinking that if you do not bring up the opposing view, your readers would not know and may then be more willing to buy into your argument. The opposite is in fact true. Informed readers are likely to dismiss your essay as biased or uninformed if you intentionally exclude the opposing views.

To discuss a topic or issue thoroughly and to convince your readers, you will need to represent (potential) objections fairly and then answer them directly and persuasively. Tackling each point of an objection enables you to put to rest opposing views, and this helps you advance your own argument. Instead of mocking the opposition or simply dismissing it as irrelevant or wrong, you need to walk your readers through your reasoning, pointing out in what ways the opposing view is wrong, misguided, extreme, irrelevant, illogical, or not tenable. In your critique of the opposing view, you need to be measured in tone and in logical reasoning so that it does not come across as brash, unreasonable, zealous, or uncivilized. The hedging devices mentioned in Chapter 3 are useful here.

Text 4-6 is an excerpt from a book chapter that promotes SFL genre pedagogy for writing (Christie, 2010, p. 64). The author acknowledges and responds to the criticism (or opposing view) that the pedagogy does not develop critical students because it induces conformity and unreflective adoption of school-based genres in writing. She first admits that critical literacy was not an explicit part of the genre-based curriculum she and her colleagues initially developed, but then counters that the omission does not mean that students should be discouraged from critically reflecting on the genres they are expected to write. She further argues that SFL genre theorists have in fact embraced and promoted critical literacy, and provides specific examples to illustrate her point.

Text 4-6

If I turn to the first of the publications where I wrote about genre pedagogy using functional grammar (Christie, 1984) in the Deakin B.Ed., course material, it is true that there was no suggestion that students be encouraged to reflect upon the genres they wrote, though equally there was no suggestion that this should be discouraged. Moreover, none of my three colleagues who designed and taught the program with me, while taking up very different theoretical positions, proposed such critically reflective activity either. The call for critically reflective practices came a little later in the decade and into the 1990s. I would suggest that SFL genre theorists actually contributed to such calls, so that the genre-based pedagogy that soon emerged actually revealed a commitment to critique and reflection (Martin, 1999). Macken-Horarik (1998, 2002) also addressed matters to do with critical literacy, stressing the importance of developing the necessary skills in recognizing and manipulating genres as a necessary step toward acquiring critical capacities, a point also noted by Unsworth (2001, pp. 14–16).

Some templates useful for introducing objections and making concessions are presented below, with key linguistic markers underlined.

- <u>Of course</u>, leading in healthcare organizations is more than managing boundaries, <u>but</u> a greater awareness of this component of healthcare leadership might assist [...].
- We <u>recognize</u> that what we are proposing may not appear radical enough to some.
- We <u>are aware</u> that each geographical and social context has certain peculiarities that have an effect on the specificity of each educational reality.
- <u>While</u> censorship is dangerous to a free society, some of the concerned citizens who are in favor of censorship <u>may have valid points</u> when they object that [...].
- It would be <u>unrealistic</u> to assert that these skills are not interrelated, <u>yet</u> there may be real merit in examining each one separately, and in developing them independently.
- <u>Although</u> the area of ethics and leadership has many strengths, it <u>also</u> has some weaknesses.
- Third, the two approaches in question are, <u>while effective</u> in distinguishing between different genres, <u>not</u> as sensitive to variations within the same text type. In other words, they <u>may not be particularly effective</u> in differentiating the quality of texts within the same genre.
- We <u>concede</u> that many bilingual students struggle in literacy learning at school. <u>However</u>, we do not believe that the language abilities of bilingual students are a problem to be solved. <u>Rather</u>, they are a resource that contributes to society. <u>Indeed</u>, the valuing and use of language can enhance the positioning of the U.S. in this global world.
- <u>Certainly</u>, there has been conceptual work on, for example, the impact of peacekeepers on state sovereignty; [...]. <u>But</u> the cartography of much of the writing on this issue has been determined by problem-solving imperatives.
- <u>Notwithstanding these limitations</u>, the present study provides an important contribution to the understanding of socialization processes.
- <u>To be fair</u>, the CCSS writers were not unaware of these limitations, as they also recommended [...]. However, they did not [...].

Based on the examples above, it appears that *of course, while, although, acknowledge, concede, admittedly,* and *certainly* are some of the more common terms for introducing an opposing view or acknowledging an existing view that is considered unproblematic. Once the opposing or existing view is presented (and a concession is made), it is then followed by *but* or *however,* which shows that the author is ready to counter the view.

Recommending

In academic writing, you may sometimes need to make recommendations for researchers, practitioners, and/or policy makers based on your arguments or research findings. Often, recommendations for future research are made in light of the limitations identified in your own work. In this case, recommendations can be considered the mirror image of limitations. What is identified as a limitation becomes the basis for making recommendations. This means that limitations and recommendations can be presented together as you ponder what to do in the future in light of what has just been done.

Some useful linguistic resources (underlined) for stating recommendations (and limitations) follow. As you can see below, some recommendations are made in a more authoritative or assertive manner through the use of boosters (e.g., *should, need*) in a somewhat hortatory style, some are made more tentatively with the use of hedges (e.g., *may, suggest*), and some show neither hesitation nor force in the recommendation. The force of recommendation needs to be proportionate to the amount of evidence you have presented in your paper.

- Policy makers <u>should</u> begin supporting research into [...].
- The numerical surge model is more efficient for [...] and <u>should be recommended for</u> quantifying the mangrove effect on [...].
- To conclude, we <u>need to</u> continue to investigate [...].
- <u>Further research is needed</u> to identify [...].
- Inclusion of garage hazards <u>should be examined in future studies</u>.
- <u>It is recommended that</u> a cohort consisting of content experts devise a system [...].
- <u>The present results urge us to consider</u> interventions aimed at challenging [...].
- We hope that <u>by articulating</u> [...], <u>we will inspire others</u> who [...].
- Policy makers concerned with improving academic outcomes <u>may want to</u> broaden their view, [...].
- Answering the question of generalization <u>is</u> therefore <u>a high priority for future work</u> on adaptation.
- The experiment and model reported here <u>leave open the question of</u> how much the changes in expectations which constitute adaptation generalize to novel situations.

- We suggest that further progress can be made by using [...] to articulate [...].
- In future iterations of standards, we hope more attention is paid to language acquisition and biliteracy.
- That being said, the review also suggests that researchers would be wise to approach investigations into [...].
- Through this process of [...], we are better placed to suggest future research that will continue to strengthen the field of social justice and teacher education.
- There are some limitations to the study that should be considered when interpreting the results and implications of the study.
- In light of these discussions, the authors offer the following recommendations to colleges and universities [...].
- Colleges are also advised to consider establishing programs which improve [...].
- While these results show important developments in [...], they should be interpreted in light of the study's inherent limitations of being a reflective enquiry relying on a small sample. However, these results provide scope for further research in similar contexts of [...].
- PISA also suffers some limitations: It assesses a very limited amount of [...]; it can adopt only a [...] design; it ignores the [...]; and the way its results are presented—in some, at least, of its tables—encourages a superficial, "league table" reading of what should be a more interesting but essentially more complex picture.
- Two limitations of this study were the quasi-experimental design and voluntary participation of treatment teachers.
- Although exploratory, the present study is not without limitations. First, the sample size [...] was small. Second, issues related to [...] were not addressed directly. Third, the sampling strategy places limits on the conclusions and generalizations about [...]. There is a need for subsequent studies to incorporate [...]. And finally, it is necessary to consider [...].
- As Pierre Bourdieu reminds us, one of the most important activities scholars can engage in [...] is to analyze critically [...]. I would urge us to take this role even more seriously than we have in the past.
- Having said this, however, we need to be cautious not to ignore [...].
- More research is necessary, however, in order to understand [...].
- There is, however, a need for more detailed studies that [...].
- Future research is required in order to [...].
- The revised conception of [...] suggests many possibilities for future work.
- Future investigations into [...] would have strong relevance to the field.
- Additional research is needed to replicate the current findings and to determine [...].
- We recommend more field experimentation on [...].
- We put forth the following recommendations for academic medical centers [...].
- As an implication, we suggest changes to [...].

- It might therefore be worth looking at ways of [...].
- The results presented here draw attention to the need for controlling [...].
- From this research, some recommendations for the field are evident. First, [...]. Second, [...].

Connecting

Academic writing has a tight texture. A fundamental job in academic writing is to stitch the pieces you have put on paper into a cohesive whole so that it conveys your message logically, clearly, and smoothly. This requires that you use effective devices to establish links among different parts of your writing. One misunderstanding about academic writing is that it is more explicit than everyday writing. This is not necessarily true, as academic writing uses both explicit and not-so-explicit means of connecting ideas. In many cases, what appears explicit to disciplinary insiders may not be so explicit to readers outside the field. The decision on whether to use a signal device depends on who your intended readers are; that is, how familiar they are with the content you are discussing. For example, to disciplinary insiders, it may be clear that one sentence exemplifies the point made in the preceding sentence. In this case, an explicit signal such as *for example* may not be needed between the two sentences. However, when the possibility exists that a non-expert reader may interpret the connection between the two sentences as anything other than an elaboration or exemplification, it is a good idea to insert some kind of signpost to indicate the logical-semantic relationship. Recognizing when connecting devices are needed and which connecting device is the most appropriate is an important skill to develop in academic writing.

Three types of logical-semantic relationship between clauses, sentences, or paragraphs are generally recognized (cf., Halliday & Matthiessen, 2014). In the first type, one clause, sentence, or paragraph enhances the meaning of the preceding clause, sentence, or paragraph by qualifying it along the dimensions of time/space (e.g., *while, when, as, meanwhile, since, before, and then, until, following, afterwards, as soon as, where*), cause/effect (e.g., *because, therefore, on account of this, for that reason, so that, consequently, accordingly, as a result, hence, therefore, so, thus*), condition (e.g., *if, unless, when, as long as, provided that, given that*), or concession (e.g., *yet, but, however, admittedly, still, granted, to be sure, naturally, of course, despite, although, even if, even though, nevertheless*), as the following examples show:

- In spite of the similarity of findings, it is important to [...].
- As a result, statistical analysis of trends [...].
- Following Arnott (1998), we set up [...].

- Hence, the decision was made to [...].
- Accordingly, she determined the state had not given sufficient notice to the plaintiff.
- Although this is less apparent from [....], much new ground was covered when [....].
- However, many people did want to rebuild relationships with family members.
- Yet, of all the risks described in this paper, the "regulatory risk" may well represent [...].
- Because the value of GoldCo is positively correlated with [...], its exposure to interest rates is essentially the opposite of the S&L's.
- Of course, some companies might be reluctant to admit that [...].
- Nonetheless, we checked our findings by running the blocks of variables in different sequences.
- If the housing market variables are entered first, they account for 30% of the explained variance.
- While this does not eliminate [...], it does suggest that [...]
- Provided (that) enough institutional investors were attracted to [...], the senior fund shares could also [....].
- Given that the largest asset classes are [...], it is plausible that [...]
- In the meantime, developed country institutional investors have long sought to [...].

In the second type, one clause, sentence, or paragraph elaborates on or distills the ideas presented in the preceding clause, sentence, or paragraph by restating, exemplifying, clarifying, specifying, or summarizing what was said earlier, using phrases such as *for example/instance, to illustrate, as an illustration, specifically, a case in point, in particular, consider this, in fact, after all, that is, that is to say, to put it more bluntly/succinctly, to put it in another way, in other words, in brief, in short, taken together, in a nutshell, ultimately, in conclusion, to conclude, to summarize,* and *in summary,* as the examples below show:

- That is, it may be possible that [...].
- For example, regulators as well as defenders of derivatives have observed that [...].
- In simple terms, it is the leader's responsibility to [...].
- In summary, experimental research [...].
- Ultimately, this research begs the question of [...].
- To illustrate the issue, they performed [...].
- Overall, this extensive body of meta-analytic research demonstrates [...].
- Taken together, these two requirements suggest [...].
- In brief, we argue that [...]
- In short, developing a rich store of domain knowledge takes time.

- Over-imitation may also be bounded by developmental factors. <u>In particular</u>, our theory predicts that [...].
- <u>In fact</u>, the probability that GoldCo will default on the swap is appreciably lower than [...].

In the third type, one clause, sentence, or paragraph extends the idea presented in the preceding clause, sentence, or paragraph by adding something new, suggesting a replacement, proposing an alternative, presenting a comparison/contrast, or giving an exception. In this case, you use words/phrases such as *also, and, but, another, apart from, besides, moreover, further, furthermore, additionally, in addition, except, first…second…third, one…another, on the one hand…on the other hand, what's more, instead, rather, indeed, or, conversely, by contrast, alternatively, next, similarly, in a different way, likewise, along the same line,* and *in the same way,* as the examples below show:

- <u>In addition</u>, in the literature on organizational tenure, there are [...].
- <u>Also</u>, the light-colored samples are softer than the dark-colored samples in the parallel orientation.
- <u>Further</u>, male proteges with female mentors were less likely [...].
- <u>But another</u> important reason is the lack of development in [...].
- An <u>alternative</u> goal is for students to [...].
- <u>On the one hand</u>, their job seemed [...]. <u>On the other hand</u>, the lessons were more [...].
- <u>One</u> of the reasons [...]. <u>Another</u> reason [...].
- Two overall findings are basic to our understanding. <u>First</u>, our data analysis suggests [...]. <u>Second</u>, the mix of contexts and languages [...].
- <u>Conversely</u>, greater dialogic contraction [...].
- <u>Like Wagner</u>, we also [...].
- <u>Likewise</u>, Benjaminsen and Andrade (2015) found that [...].
- <u>In contrast to</u> the instructional-delivery view, the constructivist view leads to [...].
- <u>Next</u>, the panel rejected the plaintiffs' additional claims [...].
- <u>Moreover</u>, this analysis has provided Wall Street with a set of practical tools [...].
- <u>What's more</u>, this shift has been achieved [...].

The devices identified above are explicit ways of signaling connections between clauses, sentences, or paragraphs. However, there is a danger of overusing connectors or transition words, with the consequence that the whole text may sound contrived. A case in point is Text 4-7 below, which was written by a graduate student for whom English is a foreign language.

Text 4-7

<u>Nevertheless</u>, due to a lack of conceptual and theoretical foundations, these strategies may achieve some effects on promoting students' critical

thinking (CT) skills. But they may hardly lead to a comprehensive development of CT among students. Even though there is agreement on the necessity and importance of teaching CT in L2 writing, there has been no consensus in researchers' understanding towards CT. However, most of them view CT as a set of separate skills that students use unintentionally in their learning. Therefore, different types of writing tasks or activities are designed for students to practice implicitly during the writing process, focusing on one or more of the CT skills. Besides, seldom has any researchers paid particular attention to the cultivation of students' CT dispositions, which according to Paul and Elder (2001) is actually the ultimate purpose of teaching CT. In addition, teaching CT in L2 writing does not mean simply including CT as part of the teaching contents or teaching objectives. Moreover, a slight modification of the traditional L2 writing approach may not guarantee significant improvement in both CT and L2 writing skills.

To avoid overusing transition words, you can omit linking devices when the logical-semantic links between sentences are reasonably clear to your intended audience. For example, in these two sentences—*The monsoon, on which all agriculture depends, is erratic. Sometimes, it arrives early, sometimes late, sometimes not at all.*, a transition device such as *for example* is not needed, as proficient readers are unlikely to have trouble figuring out the meaning relationship between the two sentences—that is, the second sentence explains or exemplifies the notion of *erratic* in the first sentence.

Another way to avoid overusing transition words is to expand your linguistic repertoires by learning other, less explicit ways of connecting clauses, sentences, or paragraphs. One such device is the pronoun (e.g., *this, these, that, such, it, they, so*), which allows you to summarize previously presented information. When using pronouns, you need to make sure they refer to clearly defined entities (concept, idea, or object) in the text and are not too far away from their referents.

- One of the most commonly observed strategies was [...]. This strategy occurred [...].
- Such opportunities for brainstorming have shown [...].
- From this perspective, the crucial questions are [...].
- These reviews, coupled with other studies, provide evidence to support [...].
- On the basis of this convincing literature, [...].
- At the 2007 survey of [...], it was shown that [...]. That means [...].
- To our knowledge, a permit system has not yet been applied to urban motorists. Such a lack of an economic tool application may be due to [...].
- By doing so, we build upon the work of [...].
- It is notable that we observed sizable sex differences in mathematical reasoning ability in 7th grade students. Until that grade, boys and girls have presumably had [...].
- Those assumptions, however, have been subsequently called into question.

An additional way of making connections within a text is through simple repetition. In the student-generated text below, the word *crocodiles* is repeated in the first three sentences and subsequently referred to as *they*, which is then repeated throughout the rest of the text.

Text 4-8

Crocodiles lived when dinosaurs lived. Crocodiles can live in water. Crocodiles can live on land or in water. They have good vision at night. They have big mouths. They like to eat in the sun. They can open their mouth really wide. [...]

Such simple repetition, if used over a long stretch of a text, can make the text sound boring to read and result in a poorly organized prose (see also Chapter 2). This is why writers are often encouraged to seek out other ways of connecting clauses, sentences, and paragraphs. One method is to use different terms to refer to the same thing. For example, severe acute respiratory syndrome coronavirus 2 can be referred to as *SARS-CoV-2, 2019 novel coronavirus, COVID-19, the pandemic, the deadly virus,* and *the respiratory disease* in the same article. Developing a constellation of terms and phrases (e.g., synonyms, antonyms, pronouns) that you can use to refer to the same entity is an effective way of creating cohesion and making your writing more varied, interesting, and informative.

A more subtle way of creating connections is through the use of nominalization, first discussed in Chapter 2. Schleppegrell (2004) observed that advanced writers privilege nominal resources over conjunctive resources in structuring text and crafting discursive flow. Consider, for example, Text 4-9, which is the abstract from Fang (2020, p. 70). In this sample text, *the engagement* in the second sentence refers to *some interaction with complex disciplinary texts* in the first sentence. The third sentence begins with *this advanced literacy ability,* which refers to *discipline-specific reading/writing skills that go beyond [...]* in the second sentence. The last sentence begins with *such a pedagogy,* which refers to *a pedagogy that is informed by [...]* in the previous sentence.

Text 4-9

Learning in secondary content areas involves at least some interaction with complex disciplinary texts. The engagement requires discipline-specific reading/writing skills that go beyond those students have mastered in the elementary grades. This advanced literacy ability, or disciplinary literacy, is best fostered through a pedagogy that is informed by sound linguistics theory, responsive to student needs, and embedded in meaningful disciplinary experiences. Such a pedagogy, with its focus on how language is used in disciplinary meaning making, has the potential to promote knowledge building and advanced literacy development at the same time.

In another example on asthma (Padilla, Miaoulis, & Cyr, 2001, p. 613), listed below as Text 4-10, *this narrowing* in the second sentence picks up what is stated in the previous sentence (*the respiratory passages narrow significantly*) and makes it become the subject of the discussion. The next sentence begins with *asthma attacks*, which refers to *wheeze and become short of breath* in the previous sentence. Here, the passive voice (*may be brought on*) is used because *asthma attacks* enables the author to establish a tighter link with the previous sentence. Had the active voice been used, the sentence—*Factors other than allergies, such as stress and exercise, may bring on asthma attacks*—would not have connected as tightly with the previous sentence. Additionally, the subject would have sounded too long, which is contrary to the preference of written English. The English language prefers to adopt the "end-focus" syntactic structure when presenting information, meaning that heavy or new information is usually placed after the main verb (i.e., in the object position of the sentence) in order to facilitate comprehension.

Text 4-10

Asthma is a disorder in which the respiratory passages narrow significantly. This narrowing causes the person to wheeze and become short of breath. Asthma attacks <u>may be brought on</u> by factors other than allergies, such as stress and exercise.

For further illustration, let's consider another sentence—*Much of Gulf Coastal Plain <u>was formed</u> from sediments deposited by the Mississippi River as it entered the Gulf of Mexico*. In this sentence, the passive voice is used because it avoids making an awkwardly long phrase (*sediments deposited by the Mississippi River as it entered the Gulf of Mexico*) become the subject of the sentence.

In short, the foregoing examples show that discussion about whether to use the active voice or the passive voice in academic writing should be done in context, taking into consideration questions such as "which option best facilitates information flow and comprehension?" and "which option enables the author to put a focus on the information that needs to be emphasized?". Absent reference to context, any discussion of which choice (the active voice or the passive voice) is better makes little sense, as neither is inherently more or less useful/ effective than the other.

Conclusion

Writing for academic purposes involves a wide range of skills. These skills include defining, describing, exemplifying, classifying/categorizing, comparing/contrasting, explaining, referencing visuals, entertaining opposition, recommending, and connecting, as well as those discussed in Chapter 3 (contextualizing, summarizing, quoting, sourcing, agreeing/disagreeing, evaluating). Developing these advanced literacy skills and a repertoire of linguistic resources and strategies for instantiating them is a challenging process that takes time, experience, and support.

Reflection/Application Activities

1 Select three to five samples of academic writing from your field of study and examine what language resources the authors of these pieces use to define, describe, exemplify, explain, classify/categorize, compare/contrast, reference visuals, entertain opposition, make recommendations, and connect sentences/ paragraphs.
2 Identify two to three pieces of writing you did before for class assignments or other academic purposes. Discuss your strengths and weaknesses with respect to the ten writing skills presented in this chapter.
3 Write an extended definition of a key concept in your field, using the linguistic resources and strategies discussed in this chapter.
4 Compare/contrast two related key concepts in your field, using, first, the block approach and then, the point-by-point approach. What do you find handy or challenging about each approach in your writing?
5 Write a short essay explaining a noteworthy phenomenon in your field or discussing the causes and effects of a significant current event. Use as many different linguistic resources for causal explanation as possible. Think about the affordances and limitations each of these resources offers for constructing the essay.

References

Anonymous (2020). The future of restitution and equity in the distribution of funds recovered from Ponzi Schemes and other multi-victim frauds. *Harvard Law Review, 133*(6), 2101–2123.

Christie, F. (2010). The "grammar wars" in Australia. In T. Locke (Ed.), *Beyond the grammar wars* (pp. 55–72). New York: Routledge.

Fang, Z. (2015). Writing a report: A study of preadolescents' use of informational language. *Linguistics and the Human Sciences, 10*(2), 103–131.

Fang, Z. (2020). Toward a linguistically informed, responsive, and embedded pedagogy in secondary literacy instruction. *Journal of World Languages, 6*(1–2), 70–91.

Faragher, J., Buhle, M., Czitrom, D., & Armitage, S. (2007). *Out of many: A history of the American people* (15th ed.). Upper Saddle River, NJ: Prentice Hall.

Gillett, A., Hammond, A., & Martala, M. (2009). *Inside track: Successful academic writing*. London: Longman.

Graff, G., & Birkenstein, C. (2018). *They say I say: The moves that matter in academic writing* (4th ed.). New York: Norton.

Halliday, M., & Matthiessen, C. (2014). *An introduction to functional grammar* (4th ed.). London: Routledge.

Kress, G., & van Leeuwen, T. (2006). *Reading images: A grammar of visual design* (2nd ed.). London: Routledge.

Padilla, M., Miaoulis, I., & Cyr, M. (2001). *Science explorer: Life science*. Upper Saddle River, NJ: Prentice Hall.

Schleppegrell, M. (2004). *The language of schooling: A functional linguistics perspective*. Mahwah, NJ: Erlbaum.

Wilson, E. O. (2014). *A window on eternity: A biologist's walk through Gorongosa National Park*. New York: Simon & Schuster.

Section II
Writing Academic Genres

5
Writing a Reading Response

What Is a Reading Response?

Reading response is an interpretive task involving summary, analysis, and evaluation of one or more stimulus texts (Christie & Derewianka, 2008). It is a popular genre in academic learning at all levels of education. Students are regularly asked in their coursework to read and react to a piece or multiple pieces of work, such as an article, a book, a film, a sculpture, or a play. The task has been demonstrated to improve understanding, learning, and remembering of content materials (Graham & Perin, 2007). More specifically, it promotes reflection and reexamination of initial understanding as well as clarification and organization of thoughts, leading to deeper learning and engagement.

To write a quality reading response, you need first to read and understand the text(s) to which you will respond. Before reading, you should think about your reasons for reading the text(s) because why you read will influence how you read. For example, if you are reading to gain background information or for general discussion in class, you are likely to read more quickly and superficially. If you are reading to obtain specific/detailed information or for critical evaluation of the ideas and themes in the text(s), you are likely to read much more slowly and closely. While reading, you should keep your purpose in mind, bring your prior knowledge to bear, attend to text features (e.g., headings, subheadings, visuals), and take careful notes. Sometimes, you may need to reread portions of the text to gain a deeper understanding.

Once an understanding of the stimulus text(s) is attained, the task of writing begins. Unlike other genres of academic writing, reading response is usually written in the first person (*I*) and uses language in a more informal and interactive way. As such, it sits at the further left end of the stylistic continuum depicted in Figure 2.2 (see Chapter 2).

Rhetorical Moves in Reading Response

A reading response typically begins with an introduction that situates the response in a context to give readers a sense of the circumstance under which the response task is undertaken. The introduction can also be used to grab the reader's attention. This can be done by describing a scenario, telling an anecdote, relating a story, citing an interesting fact or a shocking statistic, proposing a question to be answered, identifying an issue or a problem to be solved, presenting a dilemma to be addressed, or using a famous saying or an apt quote. Following the introduction, you will then briefly summarize the gist of what you have read and then give your reactions to the overall message of the text, as well as to specific ideas in the text. The focus here is usually not on a detailed summary of everything that the text says, but on thoughtful analysis and evaluation of key points that you find intriguing, well said, noteworthy, significant, relevant, surprising, controversial, or problematic. The analysis and evaluation can also concern, in the case of a literary response, the recurring motifs and central themes in the story. Sometimes, comparisons and contrasts across texts are made if multiple stimulus texts are involved. The response may also include a conclusion that recaps your overall feelings about the text regarding its utility to and impact on you. Additionally, the conclusion can address the issue, problem, or dilemma raised in the introduction. It can also make connections to the introduction by explaining how the scenario, anecdote, story, issue, fact, statistic, or quote presented at the outset of your response is relevant or significant to your point.

In your analysis and evaluation, you can comment on the big ideas, overarching themes, or recurring motifs in the text(s). You can also make observations about specific points, evidence, or examples presented in the text(s). In these comments or observations, you should go beyond simply stating whether you agree or disagree with what is stated in the text (see Chapter 3). You can, for example, make text-to-text connections, where you identify similarities and differences among the stimulus texts or between the stimulus text(s) and other texts you have read before. You can also make text-to-self connections, where you describe how a point or an example in the stimulus text resonates with something in your own personal or professional life. And you can make text-to-world connections, where you reflect on how an idea or issue discussed in the stimulus text(s) reminds you of something else that happened or is going on in the society. Specifically, you can address questions such as the following in your reaction:

- Do you agree/disagree with what was written in the stimulus text? Why or why not?
- Did the reading make you question or think about something else?
- What questions were you left with after doing the reading?

- Can you relate the reading to your experience, other texts, or the society at large?
- Did the author have a valid point? How so?
- What are the ideologies underpinning the arguments in the text?
- Did the author present his/her argument clearly and logically?
- What evidence is included or excluded? Why? How does the inclusion/exclusion impact the author's argument or your interpretation?
- Is the evidence or example provided credible and relevant?
- What would be lost or gained had the author presented his/her message in a different way?
- Whose perspectives are privileged or ignored in text? Whose voices are heard or silenced?
- Who is included? Who is excluded? Why?
- What is foregrounded? What is backgrounded? Why?
- Who benefits? Who is disadvantaged?
- How is language used to maintain or challenge existing relations of power?
- How is language used to position the reader?
- What implications do the ideas in the stimulus text(s) have for policy, research, or practice?
- Is the writing clear, fluent, coherent, and accessible to you?

It is important to have details in your response essay. This means it is not enough to just identify points with which you agree or disagree. Instead, you need to explain your thoughts and feelings about these points through careful analysis and logical reasoning using relevant, credible examples. You are allowed to use direct quotes from the stimulus text(s) to support your claims and arguments. The deeper and relevant your thoughts are, the more understanding you demonstrate of the stimulus text(s).

In the rest of this chapter, we present and analyze two very different reading response essays to show how the rhetorical moves described above unfold and what linguistic resources are maneuvered to instantiate these moves.

Reading Response Sample #1

The first sample of reading response was written by a graduate student, whom we shall call Jill. We will annotate how the response essay is constructed in a way that communicates the student's thoughts and feelings about the stimulus text(s). The essay was written in response to select chapters in three textbooks—Graff and Birkenstein (2018), Jalongo and Saracho (2016), and Swales and Feak (2018)—that the student had read over a three-week period in a course aimed at improving students' academic writing. Paragraphs are numbered for ease of reference in analysis and discussion.

Text 5-1: Reading Response Sample #1

1   Majoring in English in college led me to build a writing style that is more prose-like and creative. The texts for this course have helped me understand the more practical nuts and bolts of academic writing that I'll need as I pursue my Ph.D. This calls for writing with a greater focus on research rather than creative writing. All three books for this course are allowing me an opportunity to build my writing skills.

2   In *Academic Writing for Graduate Students*, Swales and Feak offers a task-based approach to learning academic writing. While many of the considerations are the same as my undergraduate writing (e.g., audience, purpose, style, organization), the literary elements like plot, character development, and theme are no longer needed. Swales and Feak suggest that graduate student writers need to "display familiarity, expertise, and intelligence" (p. 6). This allowed me to reflect on the idea that if I can't do this in my writing, I need to do more research and reading before I can offer anything through my writing. While academic writing may not be as entertaining as creative writing, Swales and Feak offer that there is still room for style, stating that it must "be suitable both in terms of the message being conveyed and the audience" (p. 14). Overall, the task-based approach Swales and Feak provide offers the opportunity to become fluent in the skills needed for academic writing.

3   Like what stood out to me in the Swales and Feak book regarding expertise, Jalongo and Saracho reiterate this idea of the expert in their book, *Writing for Publication*. Jalongo and Saracho address the need for "thoroughness and authoritativeness", which echoes what I reflected on while reading Swales and Feak. This comes through in who a writer chooses to cite in their writing. Jalongo and Saracho offer strategies that are applicable to the common writing tasks of a graduate student—again different from those I am accustomed to as an English Literature major. What is most helpful in Jalongo and Saracho's book is their approach to taking what you have and scaffolding it to the next level. This is especially helpful to me since I often struggle with where to start. The authors approach the work in a way that takes what you have done or are comfortable with and polish it into something more publishable and enriching.

4   Both Swales and Feak and Jalongo and Saracho paint the big picture with academic writing and still offer skills and strategies, but Graff and Birkenstein's *They Say, I Say* is the consummate resource that allows me to join "the conversation" going on in my field of academic writing. It is so practical and useful and immediately applicable. While Jalongo and Saracho and Swales and Feak provide many opportunities to practice and build skills, Graff and Birkenstein allows me to hit the ground running with the easy-to-use templates. This book has been the most helpful in making

academic writing less intimidating. It has an approach that is like putting one foot in front of the other; baby steps.

5   Even though Graff and Birkenstein's book is a quick reference, it still offers some big picture ideas in a palatable manner. One that stands out to me is this idea that you can often find yourself "talking past rather than to one another" (Graff & Birkenstein, 167). Although they are discussing online conversations, this is true in other writing as well. Now I look at my writing to decide if I am "building on what someone else has said, challenging it or trying to change the discussion topic altogether" (Graff & Birkenstein, 167). The other big picture item Graff and Birkenstein offers that has led me to change my writing is being more explicit. I have tended to assume a reader knows what I mean or understands the context. Being more explicit in my writing allows me to communicate my ideas in a clear manner. The key for me in being more explicit in my writing is take more time to write; and as we do in our pre-class exercises, read each sentence in isolation. This brief exercise has built a skill to do this as I'm writing and making my edits for clarity and explicitness.

6   The combination of all three texts offers an opportunity to build on my already existing skills and hone them for more academic and less prosy writing. I am glad I have encountered these texts early in my doctorate work rather than later and expect to reference them often over the coming years of my program.

Analyzing Reading Response Sample #1

In this response, Jill provides a candid assessment of the relevance and utility of the course readings and discusses her own strengths and needs in light of the concepts and ideas covered in these readings. The first paragraph is an introduction that establishes the relevance of the readings to the work she is doing as a doctoral student. The last paragraph sums up the value of the three textbooks to her doctoral work and recaps her overall feelings about the readings. The main body of the essay, second through fifth paragraphs, identifies key points in each of the stimulus texts that resonate with her and provides examples from her personal experience to illustrate the connections. Along the way, extensive connections are made between the three textbooks and her personal experience as a writer. Comparisons/contrasts are also made across the three textbooks in terms of their usefulness to the student. Quotes are judiciously selected to support her claims.

A variety of transition devices are used to connect paragraphs. Specifically, paragraph #2 begins with a statement that characterizes the Swales and Feak book. It then identifies and elaborates on key points in the book that the student herself finds relevant and illuminating; at the same time, it also acknowledges some of the more common perceptions about academic writing (i.e., *while many of the considerations are the same as…*, *while academic writing may not be as entertaining…*). The paragraph ends with a summary statement that provides an overall assessment of the value of the book.

Paragraph #3 begins with a linking phrase, *Like what stood out to me in the Swales and Feak book regarding expertise*, that provides a smooth transition from paragraph #2. It then identifies the main theme of the Jalongo and Saracho book and discusses how the ideas and strategies presented in the book are helpful to the student. Specific links between her own writing struggles and the book authors' suggestions are explicitly made. Pronouns such as *which* and *this*, whose references are clearly identifiable, help stitch the paragraph together and contribute to its cohesiveness.

Paragraph #4 again begins with a transition sentence that recapitulates the main points of the two books discussed in paragraphs #2 and #3 (i.e., *Both Swales and Feak and Jalongo and Saracho paint the big picture with academic writing…*) and then characterizes the third book to be discussed (i.e., Graff and Birkenstein). Comparisons between the third book and the first two books are made to buttress the student's point that she found Graff and Birkenstein more *practical* and *useful*. The use of a simile (i.e., *like putting…baby steps*) in the last sentence vividly illustrates her point about the helpfulness of the book.

To further support her expression of preference for the Graff and Birkenstein book, the student acknowledges, in paragraph 5, a potential criticism that may be leveled against the book (i.e., *Graff and Birkenstein's book is only a quick reference*), but immediately argues against the criticism by suggesting that the book is more than just a quick reference because it *still offers some big picture ideas in a palatable manner*. The rest of the paragraph illustrates this point by discussing two big take-aways from the book—the need to talk *to*, rather than talk *past*, one another and the importance of being explicit in academic writing.

This reading response essay was written for a course assignment. The style is understandably somewhat informal, with the use of the first person (*I, me*), the second person (*you*), contraction (*I'll, can't*), and colloquial expressions (*so practical*). However, as a whole, the writing has a certain degree of abstraction, objectivity, density, rigor, and tightly knit structure—features that characterize academic writing in general (see Chapter 2). The tone is obviously evaluative (e.g., *helpful, glad, creative, useful, precise, applicable, palatable, easy-to-use*). Jill tempers her judgment through the use of hedges such as *suggest, have tended to assume, often struggle, may not be as entertaining*, and *immediately applicable*. Less frequently, she uses booster such as *so practical and useful, especially helpful*, and *most helpful* to strengthen her claims. As a whole, the essay presents a thoughtful response to course readings by explicitly identifying and critically evaluating key points in the books that resonate with her and connect with her experience as a developing academic writer. In so doing, it fulfils the purpose of the reading response genre.

Reading Response Sample #2

The second sample of reading response (see Text 5-2) was written by an undergraduate student whom we shall call Larry. Similar to what we did with the first reading response essay, we will annotate how Larry's response essay is constructed in a way that communicates his reaction to the stimulus text. The essay was written in response to an American animated musical romantic fantasy film—*The Little Mermaid* (Disney, 1989)—that the student had watched as an assignment for a course designed to improve students' understanding and appreciation of children's literature and media. Each paragraph of the essay is numbered for ease of reference in analysis and discussion.

Text 5-2: Reading Response Sample #2

1   In fifth grade, Officer Brown, my D.A.R.E. instructor, asked my class to draw a picture representing the physical characteristics of a typical drug dealer. I drew an evil-looking man with snake-like eyes. He was wearing dark black clothing, and he was standing on a grungy street corner in front of an abandoned warehouse. The purpose of this exercise was to demonstrate that anyone could be a drug dealer. A drug dealer could be a sweet Suburban soccer mom who bakes homemade cookies for her children, or a drug dealer could be that evil-looking guy wearing black clothing on the street corner. Officer Brown explained that as a society, we tend to associate negative characteristics with drug dealers because the media depicts drug dealers in this manner. As a result, this negative image of drug dealers has been imbedded into our minds at a very young age.

2   Disney movies have been instrumental in influencing children's views of good versus evil. The movies place great emphasis on the characters' physical appearance. For example, in *The Little Mermaid*, Ariel is beautiful and skinny. She has long flowing red hair, big bright blue eyes, perfectly full red lips, and she seems to have a glow about her. She is very feminine, and her voice is high pitched but pleasing to the ear. The males in *The Little Mermaid* are strapping and handsome. They have big bulging muscles that can aid them to rescue mermaids if they get into trouble. The men also have a full head of hair that always stays in place. The "good" characters in Disney movies are always portrayed with good characteristics. In

fact, it is as if they are perfect. On the other hand, the "evil" characters are described as perfectly repulsive. Ursula, a sea witch, in *The Little Mermaid* is an ugly dark-looking creature with a long pointy nose, and long fingers. She has monster sharp teeth and a gruff manly voice. Ursula does not possess one positive quality. Like other "evil" characters, Ursula is on the other end of the continuum compared to Ariel.

3   The environment is also used to depict differences between the "good" and "evil" in Disney movies. For example, in *The Little Mermaid*, Ariel lives in a well-maintained golden castle. The water surrounding the castle is crystal clear. On the floor of the sea, there is green seaweed and bright-colored flowers. There are also various forms of life swimming around the castle. The fishes, shrimps, crabs, and other animals are bright vibrant colors. Ursula, on the other hand, lives in a dark dreary cave. During parts of the movie, the water surrounding the cave is black, and at other times, the water is dark blue. Ursula's cave is unkempt, and it is full of dying souls and skeletons. The only form of life near the cave is Ursula's assistances, eels. The eels are black with slanted snake-like eyes that glow a yellowish-green color. The floor of Ursula's cave is not made of grass. Instead, the floor is made of dirt and rocks. The entire atmosphere surrounding the castle represents death.

4   In the previous paragraphs, it was alluded to that the use of color also helps distinguish between "good" and "evil". Scenes involving the "good" characters contained an abundant amount of color. There are mostly bright vibrant colors, such as yellows, reds, oranges, purples, and blues. For example, Flounder, Ariel's friend, is bright yellow with a mixture of dark and light blue strips. Most of the fish in the sea are a mixture of two colors. The fishes are red with yellow fins, purple with yellow fins, blue with red fins, or blue with purple fins. Other animals are red and orange. There is also some pink mixed among the animals. The scenes involving the "evil" characters lack color almost entirely. The little color that is used is cold and dark. The most abundant color representing Ursula is black. Ursula herself is a dark purple, and there are some dark blues and greens. There is also the yellowish-green glow that comes out of the eels' eyes.

5   Officer Brown was on to something when he stated that the media influences our opinion. It may not be obvious to children as they watch *The Little Mermaid* or another Disney movie, but that movie is influencing their opinion. The movie gives children a template as to how "good" individuals should look, how they should act, and even what they should possess. Of course, the movies also give children a template for "evil" individuals. The template teaches children that "evil" individuals should look, act a certain way. It also teaches them that evil people should not

possess certain items. For example, in *The Little Mermaid*, Ariel lives in a castle, but Ursula is not even good enough to have a house. Instead, she lives in a damp dreary cave. As they grow, children take these images of "good" and "evil" and adopt them as their own beliefs. Louis Althusser coined the term interpellation, the idea that as individuals we tend to accept society's norms as our own. Therefore, in the beginning of the paper when I described my picture of a drug dealer in the fifth grade, it could be conjectured that I obtain those images from society, and not from reality. In reality, there is no such concept as a "typical" drug dealer. As officer Brown stated, anyone could be a drug dealer.

(Source: https://www.longwood.edu/staff/mcgeecw/ sampleresponsepapers.htm, accessed on July 25, 2020)

Analyzing Reading Response Sample #2

Unlike the first reading response, where Jill focuses on how the three textbooks are relevant and useful to her as a doctoral student reader/writer, this second reading response, written by Larry for an undergraduate English class, discusses and appraises a popular Disney movie by engaging in what Christie and Derewianka (2008) referred to as "thematic interpretation". It goes beyond expressing immediate feelings about or giving a simple attitudinal response to the film. It is neither a retelling of the events in the film nor an analysis of the story characters. Rather, the response essay generalizes from the specific characters and concrete events of the story to construct an interpretation of the abstract symbols and recurring motifs in the film.

The essay consists of five paragraphs, with an introduction (first paragraph), a body (second through fourth paragraphs), and a conclusion (last paragraph). The first paragraph describes a classroom activity Larry participated in as a fifth grader. The scenario is used to introduce a thesis that becomes the focus of discussion in the response essay—that is, the media influences our perception of "good" versus "evil". The last paragraph recapitulates this central theme by making a connection back to the classroom scenario presented in the introduction, explaining its significance to the discussion, and distilling, through reference to the theoretical construct of interpellation, the key points of the response essay. The main body of the essay identifies and expounds three key points, one per paragraph, related to the central theme—*Disney movies have been instrumental in shaping children's views of good versus evil*. Each point is explained and supported with specific details from the film. The technique of comparison/contrast (see Chapter 4) is used when examples from the film are presented. This increases both clarity and persuasiveness of each point discussed.

Constructing a well-crafted response like this essay is no easy task. It requires the author to make connections between the concrete motifs in the film and the abstract thematic preoccupations of the film maker and to organize and marshal information about the film in such a way that a clear focus is offered and pursued in an orderly manner. Each paragraph in the main body of the response essay begins with a topic sentence, which is subsequently explained and exemplified. Transition devices are used to connect paragraphs. Specifically, paragraph #2 begins with a thesis statement (i.e., *Disney movies have been instrumental in influencing children's views of good versus evil.*) that echoes the message introduced in the last sentence of the first paragraph (i.e., Our negative image of drug dealers is influenced by the media from a very young age.). It then presents the first key point related to the central thesis—The physical appearance of good versus evil characters are depicted differently in the Disney movie. The point is illustrated by contrasting how two sets of characters, Ariel (a 16-year-old mermaid princess representing "good") and her male companions versus Ursula (a villainous sea witch representing "evil") and her companions, are portrayed in the movie.

Paragraph #3 begins with another key point related to the central thesis, i.e., the physical environment in which good and evil characters live is depicted differently. To illustrate this point, Ariel's well-maintained golden castle is contrasted with Ursula's dark dreary cave. The adverb *also* serves as a transition device, signaling that the paragraph continues what is presented in the first paragraph by introducing an additional point for discussion.

Paragraph #4 begins with a transition sentence, *In the previous paragraphs, it was alluded to…*, that connects with the two preceding paragraphs of the essay and segues into the new paragraph. It introduces a further point for discussion, that is, color is used to distinguish between the "good" and the "evil". The point is illustrated by contrasting the scenes involving the "good" characters (an abundance of bright, vibrant colors) and those involving "evil" characters (little color, cold, and dark).

As a whole, Larry's response is written with not only the sort of rhetorical moves typical of the genre but also the linguistic features valued by the course instructor. Similar to Jill's response, the tone of Larry's essay is conspicuously evaluative (e.g., *great* emphasis, *evil-looking* man with *snake-like* eyes, *a grungy street*, beautiful and skinny, have a *glow* about her, big bright, pleasing, strapping and handsome, *big bulging* muscles, perfectly repulsive, an *ugly dark-looking* creature, *monster sharp* teeth, a *gruff manly* voice, *black with slanted snake-like* eyes, death, *well-maintained golden* castle, crystal clear, *bright-colored* flowers, *bright vibrant* color, a *dark dreary* cave, unkempt, cold and dark, obvious, a *damp dreary* cave). Larry tempers some of his evaluation through the use of hedges such as *a typical drug dealer, could be, may not be obvious, as if perfect, it was alluded to, mostly bright vibrant colors, almost entirely, tend to,* and *could be conjectured.* He also uses boosters such as *a very young age, perfectly full red lips, very feminine, perfectly repulsive, monster sharp teeth, crystal clear, of course, full of dying souls and skeletons, the most abundant color, in fact,* and *should* look to add force or focus to his claims. On the other hand, because Larry's response essay focuses not on personal feelings about the movie but on abstract interpretations of its themes and motifs, it has a higher degree of abstraction than Jill's response essay. Finally, Larry uses grammatical resources such as *on the other hand, like, instead, also, for example,* and *but* to facilitate comparison and contrast. He also uses devices such as *also* and *In the previous paragraphs,* instead of the traditional *first—second—third—finally* frame, to facilitate transitions from one point of discussion to the next. Taken together, Larry's essay deploys the rhetorical moves and linguistic resources that are functional and effective for accomplishing the purpose of the reading response genre.

Conclusion

Reading response is a popular course assignment in which you are compelled to think through the key points that you have gleaned from the stimulus text(s) and at the same time express your feelings about and attitudes toward the reading(s) or, in the case of literary reading, your analysis and interpretation of the underlying motifs and central themes in the story. It is an effective means of supporting reading comprehension and developing literate habits of mind. Learning to write the genre—with its rhetorical moves and linguistic features—is thus crucial to meaningful and effective learning of content materials across academic disciplines.

Reflection/Application Activities

1 In small groups, select a sample reading response paper and discuss whether the author accomplishes the task successfully. Provide reasons and evidence for your opinion.
2 Write a reading response to an article, a movie, a piece of artwork, a play, a professional book, or a novel of your choice, keeping in mind the rhetorical moves and grammatical resources that may be helpful as you craft the paper. Does writing the response consolidate and deepen your understanding of the article, movie, artwork, novel, or play?
3 Take a look at 1–2 reading response papers you wrote before. In light of what is presented in this chapter, discuss what you think you did well and not so well, as well as what you can do to improve your skills in writing the genre.

References

Christie, F., & Derewianka, B. (2008). *School discourse: Learning to write across the years of schooling.* London: Continuum.

Graff, G., & Birkenstein, C. (2018). *They say I say: The moves that matter in academic writing* (4th ed.). New York: Norton.

Graham, S., & Perin, D. (2007). *Writing Next: Effective strategies to improve writing of adolescents in middle and high school.* Washington, DC: Alliance for Excellent Education.

Jalongo, R., & Saracho, O. (2016). *Writing for publication: Transitions and tools that support scholars' success.* New York: Springer.

Swales, J., & Feak, C. (2018). *Academic writing for graduate students: Essential skills and tasks* (3rd ed.). Ann Arbor: Univerrsity of Michigan Press.

Walt Disney Pictures and Walt Disney Feature Animation (1989). *The little mermaid.* Orlando, FL: Author.

6
Writing a Book Review

What Is a Book Review?

A book review is a review of a newly published book or a set of newly published, topically related books that is deemed to have something valuable to offer to the field. The book can be a single-author book or an edited volume. It is usually not a piece of work that is seriously flawed or on a topic that is of little interest or importance to the field.

A book review can be considered a type of reading response, but it is usually more objective, formal, well structured, and rigorous. Like a reading response, a book review not only tells what the book is about but also analyzes and appraises it within the broader context of the field. In other words, a book review provides both a brief description of the book's key points and an evaluation of its strengths, weaknesses, and contributions. Unlike a reading response, which concerns your personal feelings about, attitudes toward, or connections to the book, a book review focuses more on an objective assessment of the book's merits and contributions to the field. It can be written in the first person (*I*) or the third person (*the book*).

A book review is not the same as a book report, either. A book report is usually short (250–500 words) and rarely involves analysis and evaluation. Instead, it reports on the content of the book, such as major plots, overarching themes, or key ideas. It is an assignment more commonly found in K-12 classrooms. A book review, on the other hand, requires you to situate the book in the field, have an opinion, take a clear stance, support your points with evidence or examples from the book or other relevant sources, and make recommendations or suggestions for potential readers of the book. Because a book review involves evaluation, cautious language (see Chapter 3), such as hedges, is often used to temper judgment, modulate claims, and show respect for the book author and the broad scholarly community.

Before writing a book review, you need to make sure you have read and understood the book well. You can keep the following questions in mind and take careful notes as you read:

- What is the author's purpose in writing this book? Is this purpose effectively achieved?
- What problem, issue, or phenomenon is addressed in the book?
- What approach or methodology did the author use to address the problem, issue, or phenomenon? Is the approach or methodology viable, innovative, or rigorous?
- What theory or perspective informs the author's approach?
- Against what sociocultural, political, economic, or educational milieu is the book written?
- What are the author's viewpoints?
- What are the author's main points?
- What are the values that underpin the book's message(s)?
- What is assumed or taken-for-granted?
- How did the author set up his/her argument(s)?
- What evidence did the author use to prove his/her points?
- How is the book related to other books on the same topic? What are their respective strengths and weaknesses in dealing with the topic?
- Does the author have the necessary expertise to write the book?
- How successful is the author in accomplishing his/her goal(s) for writing the book?
- What themes or motifs stand out?
- What makes the book good, worthy, different, unique, valuable, significant, original, innovative, or groundbreaking?
- What section or chapter of the book stands out as particularly illustrative of the author's talent or the book's contribution?
- What, if any, is missing, outdated, poorly conceptualized, or inadequately addressed in the book? Are these limitations reasonable in light of the purported goals of the book? Do the deficiencies compromise the overall quality or contribution of the book?
- Is the book written in a style that is clear, focused, coherent, fluent, convincing, and accessible to its intended audience?

Rhetorical Moves in Book Review

A typical book review contains five parts (cf., Natriello, 2000). Part I provides bibliographical information about the book—its title, author, publisher, city of publication, total number of pages, ISBN number, and, if available, price. The information is arranged in a format consistent with the requirement of your particular discipline (or publication outlet). For example, fields like psychology and education use the format stipulated by the American Psychological

Association (APA). This is the so-called APA format. MLA, the format stipulated by the Modern Language Association, is required in English and some other disciplines.

Part II introduces the book by establishing the context in which the book is situated. It makes a connection between the book and the broader scholarly literature base of which the book is a part. The section can also provide brief information about the author (e.g., his/her expertise and credential) and note its potential readership (i.e., for whom the book is intended).

Part III summarizes the content of the book. This can be done by describing the main points or overarching themes of the book; discussing the intellectual tradition in which the book is rooted or, in the case of a book reporting on empirical investigations, major methods employed in the studies covered; highlighting the overall organization or structure of the book (e.g., sections and chapters); and providing an overall sketch of the topics covered under each section and chapter. It can also mention noteworthy design features, such as inclusion of study guides, chapter abstracts, visuals and artifacts, or resources for further inquiry. How much details are included in the summary will depend on the length requirement of the review. The shorter a book review, the more concise the summary has to be.

Part IV appraises the relevance, value, significance, and contribution of the book by discussing its merits and limitations. The focus of the discussion can be on

- how well or effective the book achieves its purpose
- the soundness of the theoretical framework used
- the quality of scholarship, including the rigor of the methodology employed and the care taken in assembling, evaluating, and presenting evidence
- how the book compares with other books on the same subject
- the breadth, depth, and accuracy of the content covered
- what is left out of the book and whether that omission is reasonable
- what specific point is well or not so well presented/argued
- the connection between the evidence presented and the conclusions drawn, and
- clarity, coherence, and style of writing.

Part V provides final commentary and recommendation about the book. It can comment on the usefulness, contributions, limitations, or the overall writing quality of the book. It can also state whether you would recommend the book to its intended audience and what caveats or additional resources readers need to be aware of in order to make the book more accessible, relevant, or useful.

These parts can be given different weights and calibrated differently according to your emphasis and preference, as well as the readership and requirements of the publication outlet. Some book reviews focus on the critical appraisal of the book's overall message without providing too much detail about the content of each chapter; other book reviews present more detailed chapter-by-chapter summaries, but offer only a brief critique of the content. Some book reviews provide an introduction that situates the book in the broader scholarship of the discipline, but others delve right into the book's messages from the beginning without presenting background information that contextualizes the book.

The length of a book review also varies considerably, depending on space constraints or assignment requirements. A typical book review runs 1500–2000 words long, but it can sometimes be as short as 500 words or as long as 5000 words. A short book review is sometimes called a "book notice" and usually runs about 500–800 words long. It challenges the reviewer to be sharper and more focused in writing. An extended book review, sometimes called essay book review, usually involves a review of two or more books on the same topic and can run between 3,000 and 5,000 words. It allows the reviewer to compare across multiple books, assess the contributions of each individual book, develop ideas at greater length, and provide additional materials and perspectives. Most academic journals publish book reviews to keep their readership abreast of the significant, recently published scholarly books.

The rest of this chapter presents two book review samples from different academic fields and annotates how they are discursively constructed. For each book review, the References section is omitted to save space, and paragraphs are numbered for ease of reference in analysis and discussion.

Book Review Sample #1

The first book review essay (Fang & Robertson, 2020) was published in the *Journal of Adolescent and Adult Literacy*, a premier journal in the field of literacy education. It reviews a professional book on disciplinary literacy—reading/writing in academic disciplines, a topic of current interest and significance for literacy educators.

Text 6-1: Book Review Sample #1

Unpacking and Operationalizing Disciplinary Literacy: A Review of *Disciplinary Literacy: Inquiry and Instruction*

Ippolito, J., Dobbs, C., & Charner-Laird, M. (2019). *Disciplinary literacy inquiry and instruction*. West Palm Beach, FL: Learning Sciences International and Newark, DE: International Reading Association. ISBN: 978-1-943920-64-8, pp. 173

1   In a world where literacy practices are rapidly evolving, recent scholar-ship at the elementary and secondary levels has embraced the notion of disciplinary literacy (Shanahan & Shanahan, 2008). In secondary set-tings, specifically, an emerging shift is taking place from teaching basic language skills (e.g., fluency, vocabulary) and generic cognitive strategies (e.g., inferencing, summarizing) to teaching discipline-specific language and literacy practices (Fang & Schleppegrell, 2008; Moje, 2008). This move toward disciplinary literacy instruction places new demands on classroom teachers, who are now challenged to provide literacy instruc-tion that promotes not only the learning of disciplinary content but also understanding of how this content is produced, codified, communicated, evaluated, taught, and learned. Ippolito, Dobbs, and Charner-Laird's (2019) *Disciplinary Literacy: Inquiry and Instruction* (hereafter *DLII*) is a timely and welcome addition to the growing literature that aims to help teachers develop expertise in disciplinary literacy instruction.

2   *DLII* aims to "support teachers and leaders who are eager to help appren-tice all students across grade levels into the advanced literacy subcul-tures that exist within each of the disciplines" (p. 6). To this end, it makes a fundamental distinction between "shared literacy skills across [content] areas and highly differentiated and discipline-specific literacy skills" (p. 4), suggesting that advanced literacy development entails both the shor-ing up of cross-discipline literacy skills and mastery of discipline-specific literacy skills. It then provides a framework for operationalizing discipli-nary literacy and shares vignettes from K-12 classroom teachers who have attempted disciplinary literacy instruction. As a whole, the book is written in a voice that is pragmatic and accessible. Its use of the first person (*we*) and the second person (*you*) bridges the distance between the reader and the author, making the writing more interactive and engaging.

Inquiry and Instruction as a Cyclical Process

3   *DLII* proposes an approach to disciplinary literacy that links a collabora-tive inquiry cycle with an established model of reading comprehension. It begins by making the case for disciplinary literacy (Chapter 1), arguing that a focus on discipline-specific ways of reading, writing, thinking, and communicating is key to developing literacy for all students across all grades and all schools. This is followed by a chapter outlining a frame-work for guiding disciplinary literacy inquiry and instruction (Chapter 2). The inquiry framework outlines a cyclical process that includes defining an inquiry question, building background knowledge, generating ideas, testing ideas, and reflecting on and revising ideas. Given the newness of disciplinary literacy in the research literature, this collaborative inquiry cycle is intended to lead teachers to challenge fundamental assumptions and make "adaptive changes" to their instruction.

4   Along with the inquiry cycle, *DLII* also introduces the four elements that the RAND Reading Study Group (2002) identified as essential to the process of reading comprehension—the text, the task, the reader, and culture. The RAND model provides a heuristic to guide the types of questions teachers might explore related to the four elements of reading comprehension as they work to make adaptive changes. Teachers are encouraged to select an initial area of focus (i.e., text, tasks, students, culture) to examine their current practices and design teaching and learning experiences focused on the "language, genres, and modalities prized by each discipline" (Ippolito et al., 2019, backcover).

5   Chapters 3–6 then illustrate how disciplinary literacy work on each of the four elements of reading comprehension can be brought to life through the collaborative inquiry cycle. Each chapter provides first-person vignettes describing the instructional and inquiry contexts of actual classroom teachers. Interspersed around those vignettes are descriptions of the inquiry cycle that provide questions, activities, and resources teachers may find useful. These practical walkthroughs help the reader envision what the inquiry-instruction process can look and sound like.

6   Finally, the last two chapters of the book spotlight cautions and personal reflections that may influence the inquiry-instruction cycle. Chapter 7 offers contextual factors that may hinder or facilitate teachers' transition to disciplinary literacy instruction. Chapter 8 presents the authors' reflections on their own journeys and lessons learned as they walked the disciplinary literacy path in their own teaching and learning. As a whole, the book is coherent, practical, and relevant.

Challenges of Disciplinary Literacy Work

7   The above strengths notwithstanding, *DLII* is wanting in several aspects. First, whereas the book starts by defining and giving purpose to disciplinary literacy as an important instructional lever to help students "succeed within and beyond school" (Ippolito et al., 2019, backcover), it fundamentally shifts, from Chapter 2 onward, to an overarching focus more on fostering inquiry than on discipline-specific language, genres, strategies, and modalities. As such, the book may be particularly helpful for elementary-level teachers who are keen on promoting literacy through discipline-specific inquiries. However, for secondary-level teachers to challenge their fundamental assumptions and make adaptive changes in their instructional practices, the book may need a more detailed and indepth presentation of discipline-legitimated discourse genres, registers, strategies, modalities, and habits of mind.

8   Along the same vein, the connections to disciplinary literacy work are not always clearly made in the classroom vignettes provided (e.g., Chapter 5).

In light of the many (mis)conceptions of disciplinary literacy afloat in the literature (Hinchman & O'Brien, 2019), this lack of explication may cause confusion for readers, making them wonder about how disciplinary literacy instruction actually differs across content areas or grade levels. Although an appendix of resources is provided to help the reader delve further into these topics, it would be more helpful if concrete examples of disciplinary literacy instruction are highlighted in *all* of the classroom vignettes. For example, in making text a focus of disciplinary literacy inquiry and instruction (cf., Chapter 3), a teacher can engage students in exploring how experts use language to present information, infuse points of view, and structure text. Such explorations can include a discussion of how authorial voice is instantiated differently across different disciplines, with the language arts teacher focusing on how literary authors present their characters' feeling and emotions through showing (e.g., *Sam slammed the door.*) instead of telling (e.g., *Sam was mad.*), the history teacher on how historians embed personal biases in their interpretations of past events (e.g., *Boston Massacre* vs. *the incident on King Street*), and the biology teacher on how scientists use hedges to temper knowledge claims and show deference to experts (e.g., *The novel coronavirus may have originated from bats.*). Examples such as these can illustrate that from a linguistic perspective, disciplinary differences lie not just in technical vocabulary, but more broadly in the way grammar is used to make meaning.

9   Another issue with the book is in relation to the use of the RAND model of reading comprehension as a guiding framework for designing disciplinary literacy teaching and learning experiences. The authors surmise that the model could serve a "new and important use" with disciplinary literacy because they have found it to be "quite effective over time at helping [them] tease apart factors when a student is struggling or succeeding as a reader" (p. 24). The RAND model focuses on common factors (e.g., reader, text, activity) that impact an individual's text understanding. It gives little attention to the skills, strategies, practices, or habits of mind that may be similar across or unique to specific disciplines and discourse communities. Nor does it explicitly address other equally important aspects of disciplinary literacy such as composing, performing, and multimodal representations. This lack of explicit focus might serve to hyper-emphasize the role of reading in some disciplines where oral language, writing, viewing, or performing is privileged. Moreover, whereas the RAND model provides a static and singular model of how reading comprehension occurs for an individual in a given context and moment in time, it does not fully provide "a theory of action for teachers who would seek to engage a range of students across a range

of subject area classes" (Alvermann & Moje, 2019, p. 369). As such, the model has limited value for disciplinary literacy work because it "overlooks the complex roles of subject area teachers, their goals, and the contexts in which they work" (Alvermann & Moje, 2019, p. 369). The weaving of the collaborative inquiry cycle into the model to some extent mitigates this limitation.

Moving Forward

10   Overall, *DLLI* is a potentially valuable resource for teachers who have had some prior understanding of disciplinary literacy and are looking for ways to implement it in their classrooms. It is best used in professional development workshops and teacher study groups, where teachers read and share connections to their own classroom practices. Those who are not yet familiar with the concept of disciplinary literacy will likely find it helpful to read this book in tandem with other resources (e.g., Christie & Maton, 2011; Nelson & Ehren, 2012) that provide more comprehensive and in-depth discussions of the genesis and tenets of disciplinary literacy, as well as principles for and caveats about disciplinary literacy instruction. Readers are encouraged to access the book's appendix with resources that provide concrete examples of disciplinary literacy instruction (e.g., Brock et al., 2014; McConachie & Petrosky, 2010). Other relevant resources include Fang (2020) and Langer (2011). Taken together, these resources provide specific examples of how to integrate literacy work in disciplinary teaching/learning in a way that promotes the building of content knowledge, understanding of disciplinary ways of making meaning, and cultivation of disciplinary habits of mind.

Analyzing Book Review Sample #1

This book review has a title and a subtitle that give readers a quick sense of what the essay is about. It is written in the third person and begins with the bibliographical information about the book. The first paragraph of the review establishes a context by situating the book in the broader literature on the shift to disciplinary literacy instruction in K-12 schooling. The second paragraph highlights the purpose, central theme, and positive aspects of the book. The third through sixth paragraphs summarize the content of the book. Note that Chapter 2 is summarized in significantly greater detail than are other chapters, indicating that it is likely the most important part of the book.

Beginning with the seventh paragraph, the weaknesses of the book are discussed. The first weakness identified is that later parts of the book drift away from its initial focus on disciplinary literacy. The eighth paragraph further exemplifies this drift by noting a lack of connections between the classroom vignettes provided and the central concept of the book (disciplinary literacy). It also provides suggestions on how such connections can be made more explicitly through an example showing how teachers can engage students in discussions about discipline-specific ways of using language to construct the authorial voice. The next paragraph questions the appropriateness of the RAND reading model as a guiding framework for disciplinary literacy work, a topic that is the focus of discussion in Chapter 2. The review ends with an overall assessment of the book's worth and makes practical recommendations for readers (last paragraph).

A number of points deserve mentioning here. First, when a claim is made about the book's merit or drawback, evidence is always provided to support the claim. Evidence is given through citations of other sources, specific instances from the book itself, or examples provided by the reviewers. This makes the critique more convincing, and readers are more likely to accept as valid what the reviewers say.

Second, the reviewers are diligent in forging discursive flow across and within sections and paragraphs. The 10-paragraph essay is divided into four sections, each with a different focus—Section I (first two paragraphs) on context and merits, Section II (third through sixth paragraphs) on chapter contents, Section III (seventh through ninth paragraphs) on weaknesses, and Section IV (tenth paragraph) on summative evaluation. Within and across sections, efforts are made to connect paragraphs. For example, the end of the first paragraph introduces the book to be reviewed. The second and third paragraphs then begin with the title of the book (*DLII*). Other connectors are used to facilitate transitions from one paragraph to the next, including *along with the inquiry cycle, then, finally, the above strengths notwithstanding, along the same vein, another issue with the book*, and *overall*. These varied linguistic markers make the transitions between paragraphs/sections clear, smooth, and interesting to read.

Within each paragraph, links between sentences are likewise carefully crafted to forge a conceptually coherent and discursively tightly knit structure that makes the review easier to follow. For example, in the first paragraph, the first sentence notes the popularity of the notion of disciplinary literacy in K-12 schooling. The second sentence then exemplifies, through the use of the word *specifically*, how this notion plays out in secondary schooling, which is the primary concern of the journal in which the book review is published. The third sentence begins with *this move*, which is a nominalization that distills the "emerging shift" message conveyed in the second sentence. The last sentence then introduces the book, suggesting that it can help teachers develop expertise in disciplinary literacy instruction, a task that is called for toward the end of the preceding sentence.

The reviewers also seem judicious in selecting quotes from the book and other resources to reinforce key messages, foreground certain points, and lend credibility to argument. Moreover, evaluation is made with care through the use of cautious language. For example, the reviewers write that *the book may be particularly helpful* (paragraph #7) and *This lack of explicit focus might serve to hyper-emphasize the role of reading* (paragraph #9), instead of using more direct, unqualified statements like *the book will be particularly helpful* and *This lack of explicit focus hyper-emphasizes the role of reading*. This contrasts with statements such as *DLII is a timely and welcome addition* (paragraph #1) and *As a whole, the book is coherent, practical, and relevant* (paragraph #6), where positive evaluation is made without qualification. However, not all positive evaluations are unqualified, as can be seen in *the connections to disciplinary literacy work are not always clearly made* (paragraph #8), *the model has limited value for disciplinary literacy work* (paragraph #9), *The weaving of the collaborative inquiry cycle...to some extent mitigates this limitation* (paragraph #9), and *DLII is a potentially valuable resource* (paragraph #10).

Similarly, recommendations are given through the use of modal verbs and conditional clauses, as in *the book may need a more detailed and in-depth presentation* (paragraph #7); *it would be more helpful if concrete examples* (paragraph #8); *a teacher can engage students in exploring* (paragraph #8); *Such explorations can include a discussion* (paragraph #8); and *Those who are not...will likely find it helpful to read* (paragraph #10). Occasionally, recommendations are made with confidence through the use of boosters, as in *It is best used in professional development workshop* (paragraph #10) and *Readers are encouraged to access* (paragraph #10). Note that the passive voice is used in each of the two example sentences so that its subject is consistent with that of the sentence preceding it.

Claims are also tempered through the use of modal verbs, as in *this lack of explication may cause confusion for readers* (paragraph #8) and *Examples such as these can illustrate* (paragraph #8). However, not all criticisms of the book are modulated, as can be seen in *It gives little attention to the skills* (paragraph #9) and *Nor does it explicitly address other equally important aspects* (paragraph #9), where the reviewers show confidence in their judgment.

Taken together, the essay presents a critical yet considerate review that strives to provide readers with an unbiased assessment of the book's merits, shortcomings, and contributions. This purpose is achieved through strategic rhetorical and linguistic maneuvers.

Book Review Sample #2

The second book review (McCabe, 2018) is published in *Housing Studies*, a leading international journal and a major forum for theoretical and analytical developments in the housing field. It reviews an edited book by two sociologists (Dewilde & Ronald, 2017) that examines how housing property ownership has become central both to household well-being and to the reshaping of social, economic, and political relations.

Text 6-2: Book Review Sample #2

Housing wealth and welfare, edited by Caroline Dewilde and Richard Ronald, Cheltenham, UK, Edward Elgar Publishing Limited, 2017, 270 pp., $145.00 (hardcover), ISBN 978 1 78536 095 4

1   The relationship between housing and welfare is a complicated one. Torgersen (1987) famously referred to housing as the "wobbly pillar" under the welfare state because housing both provides shelter and serves as a commodity used by many families to build private wealth. The fact that housing serves multiple roles heightens the importance of contemporary efforts to understand housing policies as part of the changing welfare state. These efforts are more important than ever in the context of neo-liberalism, where housing policies are coalescing around the privatization of shelter, the promotion of homeownership and the solidification of asset-based welfare.

2   This intersection of housing policy and social welfare is the subject of a new edited volume by Caroline Dewilde and Richard Ronald. In a series of compelling case studies, they bring together scholars from across Europe to understand homeownership, housing wealth and the changing welfare state. *Housing Wealth and Welfare* is grounded in Kemeny's (1981) well-known thesis identifying a trade-off between the generosity of welfare policies and the level of homeownership across countries (Kemeny 1981). While this thesis provides the foundation for the volume, Dewilde and Ronald argue in the introductory chapter that subsequent research has "failed to unravel the underlying dynamics and explanatory mechanisms" (p. 13) behind housing wealth and welfare systems. Their volume seeks to provide that nuance—to understand variation in the development of post-war welfare policy regimes, including country-specific politics, and to identify the challenges households face as they build wealth through housing. The volume can largely be read from these two perspectives—a macro-level analysis of policy formation across welfare regimes and a micro-level analysis of the wealth-building that occurs within individual households.

3   On the first of these perspectives, an early chapter by Bengtsson, Ruonavaara, and Sorvoll compares the development of homeownership policies in Norway, Finland, and Sweden. Their orienting concept is path dependency—the idea that policies, once established, are difficult to alter. The chapter, like several in the volume, usefully digs into the history

of housing and social policies in a comparative context, exploring the political regimes in each of these Scandinavian countries, including the ideology of elected officials and the tax policies that reward particular types of housing behaviors.

4   The state continues to serve as the unit of analysis in several other chapters. Lennertz explores the relationship between housing wealth and welfare policies in a cross-national context, challenging previous scholarship that assumes rising homeownership rates are associated with declining welfare generosity. While housing researchers tend to view the impact of housing on welfare policies "purely on an expansion-retrenchment continuum" (p. 116), Lennertz argues that the welfare state transformations that occur alongside the expansion of asset-based policies are substantially more nuanced and complicated than previous research suggests.

5   Comparing East and West Germany, Kolb and Buchholz highlight the importance of institutional characteristics in shaping opportunities to acquire housing and build wealth. The authors show that divergent histories of East and West Germany clearly influenced homeownership opportunities and housing values (although they also report evidence of convergence among the youngest cohorts in their study).

6   While these chapters describe welfare policies and institutional characteristics at the level of the state, other chapters focus on the way asset-based welfare policies impact individuals and families. In a chapter about the experiences of low-income homeowners in Northern Ireland during the economic downturn, Wallace asks whether asset ownership generated resiliency. Although owning a home left many low-income families financially vulnerable, Wallace reports that homeownership did create feelings of ontological security and safety that bred resiliency during a period of market uncertainty.

7   While Wallace considers the experiences of low-income homeowners, Mandic and Mrzel study the housing experiences of elderly homeowners in post-socialist countries. In places struggling to provide for their aging populations, Mandic and Mrzel argue that housing assets can serve as a lifesaving resource by providing a source of wealth, a place for co-residence with a caregiver or an asset to be sold in exchange for alternative care arrangements. In post-soviet Russia, Zavisca and Geber explore a different set of challenges facing elderly homeowners. They argue that privatization created diverse forms of ownership—for example, joint ownership across multiple generation or "asymmetrical spousal ownership" (p. 224) in which only one partner owned the property—that diverge from common narratives about the value of owning a home.

8   While most of the chapters consider the housing experiences and welfare regimes in a single country (or set of countries), Koppe and Searle consider housing wealth and welfare over the life course. They usefully offer a four-pronged framework by considering how housing is *acquired*, how housing wealth is *managed*, the ways in which housing wealth is *used*, and the opportunities for housing wealth to be *transferred* across generations. This framework, which is offered in an early chapter, provides a useful bridge for the two broad themes from the book—not only the way that individuals engage with their household wealth over the life course, but also how state policies, including those designed to expand ownership, boost property values or tax household wealth, shift opportunities for building wealth and boosting welfare through housing.

9   Taken together, the volume acknowledges a growing convergence of housing policies centered on the individualization of welfare strategies through the privatization of housing. As John Doling reminds readers in the Epilogue, housing policies increasingly serve to shift the welfare burden away from the collective responsibility of the state and toward individuals. Despite this convergence, the volume usefully highlights variation across historical, social, and political contexts, reminding readers of the value of in-depth case studies to understand this important social phenomenon.

Analyzing Book Review Sample #2

The essay, also written in the third person, is preceded with some basic bibliographical information about the edited book being reviewed (e.g., title, author, publisher, publication year and place, number of pages, price). The first paragraph of the review establishes a context for the book by identifying a topic that is significant to the housing studies field—the complex relationship between housing and welfare. The second paragraph identifies the subject addressed in the book, as well as the purpose, approach, and theoretical perspective of the book. The third through eighth paragraphs summarize and comment on the individual chapters in the book. Note that the chapters are not presented in the same order as they are listed in the book, and not all chapters are included in the discussion (e.g., Chapter 1 not explicitly referenced in the discussion). Instead, the discussion is organized around two perspectives: first, macro-analysis of state policy (third to fifth paragraphs); and then micro-analysis of individual household wealth building (sixth to eighth paragraphs). Only 1–2 key points from each chapter are summarized and commented on. The last paragraph provides a concise summary that highlights the overall value and contributions of the book.

As a whole, the paragraphs are well connected, with various linguistic devices used to facilitate the transitions. For example, the second paragraph begins with *This intersection*, which refers to the complex relationship between housing policy and social welfare discussed in the first paragraph. The third paragraph begins with *On the first of these perspectives*, which refers to the two perspectives (state vs individual households) mentioned in the last sentence of the second paragraph. The fourth and fifth paragraphs follow the third paragraph in discussing chapters that use state as the unit of analysis.

Beginning with the sixth paragraph, chapters using individual households as the unit of analysis are reviewed. A comparative clause introduced by the conjunction *while* (*While these chapters …*) is used to facilitate this transition. The same linguistic device is used in the next two paragraphs to bring out the contrast between Wallace's chapter (discussed in paragraph #6) and two other chapters by Mandic and Mrzel and Zavisca and Geber (discussed in paragraph #7) and between most of the chapters in the book (reviewed previously) and Koppe and Searle's chapter (discussed in paragraph #8). The last paragraph wraps up the review with *Taken together*, a phrase commonly used for this purpose. Other phrases that can be used for the same purpose are *in all, altogether, collectively, generally, in general, by and large, in brief, in total, in sum, to summarize, in the aggregate, as a whole, on the whole, on average*, and *en masse*.

Throughout the essay, nominalizations are used to create virtual entities, which are then combined with other grammatical elements (e.g., generic nouns, prepositional phrases, participial phrase, embedded clause) to create expanded noun phrases that sound simultaneously abstract, technical, and dense. These include, for example, *the importance of contemporary efforts, the privatization of shelter, the promotion of homeownership, the solidification of asset-based welfare, the generosity of welfare policies, the wealth-building that occurs within individual households, the welfare state transformations that occur alongside the expansion of asset-based policies, a growing convergence of housing policies centered on the individualization of welfare strategies through the privatization of housing*, and *variation across historical, social, and political contexts*. Nominalization—such as *this intersection* (second paragraph), *this framework* (eighth paragraph), and *this convergence* (last paragraph)—are also used to help structure text and develop argument.

A variety of verbs are used to report more accurately what chapter authors and others say. These verbs include *referred to, argue(s), compares, explore(s), highlight(s), show, asks, reports, study, focus on, consider, offer*, and *reminds*. The simple present tense is used in most cases. Additionally, recommendations are given with caution, as in *this volume can largely be read…*, where a modal verb (*can*) and an adverb (*largely*) are used as hedging devices.

Appraisal resources are used to convey the reviewer's attitudes toward the book and its chapters, as well as the concepts and ideas referenced in the discussion.

Examples include *Torgersen (1987) famously referred to* (first paragraph), *a series of compelling case studies* (second paragraph), *Kemeny's (1981) well-known thesis* (second paragraph), *usefully digs into the history* (third paragraph), *a useful bridge* (eighth paragraph), and *usefully highlights variation* (ninth paragraph). These attitudes are almost never qualified. Compared to the first book review sample, this review appears to be less tentative in its evaluation. This is perhaps due to the fact that the evaluation in the second sample is largely positive.

Conclusion

Book review is a common academic exercise that requires you to read, dwell on, understand, and appraise a book or a set of two or more topically related books that is of potential significance to the field. It offers insights into the relative worth and contribution of the book or set of books. To compose a quality book review requires not only a deep understanding of the content of the book(s) being reviewed but also knowledge about the typical rhetorical moves associated with the genre and mastery of the linguistic resources that are functional and effective for instantiating these moves.

Reflection/Application Activities

1 Find a book review in your field and examine its rhetorical moves and the linguistic resources used to instantiate these moves. Discuss how these moves and resources contribute to the overall purpose of the genre and how they are similar to and different from the ones described in this chapter.

2 Take a look at a book review essay you wrote before. In light of what is presented in this chapter, discuss what you think you did well and not so well, as well as what you can do to improve your skills in writing the genre.

3 Write a review of a recently published book or a set of two topically related books in your field, using the rhetorical moves discussed in this chapter and drawing on the linguistic resources and strategies presented in Chapters 2–4.

References

Fang, Z., & Robertson, D. (2020). Unpacking and operationalizing disciplinary literacy: A review of *Disciplinary Literacy: Inquiry and Instruction*. *Journal of Adolescent and Adult Literacy*, 64(2), 240–242.

McCabe, B. (2018). Housing wealth and welfare, *Housing Studies*, 33(2), 338–340.

Natriello, G. (2000). For the record: Reviewing books. *Techers College Record*, 102(2), 267–270.

7
Writing a Literature Review

What Is a Literature Review?

A literature review is a review of relevant prior work on a topic of significance in order to find out what is known and not known about the topic and what can be done with the findings. It is not an annotated bibliography; nor is it just a summary of prior scholarship. Rather, a literature review involves objective synthesis and critical analysis of the existing research. Its goal is to detect emerging trends or patterns in a domain of scholarly inquiry, assess contributions of prior work, identify areas that deserve further investigation, and/or provide implications for policy, research, or practice. A literature review is often part of a longer article, such as an empirical research paper (see Chapter 9). It can also be an independent essay on its own.

Jalongo and Saracho (2010) identified four different types of stand-alone literature reviews that are commonly found in scholarly publications. These are integrative reviews, systematic reviews, meta-analytic reviews, and qualitative reviews. An integrative review synthesizes and critiques a diverse body of literature related to a topic of significance to the field. A systematic review synthesizes and appraises a narrower but reasonably well-defined body of literature in order to yield evidence-based decisions. A meta-analytic review conducts quantitative analysis of data (e.g., results, effect sizes) reported in previous studies in order to generate patterns and guidelines for future work. A qualitative review, which is perhaps the least common of all literature reviews, provides "one person's narrative interpretation of a diverse body of literature to promote further reflection and accept multiple perspectives" (p. 97).

In writing a research paper, a literature review is needed for one of the two reasons noted below. First, as indicated in Chapter 3, you need to situate what you want to do with a topic in the context of what has been done on the topic so that you can be sure you are not merely repeating what others have already done on the topic or generating knowledge that is already well known. This context is provided in the literature review. It allows you to build your work on existing scholarship and at the same time extend it in some way. Second, a literature review is needed to identify what is known, not known, or uncertain about a particular topic (e.g., effectiveness of a new drug or an instructional strategy) so that you can generate evidence-based guidelines and recommendations to inform further work on the topic. In other words, a literature review provides the justification for research, policy, or practice.

Rhetorical Moves in Literature Review

A literature review typically includes (a) introduction, which describes the context in which your topic is situated and explains its importance; (b) synthesis, which summarizes key aspects of prior studies; (c) evaluation, which analyzes and appraises prior studies in terms of their theoretical underpinnings, methodologies, results, interpretations, and conclusions; (d) justification, which identifies major themes or knowledge gaps in prior studies and provides a rationale for your intended work or guidelines for future work on the topic; and (e) conclusion, which recaps the main findings from the literature review and explains how these findings inform policy, research, and practice or how your work will address the knowledge gaps. Some literature reviews, such as meta-analytic reviews and integrative reviews, require a separate section on methodology that details the process and criteria used to locate, select, and categorize the studies included in the review and when appropriate, the methods used to calculate and analyze effect sizes.

How to Go about Writing a Literature Review?

When writing a literature review, you can follow the process described below: determining the scope → locating and selecting relevant studies → reading and analyzing the studies → constructing a coherent review. This process is not linear; rather, it is recursive, as you may need to go back and forth between certain components of the process during actual writing. Each component of the process is described below.

Determining the Scope

The first task in writing a literature review is to determine the scope of the review by identifying the parameters of the topic you are reviewing. This is indeed a challenging task, as inexperienced writers often have a difficult time figuring out how broad or narrow a territory their review should cover. One way to cope with this dilemma is to think about what questions your potential readers are likely to raise in relation to the topic you are proposing to investigate.

For example, to conduct a study that investigates the effect of reading instruction in the science classroom on middle school students' science literacy (cf., Fang & Wei, 2010), one question your readers may ask is this: how is reading relevant to science? After all, reading and science seem like two separate school subjects. This means you will need to review the literature that discusses ways reading connects with science—that is, how reading is central to both the conception of science and the social practices of scientists. This can also become the theoretical framework of the study (see Chapter 9).

Another question your readers are likely to ask is this: Why do middle school students still need reading instruction? After all, haven't students already learned how to read by the end of elementary schooling? To answer this question, you will need to review relevant literature on why reading instruction is still needed for middle school students to successfully read in content areas like science. And if reading instruction is needed in secondary content area classrooms like science, then has research been conducted in this particular area? That is, what does prior research say about the effectiveness of teaching reading in science classrooms on improving students' science literacy? This means that you will need to review what kinds of reading instruction has been provided in science classrooms and what their effects are on students' science learning.

A further question to ask in relation to the topic of investigation is this: If reading instruction is needed in science, then does it mean that science teachers are ready or willing to undertake such a responsibility in their own classrooms. After all, science teachers rarely think of themselves as reading teachers and may not have the knowledge, skills, willingness, and/or confidence to teach reading. This means that you will need to include a section that reviews what existing research says about science teachers' beliefs and practices regarding reading instruction.

In light of the discussion above, it is clear that your literature review for the proposed study needs to include at least four sections, which are (a) the relationship between reading and science, (b) the role of reading in secondary content area (especially science) learning, (c) research concerning the effectiveness of reading instruction on students' science learning, and (d) science teachers' beliefs about and preparedness for reading instruction. Including these areas in your review answers potential questions your readers may have about your topic and provides a reasonably comprehensive literature base on which you can identify what is known and not yet known about teaching reading in science, thus justifying your focus on the topic and informing your choice of research design and methodology for the study.

Locating and Selecting Studies

Once you have narrowed down the scope of the literature review, it is time to look for studies that belong to each of the areas you are about to review.

You can do this by searching university library catalogues (e.g., books, monographs, journals) using classification numbers for the subjects you are searching or looking for work by specific authors. You can use search engines such as Google or Baidu, online encyclopedias such as Wikipedia, and databases such as Academic OneFile, ProQuest, Google Scholar, JSTOR, EBSCO, Project Muse (for humanities and social science), EconLit (for economics), Medline (for life sciences and biomedicine), Inspec (for physics, engineering, and computer science), and Academic Search Complete. You can start your search with a general descriptor and refine the descriptor as needed, focusing on work by noted scholars and from reputable books and journals. The studies selected for review need to be not only relevant but also current and important. They may include unpublished conference papers or graduate (master or doctoral) theses (especially when your searches yield a small number of items), but these sources should perhaps be kept to a minimum. This search process is often, albeit not always, described in the methods section of a literature review article.

Getting back to the reading-science study mentioned earlier, you can look for research-based publications in books by noted scholars who have done work that crosses science and literacy/reading (e.g., Larry Yore, Jonathan Osborne, Jay Lemke, Michael Halliday), in quality science education journals (e.g., *Science Education, International Journal of Science Education, Journal of Research in Science Teaching, Journal of Science Teacher Education*), in respected reading/literacy education journals (e.g., *Reading Research Quarterly, Journal of Literacy Research, Journal of Adolescent and Adult Literacy*), or in top-tier general education journals (e.g., *American Educational Research Journal, Journal of Educational Psychology, Journal of Educational Research*). Searching for work in reputable journals or by respected scholars ensure that the studies you identify are of high quality and well regarded in the academic community.

Reading and Analyzing Studies

The next step in the literature review is to read and analyze the studies that have been found from your literature searches. These studies, often numbered in dozens, need to be (re)read and then organized into categories that make the most sense in light of the focus of your study. They can be organized by chronology. For example, you can group studies published before or after the release of the Common Core State Standards or the No Child Left Behind Act, with the intention to find out whether certain instructional practice or student educational outcome is impacted by the landmark document or legislation. You can also group studies by time (e.g., per decade or quarter of a century), with the intention to find out, for example, whether academic writing has become more informal over the past 50 or 100 years. Studies can also be grouped by the methodology employed (e.g., quantitative, qualitative, mixed), the population examined (e.g., young children, adolescents, adults), the context of investigation (e.g., day care, elementary, secondary, college, out-of-school clubs, summer camps), theoretical frameworks used (e.g., sociocultural, linguistic, cognitive, critical), or key findings (e.g., studies that show positive effects of intervention, studies that show negative effects of intervention, studies that show no effects of intervention, studies that show mixed effects of intervention).

Once the studies are grouped, you can then identify key findings, themes, strengths, weaknesses, emphases, similarities, and discrepancies in these studies, as well as major patterns, trends, gaps, and relationships among the studies, in each group, and across groups. At this time, it is also a good idea to select quotes or statistics that you think may be useful when writing the review. The results from the analysis are then summarized in a table or concept map that allows for better visualization (see, for example, Table 7.2 later in the chapter).

In the sample reading-science study mentioned earlier, you can, for example, group the studies that examine the effects of reading instruction on science learning into two broad categories—those reporting on the use of one single reading strategy (e.g., concept mapping) and those reporting on more systematic integration of reading (e.g., weekly reading of science texts plus instruction on the use of multiple reading strategies). Within each of these two groups, you can further differentiate studies that took place in elementary classrooms and those that were conducted in secondary (middle/high school) classrooms. Alternatively, you can group the studies by research setting first (e.g., elementary school vs secondary school) and then differentiate how reading is taught within each setting (e.g., teaching a single reading strategy vs more systematic infusion of reading). Themes and limitations within and across studies are then identified, with the goal of informing the design and focus of your proposed study.

Constructing the Review

The first step in constructing a literature review is to develop an outline, or bullet points, based on the results from the analysis discussed above. The outline sketches out the different sections of the literature review and key information (e.g., context, methods, findings, quotes, comments) to be included in each section. These main points are then developed into sentences and paragraphs, using a variety of connecting devices to help craft a logical, coherent review that flows. As discussed in Chapter 4, links between sentences and between paragraphs can be established through the use of subheadings (e.g., *locating and selecting studies, reading and analyzing studies*), references (e.g., *it, this, they*), conjunctions and conjunctive adverbs (e.g., *although, therefore*), nominalizations (e.g., *this conception, the process*), repetition (e.g., *Bolton [2017]—the researcher—the study*), metacommentaries (e.g., *in other words, for example, taken together, in essence*), and other connectives (e.g., *for these reasons, similar to Yore [2004]*). Listed in Table 7.1 are some transition devices used in Fang and Wei (2010) that help stitch their literature review together.

Table 7.1 Sample Transition Devices Used in Fang and Wei (2010)

Types of Links	Examples
Links between sections	• Subheadings: *theoretical framework, reading in second content area of science, reading instruction and science learning, science teachers and reading instruction* • Preview statement: *We review three areas of research that inform the design and implementation of the present study: reading in secondary content area of science, contributions of reading instruction to science learning, and science teachers' attitudes toward and knowledge about reading.*
Links between paragraphs	• Given the nature and character of science, it is not [...]. • Another way to improve [...]. • Similar to Romance and Vitale's (1992) study, Guthrie et al. (1998) [...]. • The research studies reviewed previously support the [...]. • Building on Yore's work, DiGisi and Willett (1995) surveyed [...]. • In summary, although [...]. they often report [...].
Links between sentences	• On one hand, science is [...]. On the other hand, science is also [...]. • For these reasons, science has been characterized [...]. • For example, Romance and Vitale (1992) studied [...]. • In short, developing a rich store of domain knowledge [...]. • However, adolescents engage in very little reading [...]. • Taken together, the existent research suggests [...]. • In other words, combining reading and science [...]. • Thus, it is important to know [...]. • Instead, the teachers reported [...]. • First, reading [...]. Second, the infusion of [...]. Third, the overall school climate [...]. • Content areas provide [...]. They also provide [...]. • CORI also had a positive [...]. It increased the students' ability to [...]. • They integrated the teaching of science, reading, and writing processes in a concept-based, problem-centered unit on a simple machine. This 10-week unit featured text reading, experiments [...]. • According to Eccles et al. (1993), middle schools [...] than do elementary students [...]. These factors make the integration of reading [...]. • Guthrie et al (1998) designed a year-long [...]. The researchers compared third and [...]. The study found that [...].

A Sample Literature Review Essay

The rest of the chapter presents and annotates a systematic literature review essay (see Text 7-1). The essay is a slightly modified version of Fang (2012), which was published in a top tier journal (*Journal of Adolescent and Adult Literacy*) in the field of literacy education. Additional examples are provided in Chapter 9, where literature review is again discussed as part of an empirical research article. Text 7-1, with the References section omitted in order to save space, was written to provide a state-of-the-art assessment of what we know and do not yet know about literacy instruction in academic content areas, with the goal of informing future work in the domain and providing classroom teachers with evidence-based guidelines for practice.

Text 7-1: A Sample Literature Review

Approaches to Developing Content Area Literacies: A Synthesis and a Critique

Adolescent literacy has emerged as a "very hot" topic in literacy education over the past few years (Cassidy, Valadez, Garrett, & Barrera, 2010). Its ascendency to the national spotlight reflects the growing recognition among policy makers, researchers, and educators that a continuing emphasis on literacy and literacy instruction beyond the elementary grades is key to ensuring that students are college and career ready by the time they graduate high school (CCAAL, 2010). A major concern in the United States is that more than 70% of students in grades 4–12 lack the skills to read and write proficiently in academic content areas (National Center for Educational Statistics, 2011; Salahu-Din, Persky, & Miller, 2008). An array of national reports (e.g., Biancarosa & Snow, 2006; Deshler, Palincsar, Biancarosa, & Nair, 2007; Graham & Perin, 2007a; Short & Fitzsimmons, 2007) and other professional resources (e.g., Bean, Readence, & Baldwin, 2011; Fang & Schleppegrell, 2008; Tovani, 2004) have offered many pedagogical recommendations for addressing this concern. These recommendations reflect four distinct approaches—cognitive, sociocultural, linguistic, and critical—each with its own epistemological assumptions, set of practices, and evidence base. Existing literacy programs for adolescents typically combine these approaches in various ways, with some adopting a more cognitive or linguistic orientation and others placing a greater emphasis on the sociocultural or critical dimension. This paper provides a brief synthesis and critique of these four approaches, suggesting that efforts to develop adolescents' content area literacies must recognize the strengths and limitations of each approach, as well as their complementarities.

The Cognitive Approach

The cognitive approach derives its theoretical support from cognitive psychology, a branch of psychology that studies how people perceive, understand, think, reason, remember, and learn. It advocates systematic, explicit teaching of mental routines or procedures for accomplishing cognitive goals such as understanding a text, writing an essay, or solving a problem. These routines or procedures are referred to, broadly, as cognitive strategies (Dole, Nokes, & Drits, 2008). They include strategies commonly used in content area reading/writing, such as predicting, inferencing, monitoring, summarizing, visualizing, concept mapping, and note taking. The approach assumes that the cognitive requirements for reading/writing are essentially the same regardless of content areas. It promotes the use of generic cognitive strategies before, during, and after reading/writing to help students comprehend and compose texts across all content areas.

Prominent since the 1970s, the cognitive approach has been operationalized or packaged in many ways, including collaborative strategic reading (Vaughn, Klingner, & Bryant, 2001), peer-assisted learning strategies (Fuchs, Fuchs, & Kazden, 1999), reciprocal teaching (Palincsar & Brown, 1984), transactional strategies instruction (Schuder, 1993), the self-regulated strategy development model (Graham & Harris, 1993), concept-oriented reading instruction (Guthrie, Wigfield, & Perencevich, 2004), and the strategic instruction model (Deshler, Schumaker, & Woodruff, 2004). These programs show that cognitive strategy instruction improves student reading, writing, and learning and that teaching a combination of strategies is more effective than teaching individual strategies in isolation from one another and from content (see Dole, Nokes, & Drits, 2008 and Gersten, Fuchs, Williams, & Baker, 2001 for reviews). Using the evidence standards established by the What Works Clearinghouse, Kamil, Borman, Dole, Kral, Salinger, and Torgesen (2008) concluded that the evidence base for cognitive strategy instruction is "strong".

Despite the solid evidence base, there are still questions regarding the nature and workings of cognitive strategies. Conley (2008) spotlighted a lack of understanding about how cognitive strategies can be meaningfully integrated into our overall efforts to improve adolescents' content learning. Catts (2009) questioned whether cognitive strategies are indeed comprehension strategies. To him, cognitive strategies such as summarizing are the product, rather than the cause, of comprehension, as providing a summary of a passage is possible only when the reader has comprehended the passage. He noted that it is possible that cognitive strategies "are not essential skills necessary for reading comprehension but rather activities that focus readers' attention on what is important in comprehension" (p. 180). Hirsch (2003) argued against an overemphasis on cognitive strategies in literacy instruction, suggesting that few school-age children have trouble using them in their daily listening comprehension. He recommended that instructional efforts be channeled instead to building students' knowledge of "words and the world". Clearly, there are serious doubts regarding whether implementing cognitive strategy instruction for adolescents would, as Conley (2008) has claimed, actually "pay big dividends in learning" (p. 103).

The Sociocultural Approach

The sociocultural approach recognizes that literacy is a complex process involving not just the cognitive dimension but social and cultural dimensions as well. The extent to which readers/writers are able to construct meaning with texts is influenced not only by background knowledge and strategy use, but also by factors such as purpose, interest, motivation, and identity. This new understanding of literacy led scholars to call for a reconceptualization of what it means to be literate and what can be done to promote academic literacy in the context of secondary schooling (Bean, 2000; Elkins & Luke, 1999). A common thread in this line of scholarship is that teachers should value the out-of-school literacies that adolescents bring to school and use their everyday funds of knowledge and cultural practices as both a bridge to and a resource for promoting the development of content area literacies.

Adolescent literacy projects that draw on the sociocultural approach include funds of knowledge (Moll, Amanti, Neff, & Gonzalez, 1992), third space (Gutierrez, 2008; Moje, Ciechanowski, Kramer, Ellis, Carrilo, & Collazo, 2004), youth media (Goodman, 2003), and cultural modeling (Lee, 2001), among others. These projects not only sought to build connections between home/community and school but also explored ways to meaningfully and strategically integrate the multiple funds of knowledge and literacy practices that students bring to school with the academic practices of disciplinary learning in content area classrooms. They reported positive impacts on adolescents' motivation, engagement, and learning (see Hull, 2012 for a brief review). However, because research involving these projects is primarily qualitative (Hull,

2012), the evidence base for the sociocultural approach is considered "moderate" at best by the What Works Clearinghouse standards (Kamil et al., 2008).

In its efforts to leverage students' knowledge, language, and literacy practices for academic learning, the sociocultural approach demystifies academic language and academic literacy, blurring the distinction between the academic and the everyday. In so doing, however, it also tends to downplay real and significant differences between academic language and everyday language that research has shown to exist. According to Halliday (2004), for example, "The discourses of science gain their theoretical power precisely because they are not translatable into commonsense terms. ... There is bound to be a certain disjunction between the grammar of scientific writing and the commonsense grammar of daily life" (p. 49). This difference is a major cause of reading and learning difficulties for many adolescents. Failure to take serious account of the difference makes language the "hidden curriculum" of schooling, further hindering the learning of disciplinary knowledge and ways of using language, which is a key goal of content area learning. Another concern with the sociocultural approach is that it requires reconceptualization of existing school structures as integral to, rather than separate from, students' home and community, a feat that may be challenging, albeit not impossible, to accomplish in the current socio-political climate.

The Linguistic Approach

The linguistic approach believes that students must master the lexical and grammatical resources of language that construct the knowledge and value of content areas to be successful in school, college, and workplace (Fang & Schleppegrell, 2008). It recognizes that the texts students read and write in early grades lack the richness, depth, and complexities found in the texts that present the more specialized, abstract, and advanced knowledge in later years of schooling (Fillmore & Fillmore, 2012).

Traditional foci of the linguistic approach have been on decoding, fluency, vocabulary, and text structure. However, there have been calls for greater attention to other grammatical elements in literacy instruction. For example, Scott (2004, 2009) noted that the syntactic properties of sentences can make a text difficult to understand. She recommended using strategies such as paraphrasing a difficult sentence periodically while reading, having students generate questions after reading a complex sentence, manipulating the structure and meaning of short sentences, and teaching students to write more complex sentences as ways to help students cope with syntactic complexity. Fillmore and Fillmore (2012) proposed a short daily instructional session in which teachers engage students in analyzing the structure of a "juicy" sentence from a content area text under study and discussing the information presented in these structural elements. The focal sentence is usually grammatically complex but interesting and conveys an important point in the text. Moats (2004) reported on a structured, systematic language curriculum that teaches the structure and use of all language systems (e.g., phonology, orthography, morphology, semantics, syntax) to poor adolescent readers. Fang and Schleppegrell (2008, 2010) described a more functional model that provides teachers with a set of practical tools for engaging students in systematically analyzing the language patterns and discussing the meanings of these patterns in a segment of text that is challenging but important for developing disciplinary understanding. These tools enable students to learn about how language is used as a creative resource for constructing different sorts of knowledge and value across different disciplines at the same time they are building disciplinary content knowledge and developing disciplinary habits of mind through language.

The evidence base for the linguistic approach is mixed. Kamil et al. (2008) determined the level of evidence to be "strong" for explicit vocabulary instruction. There is also some, albeit limited, evidence suggesting that teaching sentence complexity, text structure, and functional grammar analysis can improve reading and writing (Graham & Perin, 2007b; Locke, 2010; Moats, 2004; Schleppegrell, Greer, & Taylor, 2008; Scott, 2004). A key issue in the implementation of the linguistic approach is to make sure that language is not taught as isolated drill-like exercises devoid of functionalities and content contexts. Another concern is that many teachers lack deep knowledge about language to make the linguistic expectations of content area learning explicit to students (Schleppegrell, 2004). A lack of linguistic know-how can prevent teachers from effectively developing the language resources students need for full participation in content area learning and disciplinary socialization.

The Critical Approach

The critical approach views all texts—written, spoken, linguistic, visual, and multimedia—as inherently ideological and value-laden, suggesting that text meaning is neither natural nor neutral and must therefore be understood in relation to both the intention of the writer/designer and the social-historical-political contexts that govern its production. From this perspective, then, content area texts are both "positioned and positioning" (Janks, 2005, p. 97): They are positioned by the author's values and viewpoints, and the verbal and other semiotic choices made by the author create effects that position the reader in particular ways. The approach foregrounds the situated, constructed, and contested nature of meaning, emphasizes the development of critical consciousness about texts and language use, and promotes thoughtful critique and eventual disruption of existing social relations and hegemonic power structures (Cervetti, Pardales, & Damico, 2001). As such, it has a strong social justice agenda that goes beyond the government and business sanctioned goals of college/career readiness and workplace productivity.

The critical approach has gained growing recognition in literacy education since the 1990s, as critical consumption of texts becomes even more important in an era of information explosion and technological revolution. The approach, as exemplified in projects such as critical academic literacy (Morrell & Duncan-Andrade, 2002), critical language awareness (Janks, 1993), and critical media literacy (Alvermann, Moon, & Hagood, 1999), engages students in analyzing texts and interrogating the values, prejudices, and ideologies underpinning these texts, helping them better understand the politics of representation and the constructedness of knowledge. It encourages teachers and students to collaboratively explore questions such as "who is and is not represented in the text, and why?" "whose interest is best served by the message of the text?" "how are various people positioned by the text?" "how do particular content, discourse genres, and modes of inquiry become privileged and acquire power in particular disciplines?" and "how does such privileging affect access, equity, and learning in the classroom?" Classroom practices that promote such a critical orientation to texts include (a) reading supplementary texts that cover social issues glossed over or avoided by traditional or canonical texts, (b) reading multiple texts on the same topic to gain insights into author subjectivities, (c) reading the same text from a different perspective based on gender, race, ethnicity, sexuality, religion, or political affiliation, (d) producing texts that counter the perspective of the author, and (e) taking social action aimed at making a difference in students' or others' lives (Behrman, 2006).

In essence, the critical approach aims to empower students to read both "the word and the world" (Freire & Macedo, 1987) through analyzing, evaluating, problematizing, and transforming texts. However, this agenda appears to be undermined by increased standardized testing and government intrusion in classroom instruction. Without a canon of texts or formulaic teaching procedures, the approach does not lend itself to standardization or commercial prepackaging. This means that ways of doing critical literacies can look rather different from one classroom to another (Luke, 2000). In part because of this, the evidence base for the approach is considered "low" per the What Works Clearinghouse standards (Kamil et al., 2008). A further challenge in implementing the approach is that it requires both teachers and students to develop an understanding of how lexical and grammatical choices realize meaning in text. Absent this knowledge, it is not possible to conduct text analysis and see how texts mean what they mean; and without text analysis, it is not possible to do critical literacies (Janks, 2005).

Toward a Synergy of Approaches

Each of the four approaches—cognitive, sociocultural, linguistic, and critical—draws on a different theoretical and empirical tradition and privileges a particular set of teaching practices. They are, however, not mutually exclusive; they complement one another in ways that allow teachers to tailor instruction to student needs, curricular goals, and the specific tasks at hand. For example, the critical approach recognizes the importance of grammatical knowledge for critical reading. Such knowledge can be fruitfully developed or greatly enriched through a linguistic approach that offers a functional grammar framework for analyzing texts in context (e.g., Fang & Schleppegrell, 2008). Similarly, the sociocultural approach calls for inclusion of popular culture and multimedia texts in the school curriculum as a way to engage students' interests. These texts often require a critical approach that allows students to discern the insidious stereotypes, questionable values, hidden voices, unsubstantiated claims, and problematic ideologies behind the print and images.

Recent discussion about adolescent literacy underscores the need for adolescents to develop a repertoire of resources that enable them to effectively process verbal and visual signs (code breaker), participate in thoughtful conversation with text (meaning maker), use a variety of genres and registers for different purposes and contexts (text users), and critically analyze, challenge, and transform text (text critic) in a postmodern, text-based culture (Luke & Freebody, 1999). The discussion has been influential in reshaping the current thinking about the goals and practices of content area literacies. It also provides an impetus for integrating and revisioning the four approaches described in this review. This synergy must be harnessed and fully exploited if teachers are to optimize instruction that maximizes the development of content area literacies for all adolescents.

Analyzing the Sample Literature Review Essay

The literature review was written for a journal whose primary readership consists of both scholars and practitioners. It is based on Table 7.2, which summarizes the key findings from a critical analysis of existing scholarship on content area literacy instruction. The review starts with a paragraph that sets the context, introduces the topic, and states the purpose and central thesis of the review. In each of the subsequent four sections, one of the main approaches to content area literacy instruction introduced in the first paragraph—cognitive, sociocultural, linguistic, and critical—is reviewed. The same structure is followed in all of these sections. Specifically, each section begins with a discussion of, in order, the theoretical underpinning, key assumptions, and recommended instructional practices related to the approach. This is followed by a paragraph listing the instructional programs informed by the approach and the evidence base for the approach. It ends with a critique of prominent issues related to the approach. Such a consistent structure makes it easier for readers to compare and contrast the four approaches. The review concludes with caveats about and recommendations for content area literacy instruction.

The review is tightly knit not only in terms of the macro organization across sections and paragraphs but also between sentences within each paragraph. In addition to the use of obvious transition markers such as *however, for example, another, also, despite,* and *in essence,* more subtle linking devices are also used. For example, the second sentence in the first paragraph begins with *its ascendency,* which is a concept distilled from the idea presented in the first sentence (i.e., adolescent literacy has become a very hot topic). Later in the same paragraph, *these recommendations* refers to *many pedagogical recommendations* in the preceding sentence. In the cognitive approach section, *these routines* (first paragraph) refers to *mental routines or procedures* in the previous sentence and is referred to as *they* in the sentence that follows.

In the sociocultural approach section, *this new understanding* (first paragraph) refers to the ideas presented in the two sentences immediately preceding it. The phrase that begins the next sentence, *a common thread in this line of scholarship,* picks up an idea from the previous sentence (i.e., *to call for…*). Under the critical approach section, *from this perspective* (first paragraph) connects with the viewpoint presented in the previous sentence. As a whole, these devices contribute to the shaping of a text that is tightly woven, suggesting that nominalization is often used as an effective device in crafting cohesive texts for academic purposes.

In this literature review, summaries of prior work (see Chapter 3) are typically short and concise, perhaps due to the space limitation. However, there are also articles that are summarized in greater detail, such as *Catts (2009)* and *Fang and*

Table 7.2 Notes on Instructional Approaches to Content Area Literacy

Approaches	Theoretical Grounding	Research Tradition	Key Assumptions	Recommended Practices	Example Projects or Programs	Evidence Base
Cognitive	Cognitive theories	Primarily quantitative (e.g., experimental studies)	The cognitive requirements of reading and learning from texts are similar across all content areas. Cognitive strategies help with the extraction of information from texts, as well as the remembering and retention of content in school subjects.	Conduct systematic, explicit teaching of a combination of cognitive strategies with content-area texts	Collaborative strategic reading (Vaughn, Klingner, & Bryant, 2001); Peer-assisted learning strategies (Fuchs, Fuchs, & Kazden, 1999); Reciprocal teaching (Palincsar & Brown, 1984); Transactional strategies instruction (Schuder, 1993); Self-regulated strategy development model (Graham & Harris, 1993); Concept-oriented reading instruction (Guthrie, Wigfield, & Perencevich, 2004); Strategic instruction model (Deshler, Schumaker, & Woodruff, 2004)	Strong

Sociocultural	Sociocultural theories	Primarily qualitative (e.g., ethnographic studies)	Literacy is a complex process involving not only cognitive but also social and cultural dimensions. Students' out-of-school literacies can be both a bridge to and a resource for promoting the development of content area literacies.	Build connections between home/community and school by strategically integrating students' prior knowledge and cultural practices with the academic practices of content area learning.	Funds of knowledge (Moll et al., 1992) Third space (Moje et al., 2004) Youth media (Goodman, 2003) Cultural modeling (Lee, 2001)	Moderate
Linguistic	Linguistic theories	Primarily quantitative (e.g., experimental studies)	Content area texts are constructed in language patterns that differ significantly from those that construct everyday texts. Students must learn to cope with the specialized language that constructs the specialized knowledge of content areas to be successful in school and workplace.	Explicitly teach vocabulary and other grammatical and discursive patterns from a functional perspective in the context of challenging but significant content-area texts.	Word Generation (Snow, Lawrence, & White, 2009) LANGUAGE! (Greene, 1996) Juicy sentence (Fillmore & Fillmore, 2012) Functional language analysis (Fang & Schleppegrell, 2010)	Moderate to Strong

(Continued)

Approaches	Theoretical Grounding	Research Tradition	Key Assumptions	Recommended Practices	Example Projects or Programs	Evidence Base
Critical	Critical theories	Primarily qualitative (e.g., case studies)	All texts are inherently ideological and value-laden. Knowledge is neither natural nor neutral. Literacy should empower people to challenge social inequalities and promote social justice.	Engage students in critically analyzing, interrogating, evaluating, problematizing, and transforming all forms of text based on issues of, for example, power, gender, race, ethnicity, class, sexuality, religion, or political affiliation.	Critical academic literacy (Morrell & Duncan-Andrade, 2002) Critical language awareness (Janks, 1993) Critical media literacy (Alvermann, Moon, & Hagood, 1999)	Low

Schleppegrell (2008, 2010). This variation in summary length likely reflects the amount of attention the author wants to call to these studies or to the points made by these studies. The longer the summary, the more important, relevant, or complex the piece of work being summarized seems to be for the author. For example, under the cognitive approach section, *Catts (2009)* is summarized with greater length than *Conley (2009)*. This may suggest that the author intends to foreground Catts' point of view in the critique. It is conceivable that should the length limitation be relaxed, the author may choose to write longer summaries of certain studies to give them more weight. Additionally, signal verbs used in summarizing are varied so as to capture more precisely the true intention of the scholars whose work is being referenced and the author's attitudes toward those pieces of work. These verbs include *spotlighted, questioned, noted, argued, claimed, concluded, proposed, reported, described,* and *determined*.

Unlike novice writers, who tend to use quotes excessively and without clear purpose, the author of this literature review relies minimally on quotes. Quotes are carefully selected to complete, reinforce, support, or explain an argument. For example, the quote from *Conley (2008)* in the cognitive approach section (last paragraph) is used to complete the last sentence of the section. The quote itself seems fairly straightforward and thus requires no further elaboration or explanation. Using quotes this way gives the quoted idea an aura of authenticity and credibility. The *Halliday (2004)* quote in the sociocultural approach section (third paragraph), on the other hand, is used to support the argument made in the preceding sentence. It could have been further elaborated if space permits. The *Janks (2005)* quote in the critical approach section (first paragraph) is used to explain the key assumptions of the critical approach. The quote is subsequently elaborated because the terms *positioned* and *positioning* may sound too abstract and thus requires unpacking to make it more accessible to the reader.

Evaluation is an essential part of a literature review (see Chapter 3). This review is no exception. As each instructional approach is reviewed, it is also critiqued. Positive, negative, or neutral terms are used to convey the author's attitude toward each approach. The attitude is upgraded or downgraded depending on the degree of authorial commitment. In appraising the cognitive approach, for example, the author uses double boosting (e.g., *Clearly, there are serious doubts*) to raise questions about the benefits of the approach. The use of *claimed* suggests what Conley (2008) said (i.e., cognitive strategy instruction will pay big dividends in learning) lacks evidence and the author does not buy into the argument. When discussing the evidence base for the linguistic approach, the author shows caution when making the statement, *there are some, albeit limited, evidence*. Similarly, the author uses double hedges in *a feat that may be challenging, albeit not impossible, to accomplish* when discussing the sociocultural approach. The author also uses words like *can*, *appear to*, *tend to*, and *possible* to modulate his claims and avoid sounding arrogant or overtly confident, as in *a lack of linguistic know-how <u>can</u> prevent teachers from*, *such knowledge <u>can</u> be fruitfully developed*, *it also <u>tends to</u> downplay*, and *this agenda <u>appears to</u> be undermined*.

In other instances, the author presents his points of view without any hesitation or hedges, showing confidence in what he says, as can be seen in *a key issue…<u>is</u> to make sure*, *the approach <u>does not</u> lend itself to*, *it is <u>not possible</u> to conduct text analysis*, and *the discussion <u>has been</u> influential*. When making recommendations for future work, the author uses *must*, as in *this synergy <u>must</u> be harnessed* to emphasize the imperative for action. When rating the evidence base for each of the four approaches, both active voice (e.g., <u>*Kamil et al. (2008) determined the level of evidence to be "strong" for explicit vocabulary instruction.*</u>) and passive voice (e.g., *The evidence base for the approach <u>is considered</u> "low" <u>per</u> the What Works Clearinghouse standards.*) are used to indicate the source of the rating.

In short, Text 7-1 appears to be following the typical rhetorical moves of a literature review, and the linguistic resources deployed instantiate these moves in ways that contribute to the overall purpose of the genre.

Conclusion

Literature review involves identifying, selecting, reading, analyzing, and evaluating scholarly sources on a specific topic of potential significance to a field. It is a key academic genre that students and scholars are expected to master. Writing a literature review is a daunting task, especially for the inexperienced writer. It takes both content knowledge and language proficiency to craft a well-structured, focused, critical, and smooth literature review that either stands on its own or is ready for integration into a larger piece of work.

Reflection/Application Activities

1 Find a literature review essay in your field and examine its rhetorical moves and the linguistic resources that instantiate these moves. Discuss how effective these moves and resources are in helping the author achieve the purpose of the genre and how they are similar to and different from the ones described in this chapter.
2 Write a literature review of an important topic of inquiry in your field, using the rhetorical moves discussed in this chapter and drawing on the linguistic resources presented in Chapters 2–4.
3 Take a look at a literature review paper you wrote before. In light of what is presented in this chapter, discuss what you think you did well and not so well, as well as what you can do to improve your skills in writing the genre.

References

Fang, Z. (2012). Approaches to developing content area literacies: A synthesis and a critique. *Journal of Adolescent and Adult Literacy, 56*(2), 111–116.

Fang, Z., & Wei, Y. (2010). Improving middle school students' science literacy through reading infusion. *Journal of Educational Research, 103*, 262–273.

Jalongo, R., & Saracho, O. (2016). *Writing for publication: Transitions and tools that support scholars' success.* New York: Springer.

8
Writing an Argumentative Essay

What Is an Argumentative Essay?

An argumentative essay is a genre of writing where the author takes a position on an issue and provides the reasoning and evidence to back it up. To make a credible or convincing argument, you need to collect and evaluate evidence, making sure that the pieces of evidence selected for inclusion—anecdotes, statistics, examples, quotes, testimonials, artifacts—are closely relevant and can bolster the argument you want to make. Claims or statements made without the support of evidence have little value, as they are simply opinions and not valid arguments from an academic perspective. It is also expected that you would acknowledge and respond to opposing views in an argumentative essay. As the saying in football goes, the best offense is a good defense. Anticipating and addressing opposing views avoids the appearance of bias, shows a well-rounded understanding of the issue at hand, strengthens the argument, increases readers' trust in you, and decreases their resistance to your argument.

Evidence can be found in print and electronic sources (e.g., books, journals, websites, newspapers, documentary films, photos), as well as in personal experiences. It can also be collected through reading, viewing, observation, interview, survey, or experiment. Often, multiple and varied pieces of evidence are needed to make a truly persuasive case. Having evidence from multiple/varied sources enables the reader to check one source against the other—a process called triangulation, thus increasing the validity and strength of a claim. Whichever evidence or how much evidence is introduced will depend on its relevance to the argument, the audience of your writing (who may have preference for a particular kind of evidence), and the context of writing (e.g., writing for academic vs. mundane purposes). It also depends on whether the evidence comes from the primary or secondary source (see Chapter 3). Primary sources include original documents, interviews, and photographs. They are usually more compelling than secondary sources, which are someone else's interpretations of the primary source(s).

It is important to note that evidence does not speak for itself. Much like what happens in a court room, simply pointing to a piece of evidence or merely juxtaposing it with a claim will not do the job of convincing the reader. Rather, once a piece of evidence is introduced into the text, it needs to be elaborated or commented on so that the reader understands what the evidence suggests, how it relates to an argument, and why it is significant. What turns a seemingly innocent piece of information into evidence that supports a particular point of view is the link you establish between the information and your argument. How much explanation is given depends on the type of evidence introduced and the audience's background knowledge. When the evidence presented is commonsensical and easy to understand, little elaboration is needed. All you need is to make the connection between the evidence and your argument. When the evidence introduced is technical or less familiar to the audience, some unpacking of the evidence is needed to help the reader better understand what the evidence says and how it supports the argument you are trying to make. In this sense, introducing a piece of evidence into a text is like introducing a quote into a text (see Chapter 3): Both need to be explained and explicitly linked to the argument.

Evidence can be introduced in different ways depending on its type and its placement in the text. When a piece of evidence is a photo, a graph, a table, or an illustration, it can be inserted into the text, with explanation of its meaning and its connection to the point being argued. If a quote is used, it often needs to be paraphrased and explained. Sometimes, evidence is presented through storytelling—that is, by relating a real or imagined scenario or sharing a personal vignette. In other cases, evidence may be a summary of a piece of text or a synthesis of multiple pieces of work. Regardless of which piece of evidence is introduced, it needs to be placed strategically and explained clearly so that the link between the evidence and the argument is obvious to the reader.

Rhetorical Moves in Argumentative Writing

A good argumentative essay is complete, evidence-based, and logical. It typically begins by establishing a context that introduces the issue and the author's stance on the issue. Evidence supporting and/or refuting the position is then presented and explained. A conclusion is made that readdresses the thesis in light of the evidence provided and discusses the implications.

There are three types of argumentative essays, each structured somewhat differently from the other. In a balanced essay (or Rogerian style of argument), you introduce a position on an issue or problem (e.g., *Should animal research be banned? Does summer heat diminish coronavirus strength? Is education too commercialized nowadays?*), provide reasons for and against the position, summarize the two sides of arguments, and then state/explain your own point of view.

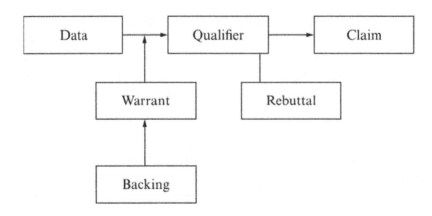

Figure 8.1 Toulmin's Model of Argument (Toulmin, 2003, p. 97)

In a persuasive essay (or Aristotelian style of argument), you introduce the issue in general terms, state a position on the issue, provide reasons for the position, acknowledge and argue against opposing views, and conclude the essay by recapping your position and its main arguments and discussing its implications. Your arguments can be enhanced through an appeal to credibility, logic, emotion, or time.

Sometimes, you can use what is referred to as a Toulmin model of argument (Toulmin, 2003). In this model (see Figure 8.1), you introduce the problem or topic (e.g., U.S. presidential election), state a claim or thesis (e.g., *The economic sanctions on Russia are justified.*), provide data (reasons or evidence) to support the argument (e.g., *The Russian government was involved in a disinformation campaign aimed at creating chaos in the 2016 U.S. presidential election.*), explore warrants (i.e., assumptions) that show how the data is logically connected to the claim (e.g., *Countries that interfere in the U.S. election must be punished.*), offer factual backing to show that the logic used in the warrants is good (e.g., *Foreign interference in the U.S. presidential election undermines people's confidence in the democratic process.*), discuss counter-arguments and provide rebuttal (e.g., *Economic sanctions are more effective and less costly than military confrontation*), and conclude by summarizing key points and discussing the implications of your argument.

Linguistic Resources for Argumentation

An argumentative essay can be written in the first person (*I/we*), the third person (e.g., *the idea, they*), or sometimes a mix of the two. Each style has its own affordances and limitations (see Chapter 2). Using the first person makes the writing sound interactive and can help reduce the distance between you (the author) and the reader, but may at times hamper the presentation of ideas and development of argument. Using the third person can sometimes facilitate the development of argument and discursive flow, but may increase the distance between you and the reader, with the consequence that the reader becomes more resistant to your argument. Whichever grammatical person you choose will depend on your needs and language proficiency.

An argumentative essay requires you to take a stance. In academic writing, such a stance is conveyed in a measured, reasoned way through judicious use of hedges and boosters, as discussed in Chapters 2–4. You also need to make efforts to minimize references to your own mental processes (e.g., *I believe*, *I think*, *I feel*) so that the focus of the writing is on the ideas presented, rather than on your emotions or feelings. It is also advisable to avoid a hortatory style in your writing (e.g., use of commands such as *You* <u>*should*</u> *avoid overquoting in writing.* <u>*Don't*</u> *overquote in your writing.*), as such a style is not typical of academic writing and comes across as immature and arrogant.

Schleppegrell (2004) identified a list of grammatical resources that you can use to construct a less personal and more carefully reasoned argumentative essay that is also well-structured and tightly knit. Specifically, to display knowledge, you can use

- abstract nouns or noun phrases to name arguments
  - *the women's suffrage movement*
  - *these protests and condemnations*
- long noun phrases to condense information
  - *a constitutional amendment that guarantees rights regardless of sex past those assured by the 19th Amendment*
  - *an integral part of the women's suffrage movement in the United States*
- technical and abstract vocabulary with appropriate collocations to encode specialized knowledge
  - *two significant women's <u>suffrage events</u> <u>took place</u> in March*
  - *the <u>constitutional amendment</u> was not fully <u>ratified</u>*
- linking verbs to connect noun phrases and construct abstractions and generalizations
  - *the kidnapping and murder of Emmett Till and the trial of his killers <u>became</u> one of the biggest news items of 1955.*
  - *The mass overnight arrest <u>was</u> proof that the military government has eviscerated the island country's freedoms and eroded the rights of its people.*

To establish an authoritative voice, you can use

- the third person and declarative sentences to realize impersonality
  - *According to public health experts, COVID-19 vaccines are the only way to stop the pandemic.*

- nominalizations and linking verbs to enable evaluation
  - *The intense media coverage of the trivial event is sickening.*
- stance markers such as hedges and boosters to attribute commitment to a proposition
  - *It might be a coincidence, but the month of "March" certainly seems fit for Women's History Month.*

To construct a well-structured text, you can

- foreground ideas in the subject position to highlight key points
  - *The disagreement between the two parties over the size of the stimulus package is widely believed to be the cause of last year's government shutdown. (vs. We know that government shut down last year because the two parties disagreed over the size of the stimulus package.)*
- combine clauses to enable condensation of information
  - *Light is so important to the survival of plants that they seem to reach toward it. (vs. Plants cannot survive if they don't have light, and that's why they seem to reach toward it.)*
- nominalizations and long noun phrases to increase informational density
  - *The intense media coverage in the weeks between Emmett's death and the trial of his killers focused worldwide attention on the legal proceedings that would be held in a sleepy little town in the Mississippi Delta, exposing to the world the cruel racial intolerance that existed in the South. (vs. After Emmett died and before his killers were tried, the media covered the story a lot. So people all over the world were very interested in finding out how the trial went. The trial was held in a sleepy little town in the Mississippi Delta. Because the story was widely reported, the world now knew that people in the South were very intolerant of other races.)*
- a range of cohesive resources to connect sentences and paragraphs
  - *Immediately after the trial, civil rights activists used the momentum from the case to cultivate support. On Sunday, September 25, Charles C. Diggs, Jr., and Medgar Evers spoke to a crowd of more than 60,000 people at a rally [...]. These protest rallies continued for several more weeks. [...] In the meantime, the national press took up the cause [...].*

The rest of the chapter presents two sample argumentative essays and annotate how each is constructed discursively. The References section of each essay is omitted so as to save space, and paragraphs are numbered for ease of reference in analysis and discussion.

Argumentative Essay #1

The first argumentative essay comes from the field of communications. It was written by Dr. Alan Kamhi, a professor in the Department of Communicative Sciences and Disorders at the University of North Carolina-Greensboro, and published in 2007 in *The ASHA Leader* (https://leader.pubs.asha.org/doi/full/10.1044/leader.FMP.12072007.28), the official monthly newsmagazine of the American Speech-Language-Hearing Association that showcases the latest research and practice advances in communication sciences and disorders and is for and about audiologists, speech-language pathologists, and speech, language, and hearing scientists. The essay argues that a "narrow view of reading", which equates reading with word recognition (i.e., decoding) only, offers a better solution to the current reading crisis than does the "broad view of reading", which considers reading as consisting of two elements—word recognition and comprehension.

Text 8-1: Argumentative Essay #1

Knowledge Deficits: The True Crisis in Education

1   There has been no shortage of explanations and solutions for the persistently poor reading levels of our nation's school children over the past 30 years. Although some progress has been made—reading levels were lower in the 1970s than they are today and the gap between Hispanic, black, and white children has decreased over the last 13 years—the proportion of children reading below the basic level has hovered around 35% in the last 25 years, and 70% never attain reading proficiency (NAEP, 2007).

2   As Congress prepares for the reauthorization of the No Child Left Behind (NCLB) Act, everyone with any interest in our nation's students is offering opinions on who or what is to blame for the continuing lack of progress and how to fix the problem. The most frequent targets are teachers (poorly trained), schools (not conducive to learning), students (large numbers who are disadvantaged, are second-language learners, or have learning disabilities), assessment instruments (low state standards), and instructional methods. The respective solutions are to provide better teacher training and school learning environments, devise more rigorous assessments, and use evidence-based instructional methods.

3   These solutions might have some impacts on reading achievement levels, but as long as the "broad view" of reading is reflected in high-stakes assessment, our efforts to dramatically improve reading levels in the United States will have the same lackluster effect as our efforts over the last 25 to 30 years. The broad view of reading is familiar to most people and accepted by almost everyone. Reading, according to this view, consists of two basic components—word recognition and comprehension (Perfetti, 1996). "Thinking guided by print" is a succinct definition of reading according to the broad view.

4   The fundamental problem with the broad view of reading is that it encompasses two very different abilities—word recognition (word-level reading) and comprehension. Word recognition is a teachable skill; comprehension

is not a skill and is not easily taught. Word recognition is teachable because it involves a narrow scope of knowledge (e.g., letters, sounds, words) and processes (decoding) that, once acquired, will lead to fast, accurate word recognition. There are numerous evidence-based instructional programs that effectively teach word-level reading to all students except those with the most severe disabilities (cf. National Reading Panel, 2000), and some of these students can be taught word-reading skills with intensive phonic programs (cf. Torgeson, Otaiba, & Grek, 2005).

5   Comprehension, in contrast, is not a skill; it is a complex of higher-level mental processes that include thinking, reasoning, imagining, and interpreting. Comprehension is difficult to teach because these processes are domain- or content-specific rather than domain- or content-general. This is why the best predictor of comprehension is familiarity with a content domain (Hirsch, 2006; Willingham, 2006), not strategy-based instruction as many believe (NRP, 2000). Familiarity with the content of a passage is, in fact, so important that poor decoders do better than good decoders when they have more knowledge of the topic (e.g., Recht & Leslie, 1998). Because comprehension is knowledge-dependent, instructional approaches that target general strategies will have limited impact on measures of reading that include diverse content domains (Willingham, 2006).

6   Hirsch's (2006) solution to address the nation's reading crisis and improve reading performance is to provide elementary-school children with a knowledge-based core curriculum. His Core Knowledge Foundation has made inroads in developing and implementing a core curriculum in schools throughout the country. The results of these programs are promising, but our nation is unlikely to embrace a core curriculum. As the response to NCLB has shown, most federal initiatives to mandate curriculum changes are met with resistance at state and local levels.

7   My solution to the reading crisis is no more likely to be embraced than Hirsch's or any other, but unlike other ones, mine costs nothing, requires no significant changes in teacher training, new measures of reading, new instructional programs, or new legislation. It simply requires rejecting the broad view of reading and embracing the "narrow view" of reading. Unlike the broad view, which conflates reading with comprehension, the narrow view restricts the scope of reading to word recognition. By limiting reading to word recognition, the focus is on a skill that can be taught to every typically developing child and to most students with language and learning disabilities.

8   By embracing the narrow view, we can eliminate our nation's obsession with something that cannot be easily taught—domain-general comprehension and reasoning. Comprehension and reasoning will remain important educational goals, but they will be taught in domain-specific content areas and called by their rightful names (American/European history, biology/chemistry, geometry/algebra, contemporary fiction/drama)

as they are in colleges and universities. If state and national assessments distinguish between word-level reading and content knowledge acquisition, the reading crisis will be over. Reading proficiency levels should reach a minimum of 90%. Anything less will not be acceptable, given the numerous research-supported instructional programs that effectively teach word-level reading (NRP, 2000).

9   The benefits of the narrow view of reading are far-reaching. Teachers benefit by being able to teach content areas without concerns about how students perform on conflated measures of reading. Students benefit by the differentiated assessment of reading and content-area learning, particularly those with adequate word-reading skills who are poor comprehenders. These students will now be viewed as attaining reading proficiency, and remediation can focus on addressing the difficulties these students have in learning specific content areas.

10   Most importantly, the narrow view will focus attention on the true crisis in American education—knowledge deficits. As a recent report (Pianta, Belsky, Houts, & Morrison, 2007) has shown, teachers spend too much time on basic math and reading and not enough time on content areas such as science and social studies. Knowledge acquisition needs to become the primary goal of education. Reading, we need to remember, is just one way to acquire knowledge. There are many others. Let our educational debates focus on the best way to assess and teach content knowledge.

Analyzing Argumentative Essay #1

The author starts the essay by establishing a context that allows him to introduce his central argument—a different view of reading is needed to solve the reading crisis in education. This context describes the reading crisis (first paragraph) and the federal response to this crisis (second paragraph). It then suggests that the largely failed federal effort to address the reading crisis is due to its embrace of the broad view of reading (third paragraph). Next, it discusses the fundamental problem with the broad view of reading (fourth and fifth paragraphs) and the challenges this view poses for instructional innovations (sixth paragraph).

Having established the context that provides the necessary background information and identified the flaws with the broad view of reading, the author then introduces the narrow view of reading, arguing that it has a better chance of solving the current reading crisis (seventh and eighth paragraphs). In making the argument, he first concedes that his solution, just like other proposed solutions, might not be embraced, and then explains what a narrow view of reading is, why it is needed, and how it can help solve the current reading crisis. The last two paragraphs (ninth and tenth paragraphs) deal with the larger implications of the narrow view of reading, discussing why it matters and who would benefit from it.

In essence, the essay follows the rhetorical moves identified by Graff and Birkenstein (2018) as central to developing an argument—establishing a territory, introducing what others say, presenting what the author wants to say in response, planting a naysayer, and saying why it matters (i.e., addressing the "so what" and "who cares" questions).

In developing his argument, the author relies heavily on print sources as evidence to support his position. More specifically, he summarizes and quotes relevant articles by respected scholars in the field (e.g., Hirsch, Perfetti, Torgesen et al.) or from reputable outlets (e.g., top tier academic journals, government reports) to help him make his case. Some sources (e.g., Hirsch, National Reading Panel) are summarized in greater length than are others (e.g., Willingham, Torgesen et al., Pianta et al.), depending on their relevance and importance to specific points of argument. The argument is further bolstered through comparisons between the two views of reading (e.g., *in contrast, unlike*).

The essay is written primarily in the third person, making the text sound more objective and more focused on ideas (rather than the author). The occasional use of "my" and "we" helps bridge the distance between the reader and the author, thus reducing the reader's resistance to the text's message. Abstract nouns are used in developing the argument. These include *some progress, the most frequent targets, the respective solutions, the fundamental problem with the broad view of reading, the benefits of the narrow view of reading, comprehension and reasoning, knowledge acquisition,* and *the focus.* Long nouns phrases with nominalizations (underlined) are used to pack a heavy load of semantic content in building the argument. These include *no shortage of explanations and solutions for the persistently poor reading levels of our nation's school children, Hirsch's (2006) solution to address the nation's reading crisis and improve reading performance, our nation's obsession with something that cannot be easily taught, the differentiated assessment of reading and content-area learning,* and *the difficulties these students have in learning specific content areas.*

Typical of fluent academic writing, the connections between sentences and between paragraphs are made primarily through resources such as nominalizations and prepositional phrases but rarely through conjunctions. For example, *these solutions* in the third paragraph summarizes the information presented in the second paragraph and becomes the subject of discussion in the third paragraph. And the pronoun *this* in the third sentence of the fifth paragraph refers to the idea presented in the previous sentence, that is, comprehension is domain- or content-specific rather than domain- or content-general. The third sentence in the seventh paragraph begins with a prepositional phrase *unlike the broad view,* which connects with the preceding sentence that advocates *rejecting the broad view of reading and embracing the "narrow view" of reading.* Similarly, the fourth sentence in the same paragraph begins with *by limiting reading to word recognition*, which is linked conceptually to the phrase *restricts the scope of reading to word recognition* in the third sentence.

The authorial stance is conveyed in a passionate but at the same time reasoned tone, depending on the amount of available evidence as well as the author's own perspective and conviction. In some cases, the author uses cautious language such as hedges to moderate knowledge claims and withhold full commitment to statements (e.g., *might have some impact*, *can eliminate*, *no more likely*, *easily taught*, *according to this view, as many people believe*). In other instances, no such hesitation is present (e.g., *Comprehension…is not a skill. The results of these programs are promising. The benefits of the narrow view of reading are far reaching. Word recognition is teachable.*). In still other cases, boosters are used to add force to claims and show confidence in statements (e.g., *Familiarity with the content of a passage is, in fact, so important that […]; teachers spend too much time on basic math and reading; It simply requires rejecting […]; Most importantly, the narrow view will […]; a recent report has shown […], Reading proficiency should reach a minimum of 90%.*). In short, a variety of linguistic resources are used to present the author's stance in a way that is measured and at the same time proportionate to the evidence presented or reasonable assumptions. They help advance the author's argument.

Argumentative Essay #2

The second argumentative essay (Text 8-2), titled "US withdrawal from WHO is unlawful and threatens global and US health and security", is a commentary written by a group of 15 world-renowned scientists in response to the Trump administration's announcement to eliminate U.S. funding for the World Health Organization (WHO). It was published online on July 8, 2020 in *Lancet*, a weekly peer-reviewed publication that is among the world's oldest and best-known general medical journals.

Text 8-2: Argumentative Essay #2

US withdrawal from WHO is unlawful and threatens global and US health and security

1   On May 29, 2020, President Donald Trump announced the USA would sever its relationship with WHO and redirect funds to US global health priorities. On July 6, 2020, the US administration officially notified UN Secretary-General António Guterres of its intention to withdraw from WHO membership. This notification coincides with record daily increases in COVID-19 cases worldwide and rising infections in more than three-quarters of the US states. In response, 750 leaders from academia, science, and law have urged the US Congress to block the president's action.

2   The US Congress, the courts, and the public all have the power to block this reckless decision. The USA entered WHO membership through a 1948 joint resolution passed by both houses of Congress and this resolution has been supported by successive administrations. Former President Harry Truman explicitly referenced that resolution as his legal basis for joining WHO. The current US administration's unilateral action notifying the UN that the USA is withdrawing violates US law because it does not have express approval of Congress to leave WHO. A Supreme Court precedent has made clear that "When the President takes measures incompatible with the expressed or implied will of Congress, his power is at its lowest ebb."

3   The US administration's decision to sever ties and terminate WHO funding violates a binding condition in Congress's 1948 resolution, which must be met before the USA may withdraw. The law mandates the USA must pay its financial obligations for the current fiscal year. Because withdrawal could not occur until next July, the USA must pay its mandatory WHO contributions through the end of 2021. And because any withdrawal could not take effect until July, 2021, a new US presidential administration could simply revoke the withdrawal upon taking office.

4   Withdrawal from WHO would have dire consequences for US security, diplomacy, and influence. WHO has unmatched global reach and legitimacy. The US administration would be hard pressed to disentangle the country from WHO governance and programs. The Pan American Health Organization (PAHO) is among six WHO regional offices and is headquartered in Washington, DC, USA. The USA is also a state party to two WHO treaties: the WHO Constitution, establishing it as the "directing and co-ordinating authority on international health"; and the International Health Regulations (IHR 2005), the governing framework for epidemic preparedness and response.

5   Various US institutions collaborate with WHO on vital work that would be harmed if the relationship is severed. There are 21 WHO collaborating centers at the US Centers for Disease Control and Prevention (CDC) and three at the National Institutes of Health, focused on US priorities, including polio eradication, cancer prevention, and global health security. The Secretariat of the 44 WHO Collaborating Centers for Nursing and Midwifery is based in the USA.

6   This autumn, seasonal influenza, and COVID-19 will pose a double burden on health system capacities. The USA could be cut out of the global system to design annual influenza vaccines. The WHO Global Influenza Surveillance and Response System aggregates data from countries around the world to track and study circulating viruses. US agencies, pharmaceutical companies, and laboratories also rely on the WHO Pandemic Influenza Preparedness Framework to gain access to new

influenza virus samples for research and development. Severing ties with WHO could impede US access to crucial tools for developing biological countermeasures to influenza.

7   A COVID-19 vaccine is urgently needed not only to safeguard public health but also to safely reopen society. WHO is conducting the Solidarity trial for COVID-19 treatments joined by more than 100 countries. WHO also leads the Access to COVID-19 Tools (ACT) Accelerator for COVID-19 diagnostics, therapeutics, and vaccines. If the USA does not participate in these WHO initiatives, Americans could have limited access to scarce vaccine supplies, and are likely to be barred from travel to foreign destinations.

8   Experienced US personnel are often seconded to WHO or embedded in outbreak response teams. US scientists gained access to Wuhan, China, as part of a WHO COVID-19 mission to China. US global health strategies to rapidly respond to international disease outbreaks will be compromised without membership of WHO. Beyond COVID-19, WHO is tracking and responding to dozens of infectious disease outbreaks around the world, including yellow fever in Togo, Middle East respiratory syndrome in Saudi Arabia, and dengue fever in Brazil. On June 25, 2020, the Democratic Republic of the Congo (DRC) Government declared the end of the world's second longest outbreak of Ebola virus disease. WHO deployed staff to a Congolese warzone, even when the White House banned CDC personnel from involvement in this effort. The DRC Government reported a new unrelated outbreak of Ebola virus disease in June, 2020, in the country's northwest, and WHO surge teams have been deployed. WHO's crucial role in curtailing infectious diseases extends beyond outbreaks to diseases. In 1980, the World Health Assembly declared smallpox eradicated, WHO's historic achievement. Today, WHO's key work in HIV, tuberculosis, malaria, and maternal mortality makes US foreign assistance effective.

9   COVID-19 has revealed shortcomings in WHO's powers and funding, warranting substantial reforms. WHO has limited authority to ensure state compliance with the IHR, including constrained ability to independently verify official state reports. But after leaving WHO, the USA would be on the outside looking in, without global influence to promote crucial reforms. Stand-alone US programs, moreover, could never substitute for a truly global agency. Absent treaty obligations, in a multipolar world, mean there are no guarantees that countries will cooperate with the USA.

10 Health and security in the USA and globally require robust collaboration with WHO—a cornerstone of US funding and policy since 1948. The USA cannot cut ties with WHO without incurring major disruption and damage, making Americans far less safe. That is the last thing the global community needs as the world faces a historic health emergency.

Analyzing Argumentative Essay #2

The persuasive essay makes rhetorical moves that are similar to those involved in the first sample discussed earlier in the chapter. It begins by providing a context, President Donald Trump's announcement to sever ties between US and WHO and to terminate funding for WHO amid rising COVID-19 cases and soaring infections across the US, that becomes the impetus for the commentary that argues the US withdrawal (a) is unlawful and (b) threatens global and US health and security. The second and third paragraphs address the first part of the argument, that is, the Trump administration's decision is illegal. To support this argument, the essay invokes the 1948 joint resolution passed by both houses of Congress, suggesting that the Trump administration's decision violates the law. It further argues, in the third paragraph, that the decision breaches a binding condition in the Congressional resolution regarding US' financial obligation to WHO for the current fiscal year.

From the fourth through ninth paragraphs, the essay addresses the second part of the argument, that is, the Trump administration's action threatens global and US health and security. To develop this argument, the fourth paragraph introduces a topic sentence—US withdrawal from WHO would have dire consequences for US security, diplomacy, and influence. This thesis is supported with examples that show why the US disentanglement from WHO is difficult to achieve (paragraph 4); harms US agencies, companies, and laboratories (paragraphs 5 and 6); and endangers public health (paragraph 7).

Besides arguing against the withdrawal from WHO, a good strategy is to state the benefits of staying with WHO. The eighth paragraph does exactly that. It flips the coin of argument by enumerating the potential benefits, to both the US and the world at large, of continuing US engagement with WHO. The ninth paragraph admits that WHO has its own shortcomings and explains the reason behind its flaws. It acknowledges as valid the main concern that the Trump administration has used to defend its action. However, the essay further argues, through the deployment of an adversative conjunction *but*, that even with all its imperfections, WHO is still worth supporting and that leaving WHO would only jeopardize the US interests and diminish the US influence. The last paragraph summarizes the commentary by reiterating the main point of the argument, which is that the US must collaborate with WHO to avoid incurring major disruption and damage, both to itself and to the global community.

In making the argument, the scientist authors draw on 20 different online and print sources as evidence to support their position. These sources, not excerpted in the sample here due to space limitation, include news reports from prestigious outlets such as *The Washington Post* and *New York Times*, documents from WHO and the U.S. government, and articles from reputable medical journals (e.g., JAMA). The authors use forceful language to express their disapproval of the Trump administration's decision. They call the decision *reckless* (second paragraph) and anticipate its potential consequences to be *dire* (fourth paragraph). They argue that the decision to withdraw from WHO requires *express* approval of the Congress (second paragraph); remark that 750 leaders from academia, science, and law have *urged* (rather than just asked) the US Congress to block the president's action (first paragraph); and encourage the new US presidential administration to *simply revoke the withdrawal upon taking office* (third paragraph). They contend that the USA *must* pay its mandatory WHO contributions for the current fiscal year (third paragraph), that a COVID-19 vaccine is *urgently needed* (seventh paragraph), and that *Health and security in the USA and globally require robust collaboration with WHO.*

On the other hand, when discussing the potential consequences of the withdrawal decision, the authors employ modals—such as *may*, *could*, and *would*—to temper their claims. Examples include *would have dire consequences* and *would be hard pressed* (fourth paragraph), *would be harmed* (fifth paragraph), *could be cut out of* and *could impede* (sixth paragraph), *could have limited* and *are likely* (seventh paragraph), and *would be on the outside* and *could never substitute* (ninth paragraph). The degree of caution conveyed in these instances contrasts with the degree of certainty expressed in other instances, such as *seasonal influenza and COVID-19 will pose a double burden* (sixth paragraph) and *US global health strategies to rapidly respond to international disease outbreaks will be compromised* (eighth paragraph).

As a commentary published in a top medical journal, the essay is necessarily formal in style. Two key markers of formality are nominalization and expanded noun phrase. Nominalizations are sometimes used to synthesize information and at the same time connect sentences. For example, *this notification* (first paragraph) summarizes the idea presented in the preceding sentence (*the US administration officially notified UN Secretary-General*). The word *withdrawal* in the third paragraph repackages the verb *withdraw* that has previously been mentioned so that the action of withdrawing becomes a concept that can be further discussed. Long noun phrases, many with nominalizations and multiple postmodifiers (e.g., prepositional phrase, the infinitive, the participial phrase, the appositive phrase), are deployed throughout the essay to both compact information and facilitate discursive flow. Samples of these noun phrases (with nominalizations underlined) include *the current US administration's unilateral action notifying the UN that the USA is withdrawing*, *the US administration's decision to sever ties and terminate WHO funding*, *the governing framework for epidemic preparedness and response*, *crucial tools for developing biological countermeasures to influenza*, *the end of the world's second-longest outbreak of Ebola virus disease*, *constrained ability to independently verify official state reports*, and *robust collaboration with WHO—a cornerstone of US funding and policy since 1948*. One informality feature, sentence initial conjunction, is also present, as in *Because withdrawal could not occur until next July […]* and *And because any withdrawal could not take [...]* (third paragraph). This suggests that occasional use of informality features is acceptable in academic writing (see also Chapter 2).

Conclusion

Writing an argumentative essay is a common academic task, as making argument is a staple of scholarly inquiry. In completing this task, you are expected to introduce the issue, state your position on the issue, present your reasoning and evidence, connect evidence and reasoning to claims, and acknowledge and respond to opposing views. Developing the linguistic resources for instantiating these moves and for projecting an appropriate stance that is proportionate to the evidence introduced is vital to crafting an argumentative essay that is clear, focused, logical, rigorously reasoned, well supported, tightly structured, and above all, powerful and convincing.

Reflection/Application Activities

1 Find an argumentative essay in your field and examine its rhetorical moves and the linguistic resources that instantiate these moves. Discuss how effective these moves and resources are in helping the author(s) achieve the goal of the essay and how they are similar to and different from the ones described in this chapter.
2 Take a look at 1–2 argumentative essays you wrote before. In light of what is presented in this chapter, discuss what you think you did well and not so well, as well as what you can do to improve your skills in writing the genre.
3 Write an argumentative essay on an important issue in your field, using the rhetorical moves discussed in this chapter and drawing on the linguistic resources and strategies presented in Chapters 2–4. You can select any of the three types of argumentative essays discussed in the chapter.

References

Goston, L., Koh, H., Williams, M., Hamburg, M., Benjamin, G., Foege, W., Davidson, P., Bradley, E., Barry, M., Koplan, J., Periago, M., Sadr, W., Kurth, A., Vermund, S., & Kavanagh, M. (2020). US withdrawal from WHO is unlawful and threatens global and US health and security. *The Lancet* (www.thelancet.com), 396(10247), 293–295. doi:10.1016/S0140-6736(20)31527-0

Graff, G., & Birkenstein, C. (2018). *They say I say: The moves that matter in academic writing* (4th ed.). New York: Norton.

Kamhi, A. (May, 2007). Knowledge deficits: The true crisis in education. *The ASHA LEADER*, pp. 28–29.

Schleppegrell, M. (2004). *The language of schooling: A functional linguistics perspective.* Mahwah, NJ: Erlbaum.

Toulmin, S. (2003). *The uses of argument* (2nd ed.). Cambridge: Cambridge University Press.

9
Writing an Empirical Research Article

One type of writing that students (especially those at the graduate level) and scholars are expected to be able to write is the empirical research article. The purpose of this type of paper is to report on an empirical study of some sort. The study can be quantitative, qualitative, or a mix of the two. A quantitative study aims at general understanding, seeking to establish relationships, explain causes of change (or lack thereof), confirm or reject hypotheses, and generalize from sample to population primarily through objective measures and statistical analysis. It involves collection, analysis, and interpretation of numerical data for the purpose of testing hypotheses or answering questions. A qualitative study, on the other hand, aims at particular understanding, seeking to generate a rich body of knowledge that is unique to the individual case(s) being studied or to develop working hypotheses about the individual case(s). It uses a variety of methodologies for gathering, analyzing, and interpreting data, including ethnography, grounded theory, oral and life stories, phenomenology, discourse analysis, and ethnology. The mixed-methods study combines quantitative and qualitative research methodologies in a single research study.

Regardless of its type, an empirical research article in an academic journal typically includes most or all of the following elements: abstract, introduction, theoretical framework, literature review, methods, findings, discussion, and conclusion. Some of these elements may be combined into a single section (e.g., introduction + literature review, theoretical framework + literature review, findings + discussion, discussion + conclusion), depending on the norms of practice within a particular discipline and the content of the specific article. Each of these elements is discussed below.

Writing the Abstract Section

The abstract provides an overview of the study and is usually written last. A complete abstract generally consists of

- background, which introduces the study by describing the context in which the study is situated and identifies the knowledge gap(s) to be filled;
- purpose, which states the purpose or goal of the study;
- methods, which reports how the study was conducted, including participant selection and data collection and analysis;
- results, which reports the main findings of the study;
- evaluation, which briefly interprets the findings, telling the reader what they mean; and
- conclusion, which identifies the key contributions of the study to the field

An abstract in a journal article can vary from 100 to 250 words in length. This means one to two sentences are typically allowed for each of the above components. In other words, one sentence in the abstract is expected to summarize the information that is normally presented in one paragraph or an entire section in the main body of the article. Learning to write in a highly distilled and compact style is, therefore, an especially critical skill in abstract writing.

Three samples are presented below to illustrate the fact that authors craft their abstracts differently, depending on the nature of the research conducted, the length requirement of the publication outlet, the complexity of ideas to be presented, and the sort of information to be foregrounded or backgrounded given the length constraint. In some cases, authors may opt to omit background or evaluation, which then gives them more space for describing methods and key findings, the two arguably most important elements of an abstract.

In the following sample abstract (Text 9-1) from a quantitative research article published in the *Journal of Educational Research* (Andrew, Hemovich, & Himelfarb, 2010, p. 253), the authors use highly condensed language to summarize, in 123 words, their study on factors predicting positions on teaching creationism in public schools. The first sentence gives background information about the context in which the study is situated. The second sentence identifies the knowledge gap to be addressed. The first half of the third sentence states the purpose of the study. The second half of the third sentence and the first half of the fourth sentence describes the methods used in the study. The second half of the fourth sentence reports the main findings. The last sentence indicates that the evaluation of results is provided in the article, which is a common strategy authors employ to avoid oversimplifying their evaluation of research findings into one sentence.

Text 9-1

[1] The federal government has repeatedly denied the introduction of creationism into public schools as it is a direct violation of the separation of church and state. [2] Little is known about those who would opt to eliminate evolution in scientific curriculum altogether. [3] The authors examined this

more extreme anti-evolution perspective in a nationally representative sample of U.S. adults (N=2,000). [4] A binary logistic regression model involving 11 relevant predictors revealed that the most important predictor of support for the teaching of creationism-only education in public schools was low educational attainment, which yielded a stronger magnitude of effect than did belief in God or importance of religion. [5] Results are interpreted and discussed in the context of implications for educational policy and science curriculum in public school.

A longer abstract, such as Text 9-2 (again with its sentences numbered), enables the authors to provide more details about their study. The abstract comes from an article (Poole & Schmidt, 2019, p. 644), published in *Developmental Psychobiology*, that investigates biological and behavioral correlates of shyness in children. The first two sentences establish a context for the study by identifying two kinds of shyness and their hypothesized correlates. The third sentence identifies a research gap to be addressed in the study. The fourth sentence describes the research design of the study. The fifth sentence reports the findings of the study. The last sentence evaluates the reported findings. Note that no explicit purpose statement is provided in the abstract, as it can be inferred from the third sentence.

Text 9-2

[1] Early theoretical work by Buss (1986a, 1986b) posited that there is an early-developing fearful shyness that emerges during toddlerhood, and a later-developing self-conscious shyness that emerges during early childhood. [2] It has been theorized that early-developing shyness is related to fear, rooted in inherited biases, and manifests in contexts of social novelty, whereas later-developing shyness is related to self-conscious emotions, may result from social ridicule or poor social skills, and manifests in contexts of social exposure. [3] Despite the hypothesized correlates of these shyness subtypes, this theory has not been empirically tested in children. [4] We tested 96 children aged 5 to 10 years old and classified them into three groups: early-developing shyness (n = 28; $M_{AgeOnset}$ = 2.4 years), later-developing shyness (n = 19; $M_{AgeOnset}$ = 4.8 years), and non-shy (n = 49). [5] Findings revealed that children with later-developing shyness had the highest relative cortisol responses in the context of self-presentation, highest levels of embarrassment, and lowest social skills relative to the other groups, while children with early-developing shyness displayed the highest relative resting right frontal brain asymmetry (a neural correlate of fear) relative to the other groups. [6] These preliminary findings provide partial empirical support for the previously theorized correlates and distinction of early-developing and later-developing shyness in childhood.

In another abstract (Text 9-3), from a qualitative research article published in the *Journal of Mathematical Behavior* (Fang & Chapman, 2020, p. 1), the authors summarize their study in 151 words. The first sentence establishes the research territory, and the second sentence states the importance of research on the topic, instead of identifying research gaps. The third sentence then states the purpose of the study. The fourth and fifth sentences describe the study's research methods (participants, data collection, data analysis). The next sentence reports the main findings of the study, which are then evaluated in the last sentence.

Text 9-3

[1] Recent scholarship on disciplinary literacy calls for an emphasis on teaching discipline-specific language/literacy practices. [2] An understanding of these practices is, therefore, essential to literacy instruction in secondary content areas such as mathematics. [3] This case study examined one mathematician's reading practices, with a focus on the strategies he used in text comprehension. [4] Data collected include the mathematician's think-alouds during reading, discussion of his reading think-alouds, and semi-structured interviews. [5] These data were analyzed qualitatively through an iterative process involving multiple readings and identification and refinement of codes. [6] The analysis revealed that the mathematician engaged in extensive reading and employed an array of strategies—rereading, close reading, monitoring and questioning, summarizing and paraphrasing, storying, drawing on prior knowledge and experience, evaluating and verifying, and note-taking and visualizing—to help him make sense of what he read. [7] These findings provide important insights that can inform mathematics teachers' efforts to support students' mathematics reading and learning.

Writing the Introduction Section

The introduction is essentially a more extended version of the first two components of the abstract. It is intended to give the reader a quick sense of what the article is about and why the topic is worth exploring. This is done by "creating a research space" (Swales & Feak, 2018), which involves a series of three moves as follows:

- establishing a research territory, which provides the necessary background information on the topic and shows the reader that the general research area is important, relevant, central, or problematic in some way.
- Establishing a niche, which identifies a gap or flaw in the existing research, raises a question about the existing research, describes the significance of the topic, detects a recent movement in the existing scholarship, or issues a call for a particular line of work, with the anticipation that the gap, flaw, trend, or question will be addressed fully or in part through additional research.

- Occupying the niche, which indicates the intention to fill the gap(s) identified, address the flaw(s) found, answer the question(s) asked, or follow/counter the trend detected. This is done by stating a research purpose. In some cases, the author may also identify the specific research questions to be addressed in the study, explain the potential contributions of the study, and provide a preview of the overall organization of the article.

Text 2-3 (see Chapter 2), the introduction to an empirical research article, follows these three moves. The first three sentences provide background information about the topic and show that the research area is important. The next two sentences establish a niche by identifying knowledge gaps in the existing research. These gaps are then filled by the last three sentences, which describe the purpose and potential contributions of the proposed study.

Text 9-4 (Poole & Schmidt, 2019, p. 644) is the introduction from an article that investigates the behavioral and biological correlates of early- and later-developing shyness in young children. The introduction begins by defining the key construct of the study—shyness. The rest of the first paragraph briefly synthesizes the research literature to identify what is known about the topic. The second paragraph identifies a research gap in the existing research literature (first sentence) and suggests a reason for the existence of this gap (second sentence). The last sentence of the paragraph states the importance of filling this gap (i.e., identify heterogeneity of shyness), which can also be understood to imply the purpose of the study. In essence, this introduction is a distillation of what is presented in the literature review section that follows and where the aim of the study is more fully described.

Text 9-4

Shyness is a trait characterized by inhibition in response to social novelty or situations of perceived social evaluation (Melchior & Cheek, 1990). There is substantial heterogeneity in the phenomenon of shyness, and several decades of theoretical writings (Buss, 1986a, 1986b; Crozier, 1999; Poole, Tang, & Schmidt, 2018; Poole & Schmidt, 2019a; Schmidt & Buss, 2010; Schmidt & Fox, 1999) and empirical research (Bruch, Giordano, & Pearl, 1986; Cheek & Buss, 1981; Colonnesi, Napoleone, & Bogels, 2014; Eggum-Wilkens, Lemery-Chalfant, Aksan, & Goldsmith, 2015; Poole et al., 2019; Poole & Schmidt, 2019b; Poole, Van Lieshout, & Schmidt, 2017; Schmidt, 1999) have illustrated that shyness is not a unitary construct. For example, social withdrawal in general can result from different social motivations (Asendorf, 1990; Coplan, Prakash, O'neil, & Armer, 2004), and shyness in particular can have different phenotypic expressions (Colonnesi et al., 2014; Reddy, 2001).

Despite the known heterogeneity in shyness, relatively little work has been conducted to understand whether there are distinct behavioral and biological correlates associated with this heterogeneity. One reason for this lack of work is that there have been few theoretical models on the heterogeneity of shyness that can help guide research questions. It is, however, important to identify heterogeneity in shyness, as this allows for greater precision in understanding the social, emotional, and biological foundations and consequences of different shy subtypes (Poole & Schmidt, 2019b).

As the samples above illustrate, the introduction is brief and compact, usually one to two paragraphs in length. It helps establish, in a succinct way, a context and a purpose (or blueprint) for, as well as the significance of, the study. As such, it is an especially important, though difficult, segment to write. This is perhaps why many writers spend an inordinate amount of time in crafting a good introduction. There is certainly some truth to the ancient Greek proverb that "well begun is half done".

Writing the Theoretical Framework Section

A complete, rigorous empirical research article is expected to include a discussion of the theoretical framework that guides the conceptualization and design of the study. A theoretical framework introduces and describes the theory, model, lens, or perspective—such as Alan Baddeley's working memory model (psychology), Murray Bowen's family systems theory (sociology), Donald Burmister's layered-elastic theory (engineering), Kimberle Crenshaw's critical race theory (law), Michael Halliday's sociosemiotics theory (linguistics), and Lev Vygotsky's sociocultural perspective (education)—that explains the meaning, nature, and challenge of the phenomenon or problem under study. It gives direction to a research study and allows the reader to conceptualize the study in a broader context. A study can be grounded in more than one theory.

Generally, a theoretical framework section includes a definition of key constructs within the theory; a description of its key assumptions, tenets, or principles; and a discussion of how it is relevant to the study. Sometimes, the section is embedded as part (often the beginning) of the literature review section.

A sample theoretical framework (Text 9-5) is presented below. It is taken from Fang, Cao, and Murray (2020), which explores the language choices (academic language vs everyday language) school children made in their factual writing. Given the focus of the study, it makes sense that register theory—a theory about how language choices reflect/construct context and shape meaning—is used as the theoretical framework to guide the study. The paragraphs are numbered for ease of reference in the ensuing discussion.

Text 9-5

Theoretical Perspective: Register Variation and Literacy Learning

1   Register is the linguistic expression of a given contextual configuration. It is "a variety of language, corresponding to a variety of situation" (Halliday & Hasan, 1985, p. 38). Each socially recognizable situation type has its own register, or ways of using language. People make different language choices in different situational contexts depending on what they are talking about (i.e., field), who they are interacting with (i.e., tenor), and the channel of communication (i.e., mode). Specifically, when the topic of discussion is specialized, we expect the use of technical terms and acronyms, that is, words only "insiders" understand; on the other hand, when the topic of discussion is commonsensical, we expect the use of everyday terms, that is, words ordinary people would understand. We also vary our language choices based on the power relationship, frequency of contact, and affective involvement between ourselves and our audience (Martin, 2012). For example, we tend to use language that is a bit more formal and tentative when interacting with people of unequal status, with whom we are rarely in contact, or with whom we have low affective involvement. When we interact with people of equal status, with whom we are in frequent contact, or with whom we show affection, we tend to use language that is less formal and more intimate.

2   Moreover, how we use language is impacted by the spatial distance between us and our audience. We make different language choices depending on whether we are writing in isolation, talking over the phone, or conversing face to face, as each situational context allows for more or less immediate feedback and use of paralinguistic cues. The experiential distance between language and the social process occurring also impacts our language use. For example, narrating a sports game in which we are playing is different from writing about the event after it is over because in the former, language accompanies or constitutes the action, whereas in the latter, language is a tool for reflecting on the experience. Such a systematic relationship between text and context means that we can infer the context that a text construes based on the language choices in the text, and conversely, we can predict the language choices for a text based on the specification of its context.

3   Recognizing how language use varies across contexts is a register ability key to school success. Formal contexts such as schooling often require that students make meaning in ways that are different from what they would normally do in informal contexts such as everyday social

interaction with family and friends. In the schooling context, students are generally expected to make meaning in ways that are informationally dense, authoritatively presented, and tightly knit (Schleppegrell, 2004). This means they must develop new language resources, beyond those they have already been using in everyday social interactions, in order to take on more technical and abstract meanings that are necessary for construing uncommonsense knowledge. For example, to display disciplinary knowledge in school, students must learn to use complex nominal groups with specialized terminology and to reason within, rather than between, clauses with nouns, verbs, and prepositions. To be authoritative in the presentation of knowledge and reasoned in the development of argument, students must learn to use declarative sentences, modal verbs, and other attitudinal resources. To create tightly knit texts, students must learn to use internal conjunctions and other cohesive devices, as well as clause-combining strategies of embedding and condensing.

4   Different tasks within the school context, likewise, call for different uses of language. In school, students engage in different activities that require them to make different language choices in order to perform the activities successfully. During a typical school day, a first-grade student may participate in "show and tell", storybook reading, free play, dictation, and writing activities. Likewise, a middle school student may conduct a science experiment, write a report on the experiment, work on geometry proofs, summarize a book chapter, write an historical explanation, discuss a literary work, and make a PowerPoint presentation about a project of interest. Successful participation in these school-based activities requires that students command a rich repertoire of language resources that enable them to select, albeit often unconsciously, the lexical and grammatical features that are functional and effective for making meaning relevant to each discipline, task, and purpose. In "show and tell", for instance, the choice of present tense (*am/are doing*), first person (*I*, *we*), and demonstratives pointing to the nonverbal context (*this*, *here*, *now*) is common. In factual writing, simple present tense and generic reference to whole classes (e.g., *Fish are ectotherms.*) are preferred. Thus, differences in language choices reflect and are shaped by differences in context.

5   Not all students are equally prepared for this sort of schoolwork, however. Some students come to school ready to engage in the various tasks of schooling, whereas others face challenges in making the transition from home to school or from one grade level to the next. British educational sociologist Basil Bernstein (1971/2003) posited that the differential preparation of children for schooling stems from the disparity in the ways they were socialized into making meaning with language. To help explain his theory, Bernstein proposed a distinction between a restricted code, or

a public language, and an elaborated code, or a formal language. The restricted code refers to the language used among people with a great deal
of shared assumptions or understandings. Because much can be taken
for granted in this type of interaction, there is little need for elaboration
and explicitness in discourse. Thus, the restricted code tends to be more
truncated and dependent on the immediate context of 'here and now'. It
is characterized "by fragmentation, by logical simplicity and by leaving
implicit notions of causality, and so on" (Halliday, 2007, p. 83).

6   The elaborated code, on the other hand, refers to the language used
among people with little shared knowledge or understanding. Due to
limited communal understandings, there is a much greater need for explicitness and elaboration in interaction. Thus, the elaborated code tends
to be more thorough in explanation and complete in detail. It embodies
"generalizations of experience removed from, not dependent on, the
immediate context of the 'here and now'" and is characterized by "an
explicit formulation of relations of space, time, and cause as well as
social relationships" (Halliday, 2007, p. 83). It is, thus, the medium
"for thinking the unthinkable, the impossible" because the meanings to
which it gives rise go beyond local space, time, and context (Bernstein,
1986, p. 209). The elaborated code has evolved in stratified industrial cultures and is increasingly realized in the abstract and technical written discourses of science/technology and government bureaucracy (Rose, 1999).

7   Bernstein found that a high proportion of lower working-class families
are limited to the restricted code, whereas middle-class families are ex-
posed to both restricted and elaborated codes. Although each code has
its own aesthetics and neither is inherently superior to the other, school
and society seem to privilege the elaborated code over the restricted
code. This means that children who come to school equipped with the
elaborated code have more linguistic capital that gives them an advantage in school learning. Bernstein's observations were further validated
by subsequent sociolinguistic work of Hasan (1989/2009) and Heath
(1983), which affirmed that people from different social strata are oriented toward different ways of meaning and that this difference in coding
orientation impacts children's literacy achievement and academic performance in school.

The section begins by defining the key concept of the theory, register. The rest
of the first two paragraphs then describes and exemplifies the key tenet of the
theory—that is, language use varies according to the context of situation (audience, topic, task, purpose, space, and mode of communication). The third and
fourth paragraphs make the connection between the theory and literacy learning, showing how school literacy learning entails mastery of register variation.

The last three paragraphs suggest that the problems students face in literacy learning and schooling are due, at least in part, to a lack of control over register. Taken together, this section helps the authors make the case for a focus on language choices in investigating student's factual writing. In other words, the authorial decision to make language choices a focus of exploration in the study of writing is informed, supported, and justified by the register theory. Readers should be able to answer the question of "why is it important or appropriate to examine language choices when studying student writing?" after reading this section of theoretical framework.

In short, theoretical framework is critically important to the conceptualization and design of an empirical study—quantitative, qualitative, or mixed methods. It determines how you perceive, make sense of, and interpret your data. It also helps readers better understand your perspective and context. All research articles should have a robust theoretical framework to justify the importance and appropriateness of their work. According to Lederman and Lederman (2015), former editors of *Journal of Science Teacher Education*, a poor or missing theoretical framework is one of the most frequently cited reasons for their editorial decision not to publish a manuscript. Quality journals usually require that theoretical framework be explicitly identified and clearly explained in any submission that reports on empirical research.

Writing the Literature Review Section

A literature review, as discussed in Chapter 7, canvasses the scholarly sources (e.g., books, journal articles, graduate theses, documents) related to a specific topic or research question. Often written as part of a research paper, it provides a survey of existing knowledge on the topic, revealing gaps, flaws, patterns, trends, questions, issues, or needs in the field that can subsequently be addressed. The research questions, problems, or hypotheses should arise naturally from the literature review. Thus, it is through the literature review that a link between your proposed study and previous research is fully established.

In writing a literature review, it is important not to make a laundry list of summaries of previous studies. Instead, these studies need to be summarized, synthesized, evaluated, and integrated. A literature review also needs to be current, focusing on up-to-date scholarship that is most important to your study as well as landmark studies that may be somewhat dated. It is important to be accurate and thorough when summarizing the literature; at the same time, it is reasonable to be selective and have a spin when summarizing specific studies so that what is summarized not only connects with but also supports the point(s) to be made (see Chapter 3). Conscious efforts should also be made to avoid plagiarizing or overquoting the literature and to ensure discursive flow when making transitions from one study (or group of studies) to the next.

One question that often surfaces when writing a literature review is this: What tense do I use when reporting others' work? A perusal of published articles indicates that there is quite a bit of confusion over the use of tense in the literature review. Some suggested using the past tense when citing an empirical study and the present tense when citing a thinker's opinion. Swales and Feak (2018) proposed the following guidelines for using tense that are worth observing:

- When referring to single studies, use the past tense, as in *Adams (2007) explored the relationship between obesity and beer consumption.*
- When referring to an area of inquiry, use the present perfect tense, as in *The relationship between obesity and beer consumption has seldom been explored.*
- When referring to the state of current knowledge, use the present tense, as in *The relationship between obesity and beer consumption is a hot topic worthy of further investigation.*

What follows (Text 9-6) is the literature review (slightly modified) from Fang and Chapman (2020), which explores one mathematician's reading practices. Paragraphs are numbered for ease of reference in analysis and discussion.

Text 9-6

Literature Review: How Mathematicians Read

1   A focus on disciplinary literacy in secondary literacy instruction requires that content area teachers understand the literate practices that experts privilege and use in their work. A particularly fruitful line of inquiry that sheds light on these practices comes from studies of how disciplinary experts read. This research has explored the reading strategies used by experts from a number of academic disciplines, including science (e.g., Bazerman, 1985), history (e.g., Wineburg, 1991), engineering (e.g., Chapman, 2015), and literature (e.g., Rainey, 2017). A comprehensive review of this body of work is beyond the scope of our paper. Therefore, we limit our review to studies of mathematicians, with the goal of identifying knowledge gaps and showing how our study builds on and extends prior research.

2   Compared to science or history, studies of mathematicians' reading practices are limited. As Weber and Mejia-Ramos (2013a) observed, "research on the reading and nature of mathematics text is sparse" (p. 90). This limited amount of work focuses almost exclusively on

the mathematical practice of proof validation and was conducted primarily by mathematics scholars rather than literacy scholars. Weber (2008) conducted one of the earliest studies on how mathematicians read purported mathematical proofs and made judgments about the proofs' validity. Using think-alouds and retrospective interviews, he found that mathematicians used different modes of reasoning in proof validation, including formal reasoning and the construction of rigorous proofs, informal deductive reasoning, and example-based reasoning. He also reported that mathematicians first examined larger chunks of logical structure (i.e., zoom-out strategy) before reading each line of argument more closely (i.e., zoom-in strategy). That is, in proof validation, mathematicians first determined the structure of the argument, primarily by explicitly checking which assumptions were being used in the argument. If they found the structure of the proof, or methodological moves (e.g., proof by contradiction, direct proof), to be acceptable, they would then check each line of the argument.

3   This finding is contradicted by Inglis and Alcock (2012), who conducted an eye-tracking study comparing the proof validation behavior of first-year undergraduate students and research-active mathematicians. They found that (a) both mathematicians and undergraduate students used the zoom-in strategy (line-by-line close reading), (b) the former used the zoom-in strategy more often than the latter, and (c) neither engaged in the zoom-out strategy. Specifically, in reading mathematical proofs, the mathematicians focused on the logical details of an argument, shifting their attention back and forth between consecutive lines of purported proofs, and devoting more effort to inferring implicit between-line warrants. They did not examine the overall logical structure of the proof.

4   The study complements self-report studies by reducing problems of re-activity and veridicality through the use of eye-tracking instrument. It is limited, however, in that it focuses on reading behavior when validating proofs instead of when reading for comprehension. It is possible that reading behavior when validating a proof is different from that when reading for comprehension, because in proof comprehension, the validity of the proof is assumed (or at least initially assumed) by virtue of its author or source, and the goal of the reader is to understand the proof and not to check it for correctness.

5   Conducting a more fine-grained analysis of Inglis and Alcock's data, Weber and Mejia-Ramos (2013b) countered Inglis and Alcock's claim, suggesting that when engaging in proof validation tasks, the mathematicians did frequently use an initial skimming strategy (zooming out) before reading individual parts of the proof more carefully (zooming in). They further noted that inferring individuals' strategy use by averaging

their reaction times across multiple trials, as Inglis and Alcock did, is problematic.

6   While mathematics researchers focused on how mathematicians solve proofs, literacy researchers Shanahan, Shanahan, and Misischia (2011) focused on how mathematicians read and comprehend texts in their discipline. Specifically, they examined how mathematicians, as well as historians and chemists, interacted with texts in their field. Drawing on the work of Wineburg (1991), the researchers examined the ways experts (2 per discipline) used sourcing, contextualization, and corroboration in their considerations of disciplinary texts. They also examined how text structure and graphic elements influenced the ways experts interacted with the text, the role of interest in their reading, and how they engaged in critiquing the text. By examining the data collected from individual inter-views, reading think-alouds, and focus group meetings, the researchers found that the mathematicians gave little regard to the author of the doc-ument (i.e., sourcing) and paid little attention to contextual factors such as time (i.e., contextualization); however, they used corroboration (i.e., checking one source against another) as a reading strategy to help them make sense of text. The mathematicians used their understanding of text structure to determine where problems and solutions were located. They placed a strong emphasis on accuracy (but not much on credibility), weighing nearly every word and evaluating each piece of information to ensure understanding. They treated both equations and prose equally and as inseparable, interpreting them in a unified manner.

7   Some of these findings have been challenged. Weber and Mejia-Ramos (2013a) argued that mathematicians do pay attention to sourcing. They cited as evidence results from two of their own studies. In an experiment conducted by Inglis and Mejia-Ramos (2009), 190 mathematicians were asked to read a mathematical argument and rate it for its level of perceived persuasiveness. Half of the mathematicians were informed that the author was a famous mathematician, and the other half were not provided an author. The group who had an awareness of the author rated the argument more than 17 points higher than the other group. In another study (Weber & Mejia-Ramos, 2011), mathematicians stated that they believed a proof to be trustworthy and correct if it appeared in a reputable journal. This finding was corroborated by results from the survey data of 118 mathematicians, where a large majority stated that if a proof was published in a respected academic journal, they felt highly confident that the proof is correct and frequently felt unnecessary to check for accuracy (Mejia-Ramos & Weber, 2014).

8   Two prominent issues have emerged from the above review of expert studies on mathematicians. First, there are inconsistencies in the

findings with regard to mathematicians' reading practices, such as the extent to which the strategies of sourcing and skimming are used. Second, the bulk of research on mathematicians' reading practices focus on proof reading instead of reading comprehension of mathematics texts in general. Although Shanahan, Shanahan, and Misischia (2011) is an exception, it asked participants to read short excerpts of disciplinary texts (1.5 pages), instead of full-length papers. Moreover, it relied on the same types of strategies identified by Wineburg (1991) in his study of historians' reading practices, which is methodologically problematic. Specifically, Wineburg (1991) reported only heuristics that were present in at least 50% of the verbal protocols, leaving out other heuristics that were less frequently used but might still be important to the literate practices of historians or other experts.

9   Our study builds on and extends this small body of work by examining in greater depth the strategies one mathematician used when reading to comprehend a text in his discipline. It offers something new that is currently not well-addressed in the mathematics reading literature. Specifically, we asked the following research question: How did the mathematician make sense of a text in his area of specialization? Answers to this question will provide insights into reading comprehension that is not explicitly related to proofs. Although the focus on one participant engaging in one reading limits the generalizability of our study, it allows us to dig deeper into the participant's meaning-making practices in ways that may not be feasible with multiple participants and multiple readings.

This review is used to justify the need for continuing research on how mathematicians read texts in their discipline. To do so, it is necessary to find out what is known, less well-known, or unknown about the topic. The first paragraph reiterates the need to investigate disciplinary experts' literate practices, acknowledges the extensiveness of the work that has been done on expert reading across disciplines, and then delimits the scope of the review to mathematics.

The second paragraph begins by stating that the reading practices of mathematicians are understudied when compared to those of other disciplinary experts, suggesting that further research in mathematics is needed. The claim is supported by a quote from a reputable source (second sentence). This is followed by identification of a key theme of research on mathematicians' reading practices (third sentence). The rest of the paragraph describes the methods and key findings of an important study (*Weber, 2008*) in this body of research. The third and fourth paragraphs present and comment on a study (*Inglis & Alcock, 2012*) that reported findings contradictory to those of *Weber (2008)*. The fifth paragraph describes a study (*Weber & Mejia-Ramos, 2013b*) whose findings contradict those of *Inglis and Alcock (2012)* and which also implicates a methodological problem with the study. Taken together, these paragraphs suggest that further research is needed because of inconsistent findings reported in prior studies.

The sixth paragraph begins with *While mathematics researchers [...],* which links back to the previous four paragraphs that focus on the studies conducted by mathematics researchers and at the same time signals the move to a study conducted by literacy researchers. The study (*Shanahan, Shanahan, & Misischia, 2011*) is summarized in some detail because it is most closely related, conceptually and methodologically, to the one being conducted by the authors themselves (Fang & Chapman), who are also literacy researchers. The next paragraph then compares the study's findings to those conducted by mathematics researchers, identifying inconsistencies in the two bodies of work and thus suggesting the need for further research.

The eighth paragraph summarizes two prominent issues that arise from the studies reviewed—inconsistencies of findings and methodological limitations. These issues justify the need for further research, thus accomplishing the main goal of the literature view. This leads naturally to the last paragraph, which states the purpose of the proposed study (first sentence), highlights the uniqueness of the research (second sentence), identifies the specific research question to be investigated (third sentence), notes the significance of the work (fourth sentence), and in anticipation of the potential reviewer bias against the use of case study, acknowledges the pros and cons of the study's research design (last sentence).

Note that the authors use the past tense when describing specific empirical studies (e.g., *conducted, compared, examined*) and the simple present tense when commenting on these studies as a whole (e.g., *are limited, is contradicted, complements*). Occasionally, the simple present perfect tense is used when referring to a line of research, as in *This research has explored the reading strategies used by experts [...].* In some sentences, both the present tense and the past tense are used because these sentences mix commentary with reporting, as can be seen in *Although Shanahan, Shanahan, and Misischia (2011) is an exception, it asked participants to read short excerpts of disciplinary texts [...]* and *This finding is contradicted by Inglis and Alcock (2012), who conducted an eye-tracking study [...].* This practice contradicts a popular misconstrued rule—tense must be consistent within the same sentence—that students at all levels of schooling are often taught to observe in writing classes.

The authors also use different reporting verbs when summarizing prior studies. Most of these verbs are neutral (e.g., *observed, conducted, found, examined, reported, focused, noted*) because they are used to summarize the results from empirical investigations, rather than to present impassionate arguments made by the researchers. This is different from the argumentative essays presented in Chapter 8, where reporting verbs are generally more colored.

Writing the Methods Section

Every empirical research article is required to include a methods section that describes the steps researchers took in conducting their study. This section contains essential details that enable the reader to assess the overall rigor of the study, the reliability and validity of its findings, and its potential for replication. It answers four main questions: where was the study conducted, who/what was involved in the study, how were data collected or generated, and how were these data analyzed. This means that a methods section will contain, at a minimum, a description of the participants involved in the study and the procedures used for collecting and analyzing data. Depending on the type of research conducted and the caliber of the publication outlet, it may also include, in varying degrees of specificity, the methodology (i.e., rationale or justification) for the specific methods used, essential information about the context (i.e., research site) in which the study was conducted, the criteria used to include or exclude participants, the informed consent process, the materials used or the program implemented in data generation, fidelity of implementation, the problems anticipated in the conduct of the research and steps taken to mitigate these problems, the strategies used to validate data and triangulate findings, and researcher positionality (e.g., beliefs, bias, experiences, and perspectives).

Methodological rigor is one of the primary criteria used in manuscript evaluation and editorial decision during the publication process (see Chapter 12 for more details), as well as in assessing the quality of thesis/dissertation and research grant proposals (see also Chapter 10). Generally, the more rigorous a publication outlet, the more methodological details are expected; and the more controversial or novel a method is, the more details about the method are needed to inform the reader about it and to justify its use (Swales & Feak, 2018). A methods section that lacks specificity or is poorly written undermines the credibility and the value of the study. Some of the questions often asked about the methods section by top tier journals include:

- Are the methodology and methods used consistent with the theoretical orientation that informs the investigation and the goals of the study?
- Are the methodology and methods appropriate for the problems, questions, or hypotheses?
- Are the methodology and methods appropriate for the type of study conducted (e.g., ethnographic, philosophical, experimental)?
- Are the methodology and methods reported thoroughly but concisely?

- Are samples and sampling procedures clearly described?
- Is information about reliability and validity provided for the assessment instruments used?
- Are data sources clearly and sufficiently described?
- Are examples of data collection tools (e.g., interview or survey questions, test items, observation protocols) provided?
- Are examples of data analysis (e.g., coding manual, coding worksheets) provided?

The methods section is written mostly in the past tense and using the passive voice. However, when describing the features of an instrument (e.g., a test, a survey, or an observation protocol), the present tense is used. And with the wide acceptance of the first person (*we, I*) in academic writing, the active voice is increasingly used to describe what researchers did in carrying out their study, especially when such use facilitates the presentation of information.

The following example (Text 9-7), again excerpted from Fang and Chapman (2020, pp. 4–6), describes the methods used in a qualitative case study of one mathematician's reading practices.

Text 9-7

Methods

Participant and Setting

The participant for our study was a male mathematician, whom we shall refer to as Kang, from a large, public, research intensive university in the United States. He was born in China and earned his bachelor's degree in mathematics from one of the top mathematics programs in the world. He earned his doctoral degree in mathematics from a flagship state university in the U.S. He specialized in nonlinear partial differential equations and geometric analysis and had numerous publications in top tier journals in his field. At the time of this study, he was an associate professor of mathematics and had worked at the university for over a decade. He was fluent and articulate in both English and Chinese.

Kang was selected based on his expertise in the field and his willingness to participate in the study. Convenience sampling was desirable for our study due to the participant's accessibility and proximity to the researchers. Although this technique has drawn criticism regarding the bias involved in including such a limited sample, the purpose of our study was to seek particular understandings and not to identify generalizable findings. In other words, it was an in-depth case study (Yin, 2014) aiming to provide rich descriptions of the participant's disciplinary meaning-making practices.

Data Collection

Task. Data for the study were collected in the form of reading think-alouds, discussion of the think-aloud video, and interviews. The participant was asked to select and read an unfamiliar text in his area of expertise with the goal of understanding the text to inform his own research. The text he chose was an article from *Annals of Mathematics* (i.e., Caffarelli, Jerison, & Kenig, 2002) that describes, explains, validates, and applies some new monotonicity theorems. He was instructed to verbalize his thought processes while reading the article. The think-aloud session was videotaped. Concurrent reporting of thinking while reading was used here because it relies on short-term memory and allows the participant to report the thought as it is being formulated (Ericsson & Simon, 1993). This method has the advantage of accurately reflecting what is currently in the consciousness of the participant and is generally preferred over retrospective reporting of thinking when high ability readers are involved (Pressley & Hilden, 2004).

Training. Prior to the completion of the task, Kang was trained on how to do verbal reporting while reading through a practice session in which we provided neutral instructions and occasionally interjected prompts. For the practice session, an article outside Kang's specialty was used. The article (i.e., Debey, Houwer, & Verschuere, 2014) reported on an experiment designed to determine if truth can also serve a function in the act of lying. It was selected because the act of lying was a universal topic likely familiar to most people; however, the complexity and technical wording of the written research would likely challenge the participant enough to cause him to slow down and make his cognitive processes less hidden or automatic. During the training, Kang was asked to follow the think-aloud principles suggested by Perkins (1981): (a) say whatever is on your mind and do not hold back hunches, guesses, wild ideas, images, and intentions; (b) speak as continuously as possible, (c) speak audibly, (d) speak as telegraphically as you please without worrying about complete sentences and eloquence, (e) do not overexplain or justify, and (f) do not elaborate past events, but instead get into the pattern of saying what you are thinking now, not of thinking for a while and then describing your thoughts.

Probing. Probing is an important technique used by researchers in the case participants fall silent during the think-aloud. We prompted Kang to continue verbally reporting by asking non-specific questions (e.g., what are you doing now?) so as not to alter his normal reading behavior. Beyond this, we did not cue or prompt him to approach the reading task in any particular way.

Discussion of Think-aloud Video. Another data source is the viewing and discussion of the video clips of the reading think-aloud task. This data source was included based on the recommendation from Olson and Biolsi (1991). By videotaping the behaviors that Kang exhibited during the reading think-aloud, we had the opportunity to show Kang the video shortly after the session ended to discuss critical points or questions about observed behaviors. It also provided us with the opportunity to question Kang about puzzling behaviors or gain a fuller understanding of what we observed during the reading think-aloud. The discussion was audiotaped for later transcription and analysis.

Interviews. Interview was also used to collect data regarding Kang's literate practices in mathematics. Olson and Biolsi (1991) noted that interview is the most common method used for drawing out knowledge from expert participants. Two "semi-structured" interviews (Seidman, 2006) were conducted, one (initial interview) at the beginning and the other (final interview) at the end of data collection. The interview questions were adapted from Chapman (2015). Both interviews took place in Kang's workplace, and they were framed in a way that closely mirrored natural conversation. The interviews were audiotaped and later transcribed for analysis.

Data Analysis

Coding of Verbal Protocols. The coding of the reading think-aloud transcripts focused specifically on the strategies Kang used as he interacted with the stimulus text. In our analysis, we heeded Bereiter and Bird's (1985) caution that "efforts to mine expert protocols for teachable content are generally informal and intuitive" (p. 133). The mining process involved cataloguing the data into tools that seemed to serve as strategies used by Kang as he tried to make sense of the text. Specifically, a team of researchers (two faculty members and two doctoral students) individually read and reread the think-aloud transcripts a number of times. This initial reading served to familiarize us with the data and to gain an overall sense of the possible emerging strategies. After the initial reading, we met as a group to refine the strategies. This is a process that involved clustering, enriching, expanding, reconciling, collapsing, or decomposing the tentative strategies each of us had developed during initial reading. We created categories for all observed reading behaviors.

Coding of Interviews and Discussion of Think-aloud Video. Transcripts of interviews and discussion of the think-aloud video were read and reread to gain familiarity and an overall sense of what the data presented. The data were then coded in two stages: initial coding and focused coding (Charmaz, 2006; Glaser, 1978). During initial coding, which is typically rapid and spontaneous, we developed provisionary codes, worded as gerunds to reflect the meaning-making behaviors of the participant. These codes were adjusted and refined during focused coding, a process that is more intense and conceptual. The coding was done line-by-line, which allowed us to sift through the detailed data while keeping us in the realm of discovery.

Validation Strategies. Two validation strategies were used in our analysis: member checking and data triangulation. Lincoln and Guba (1985) considered member checking to be "the most critical technique for establishing credibility" (p. 314). The process of member checking involves providing the study's participant with the findings and interpretations as a way to solicit his feedback on the accuracy of the findings. We conducted member checking according to what Creswell (2013) suggested—sharing with Kang results from our preliminary analysis, including descriptions of identified themes but not all the raw data or transcripts. Once preliminary focused codes were identified, they, together with the details that were used to support them, were presented to Kang to see if he agreed with the codes.

In data triangulation, researchers "make use of multiple and different sources, methods, investigators, and theories to provide corroborating evidence" (Creswell, 2013, p. 251). Triangulation allows researchers to identify evidence of a common theme across multiple data sources, thus strengthening the validity of the research. In our study, the research question was answered using multiple data sources that include reading think-alouds, discussion of the think-aloud video, and interviews.

Researcher Subjectivity. It is important to make explicit any bias or assumption that may influence research (Merriam, 1988). This information is frequently a reflection of past experiences, beliefs, prejudices, and/or orientations that are likely to shape the researcher's conception and interpretations of the study. As researchers in the study, we held a Ph.D. in language and literacy education. We had worked as language/literacy teacher, consultant, coach, and researcher in K-20 settings. We agreed that language and literacy are integral to the conception of academic disciplines and their social practices. We believed that content area teachers are best positioned to help their students develop the language and literacy skills needed to read/write complex texts in their discipline. We have designed and taught preservice and inservice courses on how to infuse evidence-based language and literacy practices into content area teaching and learning.

This excerpt provides detailed information about the participant and the setting, data collection and analysis procedures, validation strategies, and researcher positionality, which are components typical of manuscripts reporting qualitive research. Note that the section is written mostly in the past tense, except when comments about data collection/analysis methods are made (e.g., _relies_ on short-term memory, _has_ the advantage of, _is_ an important technique). Citations are judiciously selected to justify the use of these methods. The excerpt uses a mix of the third and the first person, as well as the active and the passive voice, depending on the sort of information the authors want to foreground and the need to facilitate information flow.

Writing the Results Section

The Results section is where findings (positive, negative, or neutral) are faithfully reported based on the methods described above. The term "results" is commonly used in empirical research articles. However, some scholars prefer the term "findings" over "results" when reporting on qualitative research. Results are usually presented through a thoughtful combination of linguistic (e.g., words, mathematical symbols) and visuals (e.g., figures, tables) resources. Tables and figures must be labelled logically and sequentially to allow for clarity and convenience in referencing. Any information that is not the direct finding or outcome of the study should be left out of this section.

The section typically begins with a statement that reminds the reader of the study's purpose (and research design), as well as key findings to be presented. What follows depends on the type of research conducted and is best organized alongside the research questions—for each research question, present the data addressing that research question. Subheadings can be used to improve readability and clarity. For qualitative research, themes related to each research question are presented, elaborated, and supported with data. For quantitative studies, statements showing where results can be found are presented. This is then followed by statements highlighting novel, surprising, intriguing, unusual, or potentially highly important findings that are closely relevant to each research question. References to tables and figures are often needed to illuminate the findings presented (see Chapter 4). Usually, the past tense is used to describe the results, and the present tense is used to refer to figures and tables.

One caveat here is to avoid duplicating the same data among prose, tables, and figures. In other words, it is generally a good idea not to restate exactly the same information by repeating the graphical data in the prose or by presenting the same data once as a table and once as a graph. Instead, you can use the prose to summarize what the reader will find in the table/figure or to draw readers' attention to the most important or intriguing data points. Rather than attempting to cover all the information in the table/figure, you should think about what is most important and relevant to the research question being addressed. For example, if a table shows that the test scores for Groups A and B are, respectively, 26 and 21, there is no need to repeat the same information verbatim in the prose (e.g., *Group A scored 26 points and Group B scored 21 points.*). Instead, it is better to say something to the effect that *Both groups scored in the lowest quartile, with Group A outperforming Group B by five points, and the difference between the two groups was statistically (in)significant.*

Presented below are two samples of the beginning of the Results section. Text 9-8 is from Fang, Gresser, Cao, and Zheng (2021), a quantitative study of noun phrase complexity in K-12 students' informational writing. Text 9-9 is from Aukerman and Schuldt (2015, p. 126), a qualitative study of bilingual second-grade students' perception of their reading competence and epistemic roles in two contrasting settings where texts were regularly discussed. Text 9-8 begins by reminding the reader of the focus of the study (first sentence) and of the rationale for this narrow focus (second sentence). The next sentence tells the reader where results can be found (Table 2), and the last sentence draws the reader's attention to the numerical patterns in the table. The rest of the section (not excerpted here) then reports results related to each of the four research questions explored in the study. Text 9-9, on the other hand, gives the reader a preview of what the authors plan to do in the Findings section (first sentence) and outlines the themes to be discussed in the rest of the section.

Text 9-8

Our cross-sectional study explored the lexical, syntactic, and semantic complexities of nominal expressions third, fifth, seventh, and ninth-grade children used in their informational writing. Because of the number of variables involved in this investigation, our analysis was deliberately confined to the internal structure and content of nominal expressions, without attention to their grammatical functions or semantic roles, which are part of our goals in the larger research project. The means and standard deviations for nominal complexity measures, holistic rating scores, and word counts are presented in Table 2. As can be seen from the table, the school children, regardless of grade level, scored between 1.0 and 2.0 on four measures of nominal complexity (length, abstraction, density, and quality) and between 0 and 1.0 on two measures of nominal complexity (variety and sophistication).

Text 9-9

In the following section, we unpack students' perceptions of what it meant to be a good reader by first exploring students' descriptions of good readers as they related to other students in the classroom and themselves, and then by examining their descriptions of what readers do. We specifically consider students' perspectives on three epistemic roles in textual discussions: students' roles vis-à-vis the text, students' roles vis-à-vis others (including teachers and peers), and the teacher's role vis-à-vis the text and the students.

When writing the Results section, it is important not to confuse results with explanation. Data reporting and data interpretation are not the same and should not be conflated. The Results section contains only information derived from the data collected and analyzed. Comments about or interpretations of the importance of the results belong to the Discussion section, which is presented next.

Writing the Discussion Section

The job of the Discussion section is to make sense of the results of the study and to think about what those results mean for research, practice, and/or policy in the wider context. It interprets the findings in light of what is already known about the research problem being investigated and explains any new understanding or insights that emerge from your study of the problem. It provides a space for you to comment on and explain the results, as well as to note the limitations, caveats, and implications of these results.

Discussion is arguably one of the most challenging sections to write in an empirical research article. It does not simply repeat or rearrange what has been presented in the Results section. Unlike the Results section, which contains only data, the Discussion section contains evidence-based speculations about why you find what you found and how your findings compare with expected results and those of related studies (including the ones mentioned in the Literature Review section). Rather than attempting to cover all findings, the Discussion section focuses on explaining findings that are particularly significant, intriguing, counterintuitive, or unusual, giving the reader a clear sense of how the study advances the reader's understanding of the research problem identified in the Introduction section and the research questions posed at the end of the Literature Review section. As such, the Discussion section allows you to link back to the literature review presented earlier in the paper.

Occasionally, Discussion is combined with Results into one section. This is especially the case when results are not extensive or when the writer prefers to present and interpret one set of results at a time before moving on to present and interpret the next set of results. Careful linguistic maneuvering is critical here to avoid conflation of results and interpretations, which can confuse and frustrate the reader.

The Discussion section typically begins with a reference to the main purpose of the study, a synopsis of the key findings in relation to each research question, possible explanations for each of these findings in light of the study's task/context and relevant theories, comparison with expected findings or the findings from related studies, limitations of the overall study (e.g., research design, methods of data collection and analysis, techniques for sampling participants) that may explain the findings or restrict the extent to which the findings can be generalized, and the implications of the findings for research/policy/practice (e.g., new questions that deserve further exploration; new insights that promote rethinking of established theory, common beliefs or general practice; or possible conclusions that can be used to inform policy and guide practice).

Given that Discussion involves making conjectures and explanations, a considerable amount of hedging is used to convey tentativeness of explanations or generalizations. Caution needs to be exercised to not extrapolate the results or read too much into data and make generalizations or conclusions that go beyond the scope of the study or what the data actually suggest. In other words, any interpretation or recommendation made needs to have the right amount of strength and be based strictly on the data reported. Caution also needs to be taken not to introduce new pieces of data, that is, findings that are not already reported in the Results section, as doing so may confuse the reader. The present tense is used for established facts, and the past tense is used when referring to specific work or prior studies.

Presented below is the Discussion section of Fang and Chapman (2020), a study that examines one mathematician's reading practices. Paragraphs are numbered for ease of reference in discussion.

Text 9-10: Discussion

1   Our case study explored one mathematician's reading practices, with a particular focus on his sense-making strategies when reading an

unfamiliar text in his specialization. It identified some important insights, strategies, and practices that are relevant to educators who are interested in promoting disciplinary literacy in mathematics teaching and learning. Specifically, our study found that Kang engaged in wide reading of the professional literature both in print and online. Similar to other fields such as history and science (e.g., Nokes, 2013; Wellington & Osborne, 2001), reading is part and parcel of the social practices that Kang engaged in to keep himself abreast of the field, to satisfy his wonderings and queries, to inform his own inquiries, and to gain motivation for his work. This suggests the potential benefits of making reading an integral part of the classroom activities that students engage in while learning mathematics. In other words, reading can be a way of helping students to gain ideas, building background knowledge, seek clarification, develop motivation, and increase competence in mathematics.

2   Although secondary students are not expected to read the kind of materials (e.g., academic journal articles) that experts like Kang interacted with, they can be encouraged to read textbooks, which are seldom used despite their ubiquity in mathematics classrooms (Wade & Moje, 2000). Other materials, such as online resources (e.g., videos, articles) and trade books, can also be used to promote mathematics reading, learning, and engagement. These textual resources need be carefully vetted to ensure their quality, especially given the importance that Kang (and the mathematicians in other studies) attached to the credibility and quality of sources and in light of a plethora of commercial materials available on the market.

3   At the same time, students need support in their interaction with these materials (Borasi & Siegel, 2000). Although school mathematics textbooks and related materials do not reach the level of technicality, density, abstraction, and complexity that characterizes professional journal articles, as disciplinary texts recontextualized for educational purposes, they remain daunting to read and understand for many adolescents (Fang, 2012). These students require assistance in order to effectively learn from mathematics texts and to develop mathematics habits of mind—such as those demonstrated by Kang: healthy skepticism, critical-mindedness, rigorous thinking, and close attention to logic and details—that enable them to succeed in mathematics reading and learning. Such support can be provided through, for example, encouraging multimodal learning (e.g., reading, viewing, writing, graphing) and teaching the sort of strategies that experts use in their reading comprehension (Thompson, Kersaint, Richards, Hunsader, & Rubenstein, 2008).

4   Related to reading strategies, our study found that Kang used a wide range of reading strategies to help him make sense of the text he was reading. These strategies include rereading, close reading, monitoring and questioning, summarizing and paraphrasing, storying, evaluating,

and verifying, drawing on prior knowledge and intuition, and note-taking and visualizing. They are likely a function of the type of text being read, as different types of texts (e.g., explanation, proof, theoretical essay) or texts in different areas of mathematics (e.g., geometry, calculus, algebra, number theory) may elicit different areas of focus for reading. For example, strategies such as evaluating and verifying may be used much more frequently in proof comprehension than in reading theoretical explanations, where constant summarizing and paraphrasing may be needed. On the other hand, it is worth noting that our finding corroborates those reported in earlier research. Like Shanahan, Shanahan, and Misischia (2011), whose mathematicians read excerpts of a theoretical paper and two explanations of linear equations, we found that Kang also paid great attention to formulas/equations and interpreted them and prose together in a unified manner, going back and forth between the formulas/equations (which he verified) and the explanations or arguments provided in the prose.

5   Our finding also contradicts Shanahan, Shanahan, and Misischia (2011) but concurs with Weber and Mejia-Ramos (2011), whose participants read proofs, in that Kang paid attention to the credibility of source. The reputation of the text author and the quality of the journal in which the text appears mattered in his reading and interpretation of text. Specifically, he spent less time checking and verifying information when he read texts written by reputable authors or published in high-quality journals, and was less interested in reading manuscripts authored by unknown scholars or submitted to low-quality journals. Our study also revealed that Kang used a much wider array of reading strategies than the ones reported in other studies (e.g., Inglis & Alcock, 2012; Shanahan, Shanahan, & Misischia, 2011; Weber & Mejia-Ramos, 2011; Wilkerson-Jerde & Wilensky, 2019).

6   Like the mathematicians reported in Shanahan, Shanahan, and Misischia (2011) and other studies (e.g., Inglis & Alcock, 2012), Kang read his text carefully, paying close attention to both the visuals and the surrounding prose. He spent a significant amount of time checking and verifying the accuracy and logic of each equation and explanation. He also reread, summarized, paraphrased, took notes, and diagrammed while reading. All of these behaviors slowed down the reading process considerably, with the aim of increasing understanding and remembering. Experts in other disciplines have also been found to value and practise close reading (e.g., Bazerman, 1985; Chapman, 2015; Rainey, 2017; Wineburg, 1991). As indicated earlier, school mathematics texts are generally dense, abstract, and complex, and the information in these texts is often packaged in ways different from how ideas are typically presented in the more mundane texts of everyday life (Fang, 2012). As such, they demand close attention to words, phrases, sentences, paragraphs, formulas, and equations,

requiring students to reread portions (or all) of the text and to monitor their reading. This slowing down gives students the time needed to process the highly distilled and dense language/visuals (through summarizing, paraphrasing, storying, and note taking) and to evaluate (through questioning and verifying) the information presented in the text.

7   A particularly interesting strategy Kang used is storying, that is, telling a story to help make sense of what is presented in the text. Recall that Kang used a war metaphor of two soldiers fighting on opposite sides for territorial control to gain a better understanding of equations and explanations. According to Gabriel (2000), stories are part of the fabric and life of all human experiences. We use stories to make sense of ourselves and of the world around us and to share that understanding with others. Newkirk (2014) argued that effective argument is deeply entwined with stories and that to sustain engagement with a novel, an opinion essay, or a research article, we need a "plot" that helps us comprehend specific information or experience the significance of an argument. Despite this, stories are often dismissed as a primitive form of sense making that children need to outgrow or move beyond for advanced academic learning (Newkirk, 2014). Yet, as we see in the case of Kang, stories are also a powerful tool for understanding and inquiry in disciplinary contexts. Through storytelling, we turn dense ideas and abstract symbols into concrete scenarios consistent with how we humans typically perceive, live and interpret our lives. As Wells (1986) observed, "Constructing stories in mind—or storying, as it has been called—is one of the fundamental means of making meaning; as such, it is an activity that pervades all aspects of learning" (p. 194). In other words, stories are invaluable to learning, problem solving, and sense making in disciplinary learning. They help organize, provide coherence to, and claim meaning for our experience. As such, they are a reliable means of making sense of complex issues and phenomena.

8   Given the centrality of stories to human experience in general and to mathematics meaning making in particular, the reading and writing of mathematical stories should perhaps, as Borasi, Sheedy, and Siegel (1990, p. 188) suggested decades ago, be seen as an important learning event in mathematics classrooms, rather than just an "enrichment" activity. Through the exchange of stories, teachers and students can render their understandings of abstract topics concrete and bring their mental models of mathematics (and the world) into closer alignment. One way of bringing stories into mathematics classrooms is through the use of trade books, such as stories (e.g., *Sir Cumference and the Dragon of Pi* by Cindy Neuschwander & Adam Weber, 2019) and biographies of mathematicians (e.g., *Significant Figures: The Lives and Work of Great Mathematicians* by Ian Stewart, 2017). These books tell stories (with characters, questions or problems, and solutions) about a field that students tend

to see as abstract and detached from their personal lives. They can be used to build students' interest, hold their attention, and engage them in deeper learning. They have been found effective for teaching about mathematics concepts, the process of mathematics inquiries, the impact of mathematics discoveries, and personal and professional attributes that contribute to the success of mathematicians (e.g., Capraro & Capraro, 2006; Gunbas, 2015; Trakulphadetkrai, 2018).

9   Most of the strategies Kang employed in his reading (e.g., rereading, monitoring, questioning, summarizing, paraphrasing, drawing on prior knowledge, notetaking, visualizing) have been documented in the proof reading literature. For example, Weber and Mejia-Ramos (2011) discussed mathematicians' self-reports of note-taking and visualizing while reading proofs. Mejia-Ramos, Fuller, Weber, Rhoads, and Samkoff (2012) presented a multidimensional model for assessing proof comprehension that incorporates visualizing and summarizing. In a study of the effect of self-explanation training in proof comprehension, Hodds, Alcock, and Inglis (2014) focused on rereading, monitoring, paraphrasing, and questioning as effective proof reading strategies for students to use.

10   The reading strategies that Kang and other mathematicians used belong to the repertoire of generic reading strategies that have traditionally been the staple of reading instruction across elementary, middle, and high schools. These strategies are also employed by experts in other disciplines such as science, literature, engineering, and history (e.g., Bazerman, 1985; Chapman, 2015; Rainey, 2017; Wineburg, 1991). In light of these findings, it may be reasonable to suggest that experts from different academic disciplines share some habits of mind in their literate practices. In fact, there may be more commonalities than contrasts with respect to how experts from different disciplines read. This augurs the need to challenge what Fisher (2018) referred to as the "singular notions of correct disciplinary reading" (p. 240)—that is, chemists read differently from historians, who read differently from mathematicians.

11   Similarly, our finding calls into question the wisdom of the recent recommendation by some literacy scholars that secondary content area teachers move away from generic reading strategies in their teaching. It appears that the key question facing mathematics teachers in disciplinary literacy instruction is not whether generic reading strategies are relevant or should be taught. They clearly are still very relevant in mathematics (and other disciplinary) reading, as mathematicians (and other experts) use them regularly to make meaning. The extent to which these strategies are used and the effectiveness of their use likely depend on, among other things, the nature of the text to be read (e.g., proof vs. theoretical essay, linguistic vs multimodal, formal vs informal), individual readers' technical expertise (e.g., degree of familiarity

with the topic of the text), and their purpose for reading (e.g., reading for specific information vs. reading for general understanding).

12   It follows that the right question to ask in disciplinary literacy instruction should perhaps be this: How can generic reading strategies be used in a way that is authentic to disciplinary practices and connects with the goals of disciplinary learning? Too often, generic reading strategies are considered the literacy work of "intermediate" schooling (i.e., grades 4-6), as distinct from the disciplinary literacy work of secondary or tertiary schooling (see, for example, Shanahan & Shanahan, 2008), or taught in ways that are rarely congruent with disciplinary epistemology or connect with disciplinary goals (Dillon, O'Brien, Sato, & Kelly, 2010), leading mathematics teachers to view them as irrelevant and students of mathematics to reject them as unhelpful. For these strategies to be effective in promoting mathematics learning and engagement, they need be, as the case study of Kang appears to suggest, embedded in meaningful disciplinary experiences, where students are pursuing questions that are of interest to them or exploring issues that are significant to the discipline.

The first paragraph of this excerpt reminds the reader of the study's purpose (first sentence) and summarizes the main findings (second sentence). It also specifies and interprets the first main finding (i.e., the mathematician engaged in extensive reading as part of his professional practice) in the rest of the paragraph. Two grammatical resources—*specifically* and *in other words*—are used to introduce sentences that elaborate on the idea presented in the preceding sentence.

The second and third paragraphs discuss the implications of the first main finding for mathematics literacy instruction—that is, students need to read to learn mathematics and at the same time be supported in their reading. This segues naturally into the fourth paragraph, which introduces the second main finding of the study, which is that the mathematician used a wide range of strategies to help himself make sense of the text he read (first two sentences). The authors then interpret this finding by first explaining why they found what they found (third and fourth sentences) and then comparing the finding to that of a key study cited in the literature review. The fifth and sixth paragraphs continue to interpret this main finding by comparing it to those reported in other studies.

Explanations are offered for the high degree of consistency between the findings of the study and those of similar studies. Cautious language (e.g., *are likely*, *may elicit*, *may be used*) is used to suggest tentativeness of the explanations. Words/phrases—such as *although, at the same time, related to, for example, on the other hand, specifically, like, also, as indicated earlier,* and *as such*—are used from the third through sixth paragraphs to make logical-semantic links between sentences/paragraphs clearer and to facilitate transition. Nominalizations—e.g., *such support* (third paragraph) and *This slowing down* (sixth paragraph)—are also used to facilitate discursive transition.

The seventh paragraph highlights a particularly intriguing strategy the mathematician used (i.e., storying) and provides reasons for its use. References to experts (e.g., Gabriel, Newkirk, Wells) are made to strengthen the argument about the role of stories in disciplinary learning and in everyday life. The eighth paragraph then discusses the implications of this specific finding for literacy instruction in mathematics. The discussion is reinforced by the ninth paragraph, where connections are made between the study's second main finding and what is currently recommended in the mathematics education community. The next two paragraphs raise two issues—one conceptual (tenth paragraph) and the other instructional (eleventh paragraph)—that emerge from the study's second main finding. The last paragraph proposes a way to help solve these issues.

In short, by summarizing and explaining the key findings of the study, comparing them to those of relevant prior studies, pondering over the implications of the findings, and debating about the issues arising from these findings, the Discussion section accomplishes its main goal of making sense of and interpreting the findings. Limitations and future research directions could have been included in this section, but they are sometimes left to the Conclusion section, as is the case with Fang and Chapman (2020).

Writing the Conclusion Section

The Conclusion section brings the article to a closure, giving the reader the impression that the purpose of the study has been achieved and that the study contributes in some significant way to the existing literature. Not all empirical research articles have a conclusion, however. Some authors end their article with the Discussion, as they likely have collapsed Conclusion into the Discussion section. Sometimes, authors include limitations and implications of their study in the Conclusion section. However, when limitations and implications are extensive or discussed in depth, they are often presented in the Discussion section, as the Conclusion section, like the Introduction section, is supposed to be short and succinct, usually one to three paragraphs in length.

The Conclusion section begins by recalling the problem or issue identified at the outset of the article, reminding the reader of the purpose of the study. It then draws together the key points made in the main body of the article and makes compelling concluding remarks about the significance of the study that are commensurate with, rather than overstating or understating, the results.

Text 9-11 is the Conclusion section in Hartsfield, Shelton, Palmer, and O'Hara (2020), a research-based article from the *Journal of Aerospace Engineering* that explores the thermal properties of gallium as an effective phase change material for thermal management applications. The conclusion reminds the reader of what the authors have tried to accomplish in their research (first sentence) and of key results/interpretations from their mathematical modeling and experimental testing work (second through seventh sentences). It ends by reiterating the appeal of gallium-based phase change devices. Note that *this combination* in the last sentence synthesizes the advantages of a gallium PCM based heat sink presented in the preceding sentences.

Text 9-11

[1] In conclusion, we have used gallium to produce phase change heat sinks. [2] The significant increase in density, coupled with higher mass-specific latent heat, provides a more compact PCM device than traditional materials. [3] The thermal conductivity, higher by 2 orders of magnitude, means a simpler device can be constructed. [4] These properties led to a decrease in the needed volume for the PCM. [5] The higher conductivity also allowed for the temperature change across the device to be nearly an order of magnitude lower than traditional PCM based devices. [6] A decreased temperature distribution leads to improved application reliability. [7] The high conductivity enabled very simple parametric models, using lumped parameter assumptions, to be used for initial models of the heat sink performance with reasonable accuracy. [8] This combination makes a gallium PCM based heat sink attractive for any system in which high thermal reliability is required.

Text 9-12 is a lengthier conclusion adapted from Fang, Gresser, Cao, and Zheng (2021), a study that explores noun phrase complexities in school children's informational writing. The first paragraph reiterates the significance of the study, echoing what is said in the Introduction section of the paper. The importance of the study is highlighted through word choices such as *highly valued, critical, important,* and *rarely explored.* The second paragraph discusses the implications of the study for literacy teaching. The authorial attitude toward instructional issues in literacy is conveyed through word choices such as *importantly* and *problematic.* The attitude is moderated or amplified through the use of cautious language such as *typically, little, often, likely, clearly* and *should.* Nominalizations such as *this practice* (referring to grammar instruction described in the preceding sentence) helps structure information and connect sentences in the paragraph. The third and fourth paragraphs discuss the limitations of the study and future research directions. Note that recommendations for future research are made here through the modal verb *can,* and the authors show caution in discussing the limitations through the use of hedges (e.g., *it is also possible, may not*), but confidence in discussing the benefits of the recommended future work through the use of modal verbs representing high certainty (i.e., *will, should*).

Text 9-12

The ability to write (and read) informational texts is highly valued in K-12 schooling, as it is critical to academic success in post-secondary education, where students are expected to regularly write to learn and to communicate what they have learned in disciplinary learning and socialization. Thus, it is important to examine, as our study did, how students employ one of the key linguistic resources—nominal expressions—in their construction of informational texts. Our study yielded important insights into one rarely explored dimension of children's linguistic competence in academic writing. These insights can inform future efforts to support children's language learning and literacy development.

Importantly, our findings suggest that nominal resources are an area of language that deserves greater attention in K-12 literacy instruction. Traditionally, efforts to improve students' language proficiency for academic writing has been given in the form of grammar instruction. The instruction typically focused on elaborated structures—often dependent clauses like relative clauses, adverbial clauses, and complement clauses—through tasks such as sentence combining, with little attention to nominal structures with multiple levels of phrasal modification and embedding (Biber & Gray, 2010). This practice likely reflects two common misconceptions about academic writing, that is, increased subordination is typical of academic writing and that phrasal modification is easier to master than clause embedding. It is clearly problematic in light of our findings and those from related studies (e.g., Biber, Gray, & Poonpon, 2011; Parkinson & Musgrave, 2014; Ravid & Berman, 2010). According to Biber and Gray (2010), literacy instruction should instead provide students with extensive opportunities to engage with texts rich in nominal structures of varying complexities and encourage them to use these grammatical resources in their academic writing. Pedagogical heuristics that support this sort of academic writing development work can be found in Fang (2020).

All studies have limitations, and ours is no exception. In our study, one sample of informational writing was elicited using a somewhat contrived, although not uncommon, task. It is also possible that the task does not elicit nouns of certain complexities. Moreover, our analysis scheme, although derived from prior theoretical and empirical work, may not have been sensitive enough to capture the true range of variation among the students. Future research can collect more authentic and varied samples of academic writing. Analysis of multiple samples of writing in different genres produced by demographically diverse students in natural contexts will give us more authentic and complete pictures of school children's developing competence in using nominal expressions to construct and communicate meaning for academic purposes. In this connection, it is important to continue to fine-tune the analysis scheme we have developed for nominal complexity measures, especially given the issues that have been raised about the validity and accuracy of Biber, Gray, and Poonpon's (2011) hypothesized developmental sequence of nominal modification (e.g., Ansarifar, Shahriari, & Pishghadam, 2018; Yang, 2013). A more refined tool for measuring nominal complexity will yield more nuanced, precise understanding of students' discursive competence with nominal resources.

An additional dimension worth examining in this research is the functions of nominal expressions. That is, future research can also investigate the effectiveness of children's nominal expressions in establishing reference, tracking grammatical participants, packing information, creating technical taxonomy, construing abstraction and generalization, facilitating discursive flow, or infusing authorial judgment. An equally important line of research is to investigate how—and under what condition—children's proficiency with nominal expressions of varying complexities can best be fostered. These lines of research should generate valuable information that can be used to guide the important work of developing students' linguistic competence in academic writing.

Writing Other Parts

In addition to the above sections, an empirical research paper also includes a Reference section that lists all of the work cited in the article. Disciplines differ in the ways references are written and citations are incorporated in the paper. For example, the APA style, published by the American Psychological Association, is used in Education, Psychology, and Sciences. The MLA style, published by the Modern Language Association, is used by the humanities. The IEEE style, published by the Institute for Electrical and Electronics Engineers, is used in engineering. The Chicago/Turabian style, published by the University of Chicago Press, is used by Business, History, and the Fine Arts.

An empirical research paper may also include an Acknowledgments section and an Appendix section. The Acknowledgments section gives credit to those who/that have made contributions to the research and writing but do not qualify for manuscript co-authorship. The types of contribution that merit acknowledgment typically include those who/that provided partial or full research funds, supervisory work, administrative support, technical assistance, or editing and proofreading services. They can also include research participants who willingly contributed time and effort to data collection through the process of informed consent. The participants are mentioned as an anonymous group to protect their identities. A statement about conflicts of interest, citation of previous presentation(s), and other information may also be included in the Acknowledgments section. Anonymous editors and reviewers are rarely acknowledged, as their contributions are expected in the normal peer review process (see Chapter 12). Nor does personal encouragement from friends or family typically belong in the Acknowledgments section. Sometimes, written permission may be required for the acknowledgment of certain individuals (usually the famous or influential ones) because their acknowledgment may imply endorsement.

The Acknowledgments section typically appears at the end of the manuscript. This does not mean it is a trivial component, however. On the contrary, proper acknowledgment demonstrates research integrity and encourages further collaboration between the researchers and those who/that have contributed to the research endeavor in some meaningful way. The Acknowledgments section is typically written in the first person and as succinct as possible. Some templates for the section appear below:

- This paper is based on a (keynote) talk presented at xxx. I would like to thank xxx [name and institution] and xxx (name and institution), as well as three anonymous reviewers from [journal name], for insightful comments on earlier drafts of this paper. I remain solely responsible for the content of the paper, however.
- This study was supported by a research incentive fund from [xxx]. We, the authors, are solely responsible for the content of the article. We thank our participants for their contributions to the research project and our doctoral students xxx [name] and xxx [name] for their assistance with data collection and analysis.
- The first two authors contributed equally to this manuscript and share first authorship. The research reported in this manuscript was supported (partially supported) by xxx [grant maker and grant number]. We thank xxx [name of individual] from xxx [name of institution] who provided insight and expertise that greatly assisted the research, although they may not agree with all the interpretations and conclusions of this paper.

Two samples of acknowledgment, Text 9-13 from political science (Knobloch, Barthel, & Gastil, 2020, p. 442) and Text 9-14 from engineering (Alstadt, Katti, & Katti, 2016, pp. 8–9), are presented below, each acknowledging the kind of support the researchers received during their research and writing.

Text 9-13

This essay is adapted from the first author's (K.R.K.) doctoral dissertation. For assistance with our analysis and manuscript preparation, we are grateful to Statistical Consulting Services at the University of Washington and John C. Roundtree at the Pennsylvania State University. The research presented in this report was supported by the National Science Foundation (NSF) Directorate for Social, Behavioral and Economic Sciences' Political Science Program (Award # 0961774), the Kettering Foundation, and the University of Washington (UW) Royalty Research Fund. Any opinions, findings, conclusions, or recommendations expressed in this material are those of the authors and do not necessarily reflect the views of NSF, Kettering, or UW.

Text 9-14

The authors wish to acknowledge a grant from the Department of Energy National Nuclear Security Administration (NNSA) under Grant # DE-FG52–08NA28921) and North Dakota State University Center for Computationally Assisted Science and Technology (NDSU CCAST). The authors would also like to thank the Core Research Center (CRC) in Colorado for providing Green River oil shale samples. The curator at the CRC is John Rhoades.

The Appendix section includes any supplementary material that is not essential to the text but may be helpful in providing a more comprehensive understanding of the research project. If it is removed, readers should still be able to comprehend the significance, validity, and implications of the research. Such information is usually too cumbersome to be included in the body of the paper because it could be potentially distracting to the reader and would unnecessarily disrupt the flow of writing. Examples of items that go into the Appendix section include interview questions, survey instruments, observation protocols, mathematical proofs, lists of words, coding manual, sample transcripts, sample artifacts, and samples of coded data. If there are more than one appendix, they can be labelled alphabetically (e.g., Appendix A, Appendix B, etc.) and then referenced in the main body of the text. They usually appear after the Reference section.

Concluding Remarks

Writing an empirical research paper is a complex task that demands substantial subject matter knowledge and considerable writing proficiency. It requires deployment of many of the academic writing skills and language resources discussed earlier in this book. Another noteworthy aspect of writing an empirical research article is that it involves a significant amount of repetition. For example, the research purpose is repeated a few times throughout the article—in the Abstract, in the Introduction, in the Literature Review, in the Methods, in the Discussion, and in the Conclusion—to remind the reader of what the study tries to accomplish. Findings are presented in the Results section, taken up again for interpretation in the Discussion section, and later distilled for preview in the Abstract section. This means that as a writer you will need to develop the capacity to say essentially the same thing in varied but interesting ways. This is what the templates in Chapters 3 and 4 are intended to do: to give you a repertoire of linguistic devices that you can select for deployment across the different sections of the same article.

Reflection/Application Activities

1   Find an empirical research article in your field and identify different parts of the article (e.g., abstract, introduction, theoretical framework, literature review, methods, discussion, conclusion, acknowledgment). Discuss the rhetorical moves and associated linguistic resources and strategies used in each of these parts, as well as how these moves, resources, and strategies are similar to and different from the ones described in this chapter.

2 Take a look at an empirical research paper you wrote before. In light of what is presented in this chapter, discuss what you think you did well and not so well, as well as what you can do to improve your skills in writing the genre.

3 Write a paper based on an empirical study you have conducted, using the rhetorical moves discussed in this chapter and drawing on the linguistic resources and strategies presented in Chapters 2–4 to complete each section of the paper.

References

Alstadt, K., Katti, K., & Katti, D. (2016). Nanoscale morphology of kerogen and in situ nanomechanical properties of green river oil shale. *Journal of Nanomechanics and Micromechanics, 6*(1), 1–10.

Andrew, L., Hemovich, V, & Himelfarb, I. (2010). Predicting position on teaching creationism (instead of evolution) in public schools. *Journal of Educational Research, 103*(4), 253–261.

Aukerman, M., & Schuldt, L. (2015). Children's perceptions of their reading ability and epistemic roles in monologically and dialogically organized bilingual classrooms. *Journal of Literacy Research, 47*(1), 115–145.

Fang, Z., Cao, P., & Murray, N. (2020). Language and meaning making: Register choices in seventh- and ninth-grade students' factual writing. *Linguistics & Education, 56.* doi.org/10.1016/j.linged.2020.100798

Fang, Z., & Chapman, S. (2020). Disciplinary literacy in mathematics: One mathematician's reading practices. *Journal of Mathematical Behavior.* doi.org/10.1016/j.jmathb.2020.100799

Fang, Z., Gresser, V., Cao, P., Zheng, J. (2021). Nominal complexities in school children's informational writing. *Journal of English for Academic Purposes.* https://doi.org/10.1016/j.jeap.2021.100958

Hartsfield, C., Shelton, T., Palmer, B., & O'Hara, R. (2020). All-metallic phase change thermal management systems for transient spacecraft loads. *Journal of Aerospace Engineering, 33*(4), doi: 10.1061/(ASCE)AS.1943–5525.0001150.

Knobloch, K., Barthel, M., & Gastil, J. (2020). Emanating effects: The impact of the Oregon Citizens' Initiative Review on voters' political efficacy. *Political Studies, 68*(2), 426–445.

Poole, K., & Schmidt, L. (2019). Early- and later-developing shyness in children: An investigation of biological and behavioral correlates. *Developmental Psychobiology, 62,* 644–656.

Swales, J., & Feak, C. (2018). *Academic writing for graduate students: Essential skills and tasks* (3rd ed.). Ann Arbor: Univerrsity of Michigan Press.

10
Writing a Grant Proposal

What Is a Grant Proposal?

A grant proposal is a formal written request for funding to support a research project or some other initiative. It is a call for action that invites a potential funder, public or private, to form a partnership in working to achieve a specific outcome. As such, grant proposal writing is seen by some as a form of advocacy or social activism that invests in and promotes change.

Grant writing is an important skill to acquire for students and scholars alike, who are often encouraged (or required) to compete for grants and contracts to support their research or outreach projects. Many government agencies, such as the National Science Foundation (U.S.), and private foundations, such as the Spencer Foundations (U.S.), have programs that provide funds to support dissertation research or postdoctoral work. In many jobs—such as those affiliated with universities, research institutes, or nonprofit organizations—there is a considerable amount of pressure to secure grants for research projects or other initiatives. Having some basic understanding of how to write a grant proposal is, therefore, beneficial for not only academic success but also career advancement. Some grants are internal, meaning that the source of funding is the applicant's own institution (e.g., department, college, university, institute, center, agency). These grants are usually small in amount but can sometimes be significant. More often, grants come from external sources such as professional organizations (e.g., *United Engineering Foundation, American Educational Research Association*), business concerns (e.g., *ExxonMobil, Delta Airline*), government agencies (e.g., *National Institute of Health*, federal/state departments of education, energy, defense, or transportation), or private foundations (e.g., *Bill & Melinda Gates Foundation, Carnegie Foundation of New York*). These grants range in size from a few hundred dollars to multimillion dollars.

The main body of a grant proposal is a narrative that typically consists of a statement of need and significance, project goals and objectives, the approach and methodology to be undertaken, data management plan, method of project evaluation, and project timeline. Additional materials required may include a budget that is appropriate for the scope of work proposed, justification for the budget, the credentials of the project personnel (principal and co-principal investigators), and the capacity of the institution(s) to support the proposed work if funding is awarded.

Process in Developing a Grant Proposal

Developing a grant proposal can be a lengthy and arduous process, just like writing an empirical research article (see Chapter 9). The first step in writing a grant proposal is to have a clear sense of the nature of the project you want to propose. This can be achieved by answering questions such as

- What is the purpose of the project?
- What research question does the project address?
- Does this question address a significant issue in the field or a serious problem facing the society?
- What is the scope of work involved in the project? Is collaboration with other units or agencies needed? Would they be interested in the project?
- What are the project goals and outcomes?
- What is the rough estimate of the budget for the proposed project? and
- What are the tentative timelines for the project?

The next step is to identify the funding sources that are likely to support the type of work you plan to propose in the project. Different funding agencies have different missions and tend to fund different types of work. For example, the Bill & Melinda Gates Foundation is interested in funding projects that aim at improving people's health in developing countries and giving them the chance to lift themselves out of hunger and extreme poverty, but does not currently fund projects addressing health problems in developed countries or that exclusively serve religious purposes. The National Science Foundation embraces cutting-edge proposals that feature innovation and risk taking, whereas the Institute of Education Sciences within the U.S. Department of Education appears to be more interested in clearly defined programs or previously piloted projects that have the potential for scaling up.

Once a potential funding source is identified, it is a good idea to spend some time learning about the organization that provides the funds, including its missions and priorities, the type of work funded in the past (e.g., intervention research, program/instrument development, program evaluation, personnel training), its funding cycle, the maximal and minimal amount of budget allowed, percentage of indirect cost permitted, and submission guidelines. It is also a good idea to peruse some recently funded proposals to gain a sense of what successful proposals for the organization look like. Most funding agencies have staff (or program officers) who will answer your questions; so any query regarding the potential match between your proposed project and the funding source can be directed to the contact staff provided. The goal of this preparatory work is to ensure a good match between the funding source and your proposed project, thus increasing the chances of being funded.

Once the right funding source is affirmed, the next step is to develop the proposal in accordance with the submission guidelines. Central to a research proposal is a robust research design. Grant proposal reviewers, like reviewers for journal manuscripts, will carefully scrutinize every aspect of the proposed study to be sure that it produces valid, reliable evidence that addresses the research question(s). They examine the design and procedure of the study, including its selection of participants and research site(s), methods of data collection, data analysis plans, and the measures and procedures used. While it is understood that there is no such thing as a perfect study, efforts should be made to avoid major flaws, that is, the sort of errors commonly warned against in research methods textbooks. For example, for a quantitative study, it is important that the sample is sufficiently large and representative and that confounding variables are accounted for so as to give reviewers confidence in the results. For an efficacy study of an intervention, it is crucial that the intervention has been developed and pilot tested. For a qualitative study, it is important that validation strategies (e.g., member checking, data triangulation) and researcher subjectivities are described to increase the trustworthiness of the research. If more than one theoretical framework is used, they must be truly integrated, instead of grossly juxtaposed. The scope of work must also be appropriate to the research question(s) to be addressed, not too ambitious to risk failure and not too small to be trivial.

In addition to methodological rigor, reviewers will also be looking for evidence of significance and innovation in the proposal. Proposals that address important problems in the field, are original in conceptualization and rigorous in design, and embrace an interdisciplinary approach tend to be rated higher in the review process. Reviewers are often asked to keep the following questions in mind as they review proposals:

- Does the project address significant issues in the field?
- Is the project original, interdisciplinary, and innovative?
- Is the project grounded in robust theory and methodologically sound?
- Does the project develop or employ novel concepts, approaches, methodologies, tools, or technologies?

- What will be the impact of the study on the theory, methods, technologies, treatments, practices, or services that drive this area of research?
- Does the project represent a new direction of investigation for the researcher? If so, is the researcher qualified and prepared to undertake this new work?
- Is the proposed budget reasonable given the scope of the proposed work? and
- Does the project have commercial potential?

The qualification of the researcher (or research team) is another factor that could impact the outcomes of the review process. Usually, there is one principal investigator, called PI, and one or more co-principal investigators, called Co-PIs. There can also be other project personnel, such as project manager, investigators or partners, research assistants, evaluators, and consultants. It is important to assemble an interdisciplinary team of researchers whose expertise complements one another in a way that creates synergy across the members of the project team. Sometimes, an advisory board consisting of respected scholars in the field is created to provide guidance and on-going feedback for the project.

Finally, the proposal needs to be written in a way that is accessible to reviewers, some of whom may be outside your field of specialization. Thus, it is especially important to make sure your proposal is logically organized, clearly written, and comprehensible to reviewers who have a general or superficial knowledge of your topic but may not be experts in the field. This can be done by minimizing jargons, reducing semantic leaps, providing details, adding examples and explanations, embedding visuals (e.g., table, chart, figure or diagram), making logical-semantic links explicit, and creating discursive flow (see Chapters 2-4).

In the rest of this chapter, one sample grant proposal is presented and analyzed to show how it is discursively constructed. For the sake of space, some sections of the original proposal (e.g., project personnel, curriculum vita, references, interview protocol) are not reproduced here.

A Sample Grant Proposal

The sample grant proposal presented below (Text 10–1) was written by former University of Florida (USA) doctoral student Amber Wutich (Co-PI), now a professor at Arizona State University (USA), under the supervision of her advisor, Professor Russell Bernard (PI). The funding mechanism for the proposal is the U.S. National Science Foundation (NSF) Cultural Anthropology Program—Doctoral Dissertation Research Improvement Grants (CA-DDRIG). Designed to "support basic scientific research on the causes, consequences, and complexities of human social and cultural variation", the program supports doctoral students in US institutions conducting basic science research in cultural anthropology. The proposal, submitted to NSF in 2003, was rated either "very good" or "excellent" by members of the Merits Review Committee and funded for $11,020.

Text 10-1: A Sample Grant Proposal

Dissertation Research: The Effects of Water Scarcity on Reciprocity and Sociability in Bolivia

Statement of the Problem

Reports on the state of freshwater reserves warn that severe local shortages are imminent, and predict that violent conflicts will emerge in water-scarce regions (Elhance, 1999; Ohlsson, 1995). Water scarcity has been shown to cause civil conflict, particularly when accompanied by high population density, poverty, and income inequality (Hauge & Ellingsen, 1998; Homer-Dixon, 1994, 1996). Urban migrant communities, where ethnic, religious, and class differences can exacerbate tensions, and community-wide patterns of adaptation to environmental scarcities are not well-formed, may be particularly vulnerable to water conflicts (Moench, 2002). To better understand how conflicts develop in water-scarce regions, research is needed on the social and economic factors that mediate cooperation and conflict (Ronnfeldt, 1997). I propose to do an in-depth study of Villa Israel, a barrio of Cochabamba, Bolivia, where conflict over water is an established part of life. Every winter, seasonal water shortages threaten the lives of the people of Villa Israel, forcing them to make choices in how they use their economic and social resources.

One factor that mitigates the incidence and intensity of conflicts is the existence of cooperative ties within a community (Ross, 1993). In marginal urban settings, poverty and mutual assistance foster social support networks (Low, 1999) that strengthen community ties. However, Laughlin and Brady's model (1978) of adaptation to environmental stress predicts that, in times of severe resource scarcity, individuals will withdraw from the generalized reciprocal exchange relationships and social relationships that characterize urban social support networks. The proposed research in Villa Israel will test the Laughlin and Brady model to determine whether severe water scarcity erodes reciprocal exchange and social relationships.

Research Objectives

The overall objective is to understand how severe water scarcity affects reciprocal exchange relationships and social relationships in a marginal urban setting. The five specific objectives are:

- to document the incidence of water scarcity in the research community. This involves the development and testing of a scale to assess water consumption, as well as conducting interviews to document variation of water use in a sample of households.

- to determine how water scarcity affects the frequency and quality of reciprocal exchanges between households. This involves documenting the reciprocal exchanges that a sample of households engages in over a nine-month period.
- to determine how water scarcity affects the frequency and quality of social interactions between households. This involves documenting the social interactions that a sample of households engages in over a nine-month period.
- to determine if community norms exist for determining the order in which households withdraw from reciprocal exchange relationships. This involves testing how economic interactions change under a variety of hypothetical conditions in an experimental game.
- to determine if households withdraw from reciprocal exchange and social relationships in the order established by community norms.

Literature Review

The existence and quality of intracommunity ties has long been recognized as a factor that determines how conflicts evolve over scarce resources and other threats (Coser, 1956; Mack, 1965; Simmel, 1904 [1955]). The degree of connectedness and the presence of ties that cross social segments are both elements of social structure that inhibit conflict development (Gluckman in Ross, 1993; LeVine & Campbell, 1972). Although early conflict theorists called for empirical research to investigate when and in what order social ties are broken (Coleman, 1957), such studies have been conducted in only a few geographic regions and on a few environmental scarcities.

Laughlin and Brady's (1978) model of adaptation describes how economic and social interactions fluctuate with seasonal patterns of resource scarcity. They hypothesize that during times of widespread (but non-lethal) deprivation, households will increase generalized reciprocal exchanges and social interactions. When resource scarcity becomes more severe, households will shift to balanced or negative reciprocal exchanges and will withdraw from social relationships. Dirks (1980) demonstrated that, whether famines are seasonal or unpredictable, societies pass from an initial stage of alarm (characterized by intensified sharing and sociability) to resistance (characterized by economic and social withdrawal into households and kin groups) to exhaustion (in which kin-based alliances to find food disintegrate) as scarcity worsens. Laughlin and Brady's model was validated by a series of African famine case studies (Cashdan, 1985; Corbett, 1988; Laughlin, 1974; Walker, 1989).

Similar to the survival tactics documented in rural African households, urban Andean households engage in frequent reciprocal exchanges to guard against privation. For the purposes of this research, the social support networks of impoverished urban communities are considered to be characteristic of the first stage of response to deprivation. The anthropological literature on Andean survival strategies indicates that people form mutual support relationships based on five major kinds of ties: kin, compadrazgo, paisano, work, and church.

One of the most powerful cooperative strategies that urban migrants use to survive is to form kin-based groups (Halebsky, 1995). In the Andes, the basic units for such groups are nuclear and extended households (Lobo, 1995 [1982]). Beyond the household, ties with extended families and fictive kin constitute the heart of Andean support networks. In Lima, groups of siblings and cousins migrated together from the highlands. These siblings formed powerful core groups, which they later augmented with marriage alliances (Lobo, 1995 [1982]). Familial support is also enhanced with compadrazgo ties, in which ceremonial parents establish relationships for mutual aid with their fictive children (Isbell, 1985 [1978]). In addition, paisanos, or people who came from the same highland district, are relied upon to help and defend each other in urban settlements (Lobo, 1995 [1982]). Similarly, in Mexico City, kinship, compadrazgo, and informal social networks provided services, goods, and information that were crucial to the survival of residents of a shantytown (Lomnitz, 1977).

Andean communities also tend to have strong traditions of mutual support founded on work-based solidarity (Buechler & Buechler, 1971). In urban settlements, such ties of mutual support may be formed around cooperative welfare projects (McFarren, 1992), union membership or shared professions (Nash, 1993 [1979]), and camaraderie established while women do housework or work in markets (Weismantel, 2001).

Churches provide another setting in which mutual support relationships are formed (Krause et al., 2001). Regardless of the denomination, parishioners generally belong to church organizations that provide assistance to needy community members, and form informal assistance networks among themselves. One particularly important form of reciprocity is the obligation to provide goods and labor to kin and fictive kin during Catholic festivals (Isbell, 1985 [1978]). Protestants, lacking a system of festival-based reciprocity, form informal social support networks to provide goods and services to churchgoers (cf. Stewart-Gambino & Wilson, 1997).

While the supportive elements of Latin American urban networks have been extensively documented, the effects of severe resource scarcity on urban networks remain unexplored. Lomnitz (1978) suggested that extreme deprivation would likely cause decrement of generalized reciprocal exchanges and social interactions in urban areas. Still, no empirical research has tested the effects of drought or severe water scarcity on urban support ties.

Hypotheses

Assuming that all households engage in exchange and social relationships, and that the amount of water available to the households varies, I propose ten hypotheses:

- H1. Generalized reciprocal exchanges will occur more frequently in the wet season than in the dry season.
- H2. Social interactions will occur more frequently in the wet season than in the dry season.

- H3. During the dry season, households with more water will engage in more generalized reciprocal exchanges than will households with less water.
- H4. During the dry season, households with more water will engage in generalized reciprocal exchange relationships with more households than will households with less water.
- H5. During the dry season, households with more water will engage in more social interactions than will households with less water.
- H6. During the dry season, households with more water will engage in social relationships with more households than will households with less water.
- H7. People will trust partners to reciprocate under experimental conditions most if they believe partners are kin, followed by compadres, then paisanos, then co-workers, and finally co-parishioners.
- H8. People will reciprocate under experimental conditions most if they believe partners are kin, followed by compadres, then paisanos, then co-workers, and finally co-parishioners.
- H9. During the dry season, households will withdraw from generalized reciprocal exchange relationships in the order predicted by the experimental game.
- H10. During the dry season, households will withdraw from social relationships in the order predicted by the experimental game.

Research Plan

The research will proceed in two phases. During the first phase, I will use a sampling frame to choose a 60-household purposive sample, create and test interview protocols, choose key informants, and train a research assistant. The first phase will lay the groundwork for the second, so that I will be prepared to complete a baseline assessment of exchange and social interactions before the dry season begins in May. During the second phase, I will conduct in-depth interviews with key informants and four ethnographic interviews with each household in the sample. At the end of the second phase, I will conduct a series of experimental economic games to determine the norms of trust and reciprocity in the community.

The research design has several strengths. First, ethnographic study will yield data with high internal validity about how responses to water scarcity evolve over the wet-to-dry cycle (Kirk & Miller, 1986). Second, the household interviews allow me to document change by collecting repeated measurements of household characteristics over time. Third, interviews with key informants allow me to collect information with more time depth than would be available with only the household interviews. Fourth, the experimental game allows me to determine how certain ties affect trust and reciprocity, controlling for other factors like history. Finally, the use of three forms of data collection—household interviews, interviews with key informants, and an experimental game—will enable me to check the results of each method against the other, facilitating identification of sample biases, hoax answers, or other data problems.

Research Schedule

Phase 1	
Activities	**Duration**
Review household census data, choose purposive sample	January–February
Train research assistant	January–February
Translate household interview protocol	January–February
Create water scale-preliminary research and testing	February–March
Choose key informants	February–March
Pre-test household interview protocol	February–March
Phase 2	
Activities	**Duration**
Conduct semi-structured household interviews	April–November (4 two-month cycles)
Conduct interviews with key informants	April–November (4 two-month cycles)
Investment Game	November–December
Transcribe narrative	Ongoing (February–December)
Convert narrative data into profile matrices	Ongoing (February–December)
Record data in Excel format	Ongoing (February–December)

Research Site: Villa Israel, Cochabamba, Bolivia

Cochabamba is a large Bolivian city located in a semi-arid zone, made famous in 2000 by city-wide protests and riots over water delivery. There, a rapid increase in water demand caused by urban growth, groundwater scarcity, and topography that drains water away from the city has intensified pressures on the municipal water distribution system (Laurie & Marvin, 1999). Lacking the capital to extend water services to its growing periphery, Cochabamba contains a large population of marginal urban residents that lack access to the municipal water system.

Villa Israel, a neighborhood on the outskirts of Cochabamba, is an impoverished community of 565 migrant families. The population contains people of Quechua and Aymara origin, and members of four different Catholic and Protestant churches. Currently, Villa Israel has no municipal water or sanitation services. Most households buy drinking water from a truck, which is operated by a private vendor. Private vendors typically charge 10 to 20 times the fee charged by public utilities, and people living in marginal urban areas pay between 10 and 40 percent of their incomes to acquire water in this way (Marvin & Laurie, 1999). Households may purchase between

20 and 40 liters of low-cost, untreated water a day through thirteen public faucets controlled by the Unión Cristiana Evangélica, a Protestant church (Trujillo, 2002). During the wet season, households also collect rainfall and water from canal beds used to drain sewage and wastewater. The ability of a household to acquire sufficient water depends on its per capita income and its exchange relationships with other households. Throughout the year, all households lack sufficient water for daily sanitation tasks in Villa Israel. As the winter dry season progresses, the impacts of water scarcity become increasingly severe. For example, between April and July of 2002, fourteen children under the age of one died from water-related illnesses (Trujillo, 2002).

Data Collection

Sampling and Choosing Key Informants

Using the Unión Cristiana Evangélica census of Villa Israel as a sample frame, I will select a purposive sample of 60 households. Households will be selected to maximize variation on the following variables: ethnicity, religious affiliation, head of household's profession, number of members, and geographic location of the house (distance from water sources). Although choosing a purposive sample renders generalization from the study impossible, the purposive sample will enable me to choose households that maximize variation on the independent variables (Bernard, 2002). A sample of 60 is small enough so that, with the help of a research assistant, I can do rigorous, in-depth study of the sample, and I also have enough observations to do inferential statistics to test the hypotheses.

Upon entering the field, I will also begin to look for key informants through word-of-mouth recommendations. I will attempt to find key informants using an a priori analytic framework (Johnson, 1990), that is, based on the characteristics that will give informants access to different experiences in the community (ethnicity, religion, profession, age, and gender). Having several key informants will allow me to check their recollections and assessments of norms against each other.

Measurement of Water Availability

To determine when the wet and dry seasons begin and end (independent variables H1–2), I will consult published records of precipitation in Cochabamba for 2004. To determine the amount of water available to each household at each interview time (independent variables H4–6), I will use a Guttman scale. Attempts to physically measure the volume of water acquired by the household from all sources may result in serious measurement errors. Instead, I will develop a Guttman scale of water use (Guttman, 1950). First, I will elicit free lists of water uses from adult women and prepare a list of, say, the 20 most commonly listed items (the exact number will be determined by examining the data, of course, for repetitions of items.). Next, I will determine which tasks appear to be part of a common water use domain. To do this, I will ask 20 women to indicate which of the tasks on the streamlined list (e.g., drinking, washing windows, bathing, watering plants, and cooking) each household member has completed in the last day and in the last week. I will then create two scales (for weekly and daily use), calculating the coefficient of reproducibility (CR—the statistic that summarizes errors in the scale), for each. If the CR is greater than .85, I will consider water use to scale sufficiently (Bernard, 2002). I will then use the modal household water use to represent overall water availability in the household. If water use does not scale, I will collect measures of the volume of water acquired by each household from all sources at the time of each interview, and will also ask the person responsible for collecting water to assess how much water was collected that day.

Household Interviews

Household interviews will produce data for the following variables: number of reciprocal exchanges (H1,3), number of reciprocal exchange relationships (H4), number of social visits (H2,5), and number of social relationships (H6) that each household has reinforced (through visits, for example) during the week preceding each interview; and the order in which households withdraw from exchange and social relationships (H9–10). I will conduct one interview every two months with each of the 60 households in the purposive sample. The interview will be conducted primarily with the adult responsible for housekeeping, but I will verify responses with other household members during the interview. Each household will be allocated 4 to 8 hours per meeting for interviewing and observation. Because residents of marginal Cochabamban neighborhoods tend to mistrust and avoid researchers with structured survey protocols (Goldstein, 2002), I will conduct informal, semi-structured interviews with household members. With respondents' permission, I will record interviews using a digital sound recorder (Maloney & Paolisso, 2001). I will take detailed field notes and observations using Spradley's (1980) method for note-taking. In interviews with key informants, I will also supplement field notes with digital sound recording whenever possible.

For the semi-structured interviews, I will adapt the interview protocol from Stack's (1970) classic study of urban survival strategies for use in Cochabamba (see appendix). To do so, I will translate the protocol with a bilingual Spanish-English speaker, and pre-test the protocol with households outside the sample. The protocol includes questions about daily life, the acquisition of goods, finances, and leisure time. The advantages of using a modified version of the Stack protocol are that it has been pre-tested for research on urban survival strategies, it is flexible enough to accommodate Andean social structure, and successful replication of Stack's results will enhance the external validity of previous findings about how urban support systems function. In interviews with key informants, I will expand on the household interview protocol, and will probe for anecdotes about times when ties have been broken or when people have come into conflict over water.

Experimental Game

Following anthropologists who have modified experimental economic methods to study economic behaviors in 15 small-scale societies (Henrich et al., 2001), I will use an investment game (Berg et al., 1995) to discover the social norms that determine when and with whom households trust (dependent variable H7) and reciprocate (dependent variable H8). I will set up the games using Barr's (2001) adaptation of the investment game protocol and script for developing nations. The game is an anonymous, one-time economic interaction between two people that uses real money. Player A is given a sum equal to one day's labor (about US $3), and the option to keep the money or send some of it to the player B. If the money is sent to player B, it triples and player B determines how much of the money should be returned to player A. The amount of money offered by player A indicates how much A trusts B, and the amount B returns to A is a measure of reciprocity (Berg et al., 1995). By informing players A and B that the otherwise anonymous opposing player shares kin, compadrazgo, paisano, work, or religious affiliation, the experiment can be manipulated to test the strength of trust and reciprocity for each tie. I will conduct 60 repetitions of each interaction for each scenario, totaling 360 repetitions.

Data Analysis

Data Entry and Coding

Interviews will be transcribed by the field assistant as they are conducted. Data from the interviews will be used to construct an ordinal measure of water use (H4–6) and four interval-level dependent variables: the number of generalized reciprocal exchanges that occurred in the last week (H1,3), the number of households with which the respondents exchanged in the last week (H4), the number of social visits that occurred in the last week (H2,5), and the number of households with which the respondents visited in the last week (H6). The amount of offers (H7) and counter-offers (H8) made during the investment game will be recorded in Bolivianos. Quantitative data for households will be entered directly into Excel spreadsheets.

Inferential Statistics

I will use t-tests to compare mean numbers of exchange and social interactions for the wet and dry season (H1, H2), and ANOVA to determine whether levels of household water availability are associated with differences in mean levels of exchange and interaction (H3–H6). Analysis of variance tests will also be used to determine whether different social ties are associated with differences in mean monetary measures of trust and reciprocity (H7, H8). I will use repeated measures ANOVA to test hypotheses 9 and 10.

Analysis of Ethnographic Data

Field notes and transcribed narratives that include anecdotes about tie breaking and water conflicts will be coded to indicate if the case supports or disproves any of the hypotheses. I will examine each case to better understand the dynamics of tie breakage and water conflicts.

Preliminary Studies

In summer 2002, I traveled to Bolivia to conduct preliminary fieldwork and establish relationships with institutions that support this study. I interviewed project coordinators in USAID, CARE, the Peace Corps, and Bolivian NGOs to learn about how communities adapt to conditions of water scarcity. After the interviews, I determined that Villa Israel would be an ideal site to test the research question.

In Cochabamba, I became associated with three organizations that are working on local water problems. The first, The Democracy Center, is a Cochabamba-based organization that works to strengthen the advocacy efforts of community groups. The second organization, Water for People, is an international NGO that helps communities in Cochabamba that lack adequate water delivery install wells, hand pumps, and sanitation systems. The third is the Unión Cristiana Evangélica church, which manages the distribution of water through tap stands in Villa Israel. Each of these organizations has provided me with valuable information about the water situation, introductions to key community leaders in Cochabamba and Villa Israel, and has pledged to support me during the year-long data collection project. Since my return from Bolivia, I have stayed in frequent contact with representatives of the three organizations, and continue to receive data and consult with them on logistics of conducting research and living in Villa Israel. During summer of 2003, I will return to Villa Israel to introduce myself formally to community members, hire a research assistant from the sociology department at the Universidad Mayor de San Simón, and finalize living arrangements for the following January.

Research Competence of the Student

Over six years of coursework, I have acquired a solid four-field education in anthropology that enables me to understand the cultural, biological, historical, and symbolic aspects of water scarcity and conflict. My preparation for this research includes coursework in the following subjects: research design and cognitive research methods with Dr. H. Russell Bernard, economic anthropology and studies of race and ethnicity with Dr. Anthony Oliver-Smith, political ecology and development in the tropics with Dr. Marianne Schmink, and anthropological theory with Dr. Maxine Margolis. During spring 2003, I will take a fourth course in statistics, as well as a course in hydrology. I supplemented graduate coursework with an intensive six-week language course in Oaxaca, Mexico during the summer of 2000, in which I polished the Spanish skills I acquired studying and working in South Florida between 1992 and 1996.

While assisting Drs. H. Russell Bernard and Christopher McCarty in research projects between 1997 and 2002, I honed my skills in sampling, questionnaire design, data collection, and data analysis. Under Dr. Bernard's direction, I have conducted ethnographic interviews, transcribed narratives, and done text analysis, social network analysis, and multivariate analyses. I currently manage data collection and analysis for the Survey Research Center at the UF Bureau of Economic and Business Research under the supervision of Dr. McCarty. My responsibilities include overseeing a four-survey evaluation of health care in the state of Florida, which involves 300 interviewers and 13,500 interviews. After five years of practice and hands-on instruction in ethnographic and survey research methods, I have become an experienced and capable researcher.

I have also conducted three independent research projects in cities and marginal urban areas. Two of these projects took place in Mexico and Bolivia, where I honed my ability to do research in Spanish. In 2001, I conducted a study on the effects of social support networks on child-feeding decisions with the Mexican Social Security Institute in Oaxaca. In 2002, I traveled to Bolivia to conduct preliminary fieldwork and establish relationships with institutions that support my work. When I return to Bolivia in January 2004, I will have the experience, knowledge, and local support to successfully conduct the proposed research.

Significance of Proposed Research

Intellectual Merit

This research will contribute to two areas of social science inquiry: urban anthropology and environment-conflict theory. The research will be the first study to examine if and how urban social support relationships are transformed by severe water scarcity. Understanding how reciprocal exchange and social ties are strained during periods of severe deprivation will contribute to efforts to understand the dynamics involved in conflict over environmental resources.

Through in-depth study of one case, the research will produce data with high internal validity. This is particularly important because the research examines the process of withdrawal from reciprocal exchange and social relationships. In using Stack's ethnographic interview protocol and Berg et al.'s experimental investment game, the proposed research replicates well-known research and facilitates future replications to establish the external validity of the findings.

Broader Impacts

In addition to testing the effects of water scarcity on reciprocity and sociability, the research will facilitate the learning of two students. The proposed research will contribute to the doctoral training of a female graduate student, as well as the methods training of a Bolivian undergraduate from the Universidad Mayor de San Simón in Cochabamba.

The study also has practical applications for those seeking to anticipate and manage coming conflicts over scarce freshwater. In many Latin American cities, the arrival of new immigrants strains the ability of the local government to provide municipal services to all city residents (Gilbert, 1998). By determining when and how social ties become vulnerable during periods of severe water scarcity, the research will point to possible avenues for conflict prevention in marginal urban communities. In Cochabamba, the study's findings will be disseminated through partnerships with three local NGOs, along with suggestions regarding ways in which the research might contribute to the success of future water delivery projects.

Budget and Budget Justification (Revised)

Personnel ($7040)

Two Full-time Undergraduate Student Research Assistants (10 months each) $7040: The research assistants are needed to assist in completing 60 interviews every two months, transcribing the interviews, coding the transcriptions, and conducting the investment game. It is crucial that the interviews be transcribed and coded in Villa Israel, so that the Co-PI can perform preliminary analysis and use findings to conduct follow-up interviews with respondents, as needed, before she leaves the field.

Assuming that semi-structured interviews last, on average, 6 hours each, each two-month cycle would involve: 360 hours of interviewing, 720 hours of transcription (at 12 hours per interview), and 120 hours of coding (at 2 hours per interview). This totals 600 hours of work per month. Two full-time field assistants and the Co-PI (working 60 hours per week) can work about 560 hours a month. This would leave a residual 320 hours of transcribing and coding work to complete in December, after the monthly interviews end. The research assistants will be trained in March, and will be occupied full-time with research tasks between April and December.

The research assistants' salaries are calculated at $2.20 an hour, 40 hours a week, totaling $3520 per assistant over the 10-month period. Because the students will be hired from the sociology department from the local university (Universidad Mayor de San Simón), and will be offered internship opportunities with intensive methods training, this will likely be a sufficient wage to attract two dedicated research assistants.

Travel (foreign) ($1050)

Living expenses for Co-PI (12 months) $1030: Living expenses were calculated for the Co-PI to reside and work in Villa Israel, Cochabamba for two months. Because the Fulbright program will be funding ten months of living and travel expenses, this item has been revised to request living expenses to cover only the remaining two months. The requested amount is 46% of the State Department estimate for the cost of living in Cochabamba, and totals about 85% of an average factory worker's salary in Bolivia. Because she will be living in a working class neighborhood, $1030 will be sufficient for the Co-PI to subsist at a standard of living similar to that of the other community members for two months.

Transportation $20: Bus fare will be needed to travel from Villa Israel to any other part of Cochabamba. Trips to the Cochabamba center will be necessary for the Co-PI to make photocopies, purchase food, and acquire research supplies. The transportation budget also includes funds for occasional taxi rides to and from the airport, to carry large loads, and in the evening when buses stop running to Villa Israel. This revised item now requests travel funds to cover only two months.

Other Direct Costs ($770)

Pre-owned laptop computer $600: A laptop computer is essential for data entry, management, transcription, and analysis. The $600 estimate is for a bottom-of-the-line pre-owned laptop with the capacity to run Excel, A-3000, and SYSTAT.

Digital sound recorder $70: A digital sound recorder is needed to record semi-structured interviews, so that they can be transcribed by the research assistant. The $70 estimate is for a new, low-end digital recorder on sale.

A-3000 transcription kit $100: The transcription kit will speed the transcription work of the research assistant, so that he or she will also be able to participate in the data collection. The A-3000 transcription kit includes software, a headset, and a foot pedal.

Participant Support Costs ($2160)

Investment game $2160: The investment game must be played with a substantial starting bid (Berg et al., 1995). A common measure of an appropriate starting bid is one day's wages. In Bolivia, the average day's wage for a factory worker is $3.50; the Co-PI will set the starting bid at $3. The estimate of $2160 assumes that half of the players will send nothing (so that the cost of the interaction is $3) and half of the players send the full amount (so that the cost of the interaction is $9).

TOTAL EXPENSES: $11,020

Analyzing the Sample Grant Proposal

The dissertation grant proposal includes sections required by the funding agency. In the first section, *Statement of the Problem*, the first paragraph identifies the problem/phenomenon to be addressed in the study—water scarcity causes civic conflicts (first three sentences), states the need to better understand the problem (fourth sentence), declares the purpose of the study (fifth sentence), and highlights the pervasiveness of the problem (last sentence). The seriousness of the problem to be investigated is conveyed through word choices such as *warn, imminent, violent conflicts, water scarcity, poverty, inequality, exacerbate, tensions, vulnerable,* and *threaten*. In this way, the urgency for the study is established. Statements that summarize others' work are presented without qualification (e.g., <u>are</u> imminent, <u>is</u> an established part of life), moderated (e.g., <u>can</u> exacerbate, <u>may</u> be particularly vulnerable), or reinforced (may be <u>particularly</u> vulnerable), depending on the amount of evidence from the existing literature. Note also that the last sentence exemplifies the idea conveyed by *where conflict over water is an established part of life* in the preceding sentence, but does not use *For example* or *Specifically* to signal the logical-semantic connection between the two sentences because the meaning relationship between them seem quite clear. Overuse of linking devices can, as discussed in Chapter 4, result in texts that sound contrived.

The second paragraph begins with *one factor*, which defines and narrows the scope of the study to be about cooperative ties within a community with water scarcity. This leads to the identification of a theoretical model (i.e., *Laughlin & Brady, 1978*) that explains how such ties evolve in times of severe resource scarcity. The paragraph ends with a more specific statement about the purpose of the study. This is followed by a subsection, titled "Research Objectives", that unpacks the purpose of the study into five actionable and measurable objectives. The first sentence of this subsection is a rewording, rather than verbatim copying, of the purpose statements in the first two paragraphs. Being able to repeat the same meaning with a different wording is, as noted throughout the book, is an essential skill in academic writing.

The next section, *Literature Review*, provides a clear, focused synthesis of the relevant literature in support of the proposed research. The review focuses on research and scholarship related to the topic (intracommunity ties) and the theoretical model (i.e., Laughlin & Brady) identified earlier. Specifically, the first paragraph identifies the focal research area as important but suggests that work in this area is limited in terms of geographical regions and the number of environmental scarcities studied. The second paragraph describes the theoretical model, suggesting that it is appropriate for the proposed project because it has been successfully applied in other studies, notably those conducted in African contexts.

Beginning with the third paragraph, the review shifts to focus on prior research conducted in the same geographical region (i.e., the Andes) as that of the proposed study. The comparative phrase, *similar to the survival tactics [...]*, facilitates a smooth transition from the second to the third paragraph. The five kinds of ties identified in the last sentence of the third paragraph—kin, compadrazgo, paisano, work, and church—are then elaborated in the subsequent three paragraphs. Words such as *similarly* (*Similarly, in Mexico City,...*), *also* (*Andean communities also tend to...*), and *another* (*Churches provide another setting in which...*) help connect sentences or paragraphs. Note that these transition devices do not always occur at the beginning of the sentence. The definition for the term *paisanos*—*people who came from the same highland district* (fourth paragraph)—is indicated through the preposition *or*. Cautious language, such as *tend to* and *may*, is used when reporting research involving Andean communities. The last paragraph of the section summarizes the literature review, again highlighting the need for the proposed study. A contrastive linking device (*while*) in the first sentence of the paragraph allows the author to move from review summary (i.e., *...have been extensively documented*) to identification of knowledge gaps (i.e., *...remain unexplored*). Note also that an informality marker, *still*, is used to start the last sentence. The sentence (i.e., *...no empirical research has tested...*) alludes to the hypotheses to be tested in the study, which are described in the section that follows.

The section titled *Research Plan* is another major component of a research grant proposal. The first paragraph describes two research phases in sequence, using phrases like *during the first phase* and *during the second phase*. The connections between the two phases are also explicitly stated (i.e., *the first lays the groundwork for the second*). The use of the first person and the active voice facilitates the description here and in other sections of the proposal. The strength of this research design is then explicitly discussed in sequence in the second paragraph, using adverbs *first*, *second*, *third*, and *finally*. A detailed schedule is next presented, identifying the specific activities involved in the research and a timeline for completing them.

The next section describes the research site—first, the city of Cochabamba (first paragraph), and then the neighborhood (Villa Israel) within the city (second paragraph). The description is dense, centering on issues related to water resource, which is the topic of the study. Many long noun phrases with embedded clauses, prepositional phrases, and participial phrases (see Chapters 2 and 4) are used in the description. These include, for example, *a large Bolivian city located in a semi-arid zone, a rapid increase in water demand caused by urban growth, topography that drains water away from the city, a large population of marginal urban residents that lack access to the municipal water system, a neighborhood on the outskirts of Cochabamba, an impoverished community of 565 migrant families, 13 public faucets controlled by the Unión Cristiana Evangélica, rainfall and water from canal beds used to drain sewage and waste water, the ability of a household to acquire sufficient water,* and *14 children under the age of one.*

The section titled *Data Collection* consists of four subsections that detail data sources and how they will be collected. The first subsection, *Sampling and Choosing Key Informants,* describes and defends the sampling technique to be used in selecting participants for the study. Although the active voice is dominant, the passive voice is also occasionally used to facilitate transition between sentences, as can be seen in the first two sentences of the first paragraph (i.e., *I will select a purposive sample of 60 households. Households will be selected to maximize...*). The next two subsections provide a step-by-step description of how water availability will be measured and how household interviews will be conducted. Such details are often required in research proposals to give reviewers a concrete sense of how the research will be executed (see Chapter 4 for process description). The use of the active voice (*I will...*), as well as transition markers (e.g., *first, instead, next, then, to do this, if...then, also*), helps make the narrative flow. The active voice (e.g., *I will conduct...*) and the passive voice (e.g., *Each household will be allocated...*) are sometimes mixed in the description depending on what the author chooses to foreground and whether the choice facilitates the discursive flow. In the "Experimental Game" subsection, a similar narrative style is used. Note also that a definition of the experimental game is given, using the linguistic resources that enable the compacting of information (see Chapter 4)—*The game is an anonymous, one-time economic interaction between two people that uses real money.*

Again, the next section, *Data Analysis,* uses a mix of the active voice and the passive voice. In the "Data Entry and Coding" subsection, for example, the passive voice is used (e.g., *will be used, will be recorded, will be entered*), perhaps to foreground the data sources to be analyzed, rather than the agent doing the analysis. The active voice would have worked just as well here, as it is also used in the next subsection (inferential statistics). The last subsection, *Analysis of Ethnographic Data,* uses both the active voice and the passive voice.

The section following data analysis is titled "Preliminary Studies". Information about prior work on the proposed topic is important because it shows that the researcher is familiar with the research context, has established rapport with relevant people in the community (research site), has the connections and contacts needed when problems arise, and has tried out data collection tools. These sorts of information give reviewers greater confidence that the proposed project will be successful if funded.

The next section, *Research Competence of the Student*, speaks to researcher (Co-PI in this case) qualifications. The first paragraph focuses on the researcher's breadth of knowledge and grasp of research methodology relevant to the proposed project. It also highlights her Spanish language skills, as the proposed research is to take place in a Spanish-speaking community. The second paragraph highlights the author's research experiences (e.g., data collection and analysis) under the supervision of the university faculty. The last paragraph describes the author's own independent research experience. These pieces of information are presented to show that the author has the knowledge, experience, skills, and support to conduct the proposed research, as funding agencies are unlikely to award funds to individuals who are perceived to lack the credentials, capabilities, or support to carry out their proposed research.

The ensuing section discusses the significance of the proposed research. This includes a discussion of the intellectual merit of the proposal. The author addresses this by highlighting two contributions her proposed study can make to the field. The next area of significance relates to broader impacts of the research. NSF and many other federal programs in the U.S. have placed an emphasis on making sure that funded projects broaden participation to groups traditionally underrepresented or marginalized and address real societal problems. The author indicates this by stating that her proposed research will not only provide training opportunities for her and her assistants but can also offer suggestions and strategies to help solve problems in communities impacted by water shortage.

The last section of the proposal presents an itemized budget for the proposed research, as well as the justification for each budgeted item. Budgeted items include personnel, travel, and materials and supplies. Reasonable expenses for each item are estimated and detailed explanations are provided that justify both the item and the dollar amount.

The sample grant proposal was written according to the guidelines provided by the funding agency. It contains components typical of a proposal written for research purposes. It also deploys many of the linguistic features commonly found in academic writing and discussed in this book. These components and features enable the author to construct a clear, focused, organized, rigorous, and convincing proposal that wins the award for her research project.

Conclusion

Writing a grant proposal is a task that students and scholars are increasingly expected to undertake as part of their education, research apprenticeship, or work contract. To write a successful grant proposal, you need to know the grant agency well (e.g., its mission, priorities, requirements, deadlines), give yourself sufficient time to prepare the proposal in order to avoid any last-minute crunch, describe in detail what you propose to do (e.g., goals, design, tasks, procedures, timeline), provide convincing rationale for your proposed work, highlight the most important points or the most innovative/meritorious aspects of the proposed project, emphasize your qualifications for the proposed work, and write in a clear and accessible style. These skills take time to build, but can be attained through repeated practice and expert guidance.

Reflection/Application Activities

1 Identify two to three regular sources of funding in your field. Familiarize yourself with these sources in terms of their missions, priorities, and submission guidelines. Peruse sample funded proposals from these sources to get an idea of the nature of funded topics and research, and discuss how they are constructed discursively.
2 Find a winning grant proposal in your field of study. What are the different components of the proposal? What linguistic resources are deployed to help realize the purpose of each component? Discuss how/why these components and resources are similar to and different from the ones described in this chapter.
3 Take a look at a grant proposal you wrote before. In light of what is presented in this chapter, discuss what you think you did well and not so well, as well as what you can do to improve your skills in writing a grant proposal.
4 Write a grant proposal seeking funding for a research study, personnel training project, or another initiative you plan to undertake. Be sure to draw on the rhetorical moves and linguistic resources discussed in this book.

Reference

Wutich, A. Y., & Bernard, H. R. (2003). Dissertation research: The effects of water scarcity on reciprocity and sociability in Bolivia. Unpublished grant proposal funded by the Division of Behavioral and Cognitive Sciences, National Science Foundation, USA. https://www.nsf.gov/sbe/bcs/anthro/samples/bernprop.jsp (accessed on July 10, 2020).

Section III
Maximizing Success in Writing and Publishing

11

Building Capacity for Academic Writing

Introduction

Academic writing is unlike other types of writing. It requires more rigor and thus planning. This means it will take time and effort to craft a quality piece of academic writing. This is a process that can be agonizing at times but ultimately rewarding. My students have come up with many metaphors and similes to describe the process and/or product of writing for academic purposes. Some of these metaphors and similes are presented below:

- Writing is like cooking a meal. Even though the same ingredients are used, the meal can still look or taste different because of the ways these ingredients are used. The meal prepared with the perfect combination of ingredients looks and tastes the best.
- Writing is like a traffic light. Sometimes you write more briskly (green light); sometimes you have to stop writing (red light); and sometimes you go slow on your writing (orange light).
- Writing is like talking with yourself, during which process the ideas in your mind become clearer, more coherent, and more logical.
- Writing is paddling upstream until you realize you were going in the wrong direction.
- Writing is like drawing a map of specific areas of our brain. Since other people cannot see the inside of our brain, we need to make it understandable for the user of the map, using labels that are helpful for them.
- Writing is a piece of art. It takes time, effort, and skills to build a masterful piece that not only means something but also looks appealing.
- Writing is either building what others haven't built or completing what others have already started.
- Writing is like gardening. It involves planting seeds, fertilizing, watering, and pruning on a consistent basis. The quality of garden all depends on your efforts and gardening techniques.

- Learning to write academically is like running a marathon. It takes a long time to be a good writer.
- Writing is like drawing a pencil sketch. It involves referencing, outlining, refining, toning, foregrounding, backgrounding, highlighting, erasing, trimming, etc.
- Writing is like constructing a bridge between author and audience, between author and sources, and between current author and past authors.

Each of these metaphors/similes says something about writing that probably resonates with you. For example, if you think writing is an act of communication between the author and the audience, then you likely agree with the analogy of writing as building a bridge between the writer and the reader. If you think crafting a masterpiece of writing is a laborious process that involves generating ideas, drafting, multiple revisions, and publishing, then you will appreciate likening writing to gardening. If you nod your head at the comparison of writing to a traffic light, you likely have experienced moments when you write productively, moments when you write at a slower-than-normal pace, and moments when you get stalled in writing. In short, writing is a complex and demanding process involving many factors, and the manner in which this process unfolds impacts the quality of the product you create at the end of the process.

Developing expertise in academic writing is, likewise, a lengthy and challenging process that can take many years and involves constant mental and emotional struggles. It is simply not realistic to expect one to become a good writer overnight, let alone a good writer for academic purposes, by just attending one workshop, taking one course, reading one book, or completing one set of exercises. It takes time, effort, awareness, experience, reflection, stamina, and support to become proficient in academic writing. In the rest of this chapter, I share a few ideas and tips that I have found helpful for improving academic writing.

Fostering Writing Habits that Work for You

To be a prolific writer, you need to develop good writing habits. However, what these habits look like differ from one person to another. We all have our own habits in life. Writing is no exception. We have our own rituals and preferred time and space for writing, and what works for others may not always work for you. Some writers, for example, can work for an extended period of time in one sitting; they write in binges. They take writing retreats, renting beach condos or ranch cabins and isolating themselves from friends and family members to write productively. Others write and edit on the run for short intervals as they pick up and drop off their child/ren for extracurricular activities or shuttle between doing their own work and attending to their child(ren) at home. Some write better during the early morning hours, whereas others are more productive during midnight. Some spent hours perfecting an introduction, whereas others dump everything from memory onto paper before taking time to "wordsmith" individual words and sentences. Some have a notepad on the nightstand next to their sleeping bed so that they can jot down emerging ideas before these thoughts fade into oblivion the next morning. Others have a recorder in the car so that they can record their thoughts and ideas while driving to/from work or taking their child(ren) to/from extracurricular activities.

Given the multiple roles each of you plays in your daily life (e.g., student, parent, friend, working professional, volunteer, athlete), it is important to find out the time and environment that work best and is most feasible for you (given your circumstance and preference), and use every opportunity available to write or get ready for writing (e.g., pondering over the topic, reading for ideas, listening to podcasts, developing an outline for writing). The more diligent and persistent you are with your schedule, the more productive and successful you are likely to be.

Reading Deeply and Widely

To be a good writer, you need to know what you are talking about. In other words, you must be knowledgeable about the topic or issue you will be writing about. This knowledge is gained primarily through wide and deep reading/viewing of journals, books, magazines, newspapers, and online resources (e.g., blogs, websites, YouTube). It is also beneficial to talk with peers in the class, down the hallway, or at conferences about the topic to gain their perspectives. It is important to be immersed in your area of specialty and steep yourself in the scholarly literature so that you are familiar with what scholars in your field have said about the topic/issue because ultimately, what you say will need to connect in some way with what they have said (see Chapter 3).

As you read, make sure you keep in mind these questions: (a) what is the substance or gist of the topic? (b) why is the topic important? (c) who cares about the topic? (d) what are the issues or controversies surrounding the topic? (e) how have other scholars approached the topic and tackled the issues related to this topic? (f) what are the links and gaps in the existing literature on the topic? (g) what can I contribute to the conversation? and (h) how can I contribute in a new or substantive way? Becoming well-informed about the topic and related issues is key to writing knowledgeably, intelligently, and fluently about it.

At the same time, it is also necessary that you read widely beyond your area of specialty so that you are attuned to the viewpoints and approaches of scholars outside your highly specialized field. Scholars from other disciplines often have important theories, methodologies, or insights that can help shed light on the problem or issue you are exploring or trying to tackle. For example, in studying reading difficulties, contributions have come from not just literacy scholars, but also from scholars in disciplines as diverse as medicine, psychology, linguistics, engineering, sociology, fine arts, communications, and anthropology. Interdisciplinary or transdisciplinary work is highly valued and often needed in scholarly inquiries as it can generate fresh insights and create new research areas that can help solve many of the intractable problems in our society. Thus, becoming acquainted with the assumptions, perspectives, methodologies, concerns, approaches, and findings of scholars outside your specialty will help you become better prepared to discuss the topic or issue of interest with both depth and breadth.

In short, reading avidly national and international publications within and outside the narrow confines of your own field makes you well informed, well-tempered, and less prone to bias. A good habit during reading is to keep the purpose of your writing in mind, take copious notes, think deeply about key issues, read against the grain, attend to language choices, search for patterns and trends, identify discrepancies and commonalities across fields and among scholars, and seek new perspectives or fringe viewpoints.

Developing Linguistic Awareness

Writing is a process of making meaning through language (and other semiotic) choices. Language is not a set of grammatical rules, but an interlocking system of lexical and grammatical choices. Having an acute awareness of how these options make meaning can empower you to present information, structure message, infuse value, and position the reader in a way that is appropriate for the particular context of communication and at the same time conforms to discipline-legitimated discursive conventions. When you are reading, you may want to take note of how the author uses language to construct content, embed points of view, develop argument, structure text, and interact with the reader, paying close attention to unfamiliar or unusual ways particular words, phrases, sentences, or other grammatical structures are used in the text. This noticing has been shown to quicken the speed of language acquisition (Sharwood-Smith, 1981). It also helps you become a more conscious and effective language user. There are several things you can do to increase your linguistic awareness. These are discussed below.

Note How Familiar Grammatical Resources Are Used in Novel Ways

From time to time during reading, you likely encounter some familiar words or phrases that are used in a way you have not seen or tried before. For example, the word *or* is familiar to practically all learners of English. It is often used as a conjunction to indicate an alternative, as in *coffee or tea*. However, it can also be used as a preposition to introduce a definition or a paraphrase, as in *A region's elevation, or distance above sea level, also has an influence on temperature.* and *Volcano is a weak spot in the crust where molten material, or magma, comes to the surface.*

In another example, you may be familiar with the word *prospect* in its usual sense of "the possibility or likelihood of some future event occurring", as in *There was no prospect of a reconciliation between the two warring tribes.* However, in a sentence like *In the wake of geological team searching for oil have come smaller field crews of paleontologists prospecting for fossils*, the word *prospecting* means something different; it becomes a verb synonymous with *searching*, especially when the search involves discovery of minerals or other deposits by means of experimental drilling and excavation.

In yet another example, you may have been told how to give credit to other people's ideas through the explicit use of citation (see Chapter 3), but sometimes other peoples' voice can be infused into your text in more subtle ways, through the use of an interruption construction (see Chapter 2), such as *what geologists call*, that is seldom seen in everyday writing, as in *The scientific explanation of the rock formations in central Australia goes back to events that occurred about 550 million years ago, during what geologists call the Cambrian period.* Here, the author attributes the source of a technical terminology (*the Cambrian period*) to geologists in a way that enables the construction of a compact sentence. In this way, the author does not have to start a new sentence, such as *The term Cambrian period was coined by geologists*, that explicitly identifies the source of the term but may diffuse the focus or disrupt the discursive flow.

Similarly, in *President Trump is still promoting the purportedly research-driven notion that hydroxychloroquine is an effective treatment for COVID-19*, the word *purportedly* suggests that the author does not think the claim about hydroxychloroquine's effectiveness is supported by research-based evidence. Making the same meaning without the word *purportedly* would require two to three sentences (and perhaps more verbose wording), as in *President Trump is still promoting the idea that hydroxychloroquine is an effective treatment for COVID-19. He asserted that the idea is supported by research. However, I (the author) do not believe that the idea is research-based.* In essence, the use of *purportedly* here enables the author to eliminate the last two sentences without losing meaning. Linguistic maneuvers like this are thus intriguing phenomena to be reckoned with in learning to write for academic purposes. They give you additional tools for making meaning in ways that are valued in academic writing.

In short, the above examples are some of the linguistic phenomena that you likely have encountered periodically but may not have been fully aware of their functions or have actively used them in your own writing. So, the next time you encounter a novel use of a familiar word, phrase, or another grammatical structure, be sure to pause for a moment, reread the sentence in which the word/phrase/structure is used, write it down in your notebook, reflect on the new usage's meaning and function, and be prepared to try it out later in your own writing.

Observe How the Same Meaning Is Expressed in Different Ways

It is often the case that the same meaning can be expressed in different ways, but the decision about which expression to use depends on the context of its use, such as topic, audience, authorial attitude, focus, and flow. For example, as discussed earlier in this book (e.g., Chapter 4), causation can be expressed in different ways through conjunction (*because*), preposition (*with*), noun (*reason*), verb (*trigger*), or non-finite clause (clause where verb does not show tense). In an environmental science textbook, you may come across a sentence like <u>Unable to grow or repair themselves</u>, *the corals eventually die* <u>unless</u> *the stress is removed* <u>and</u> *algae recolonize them.*, where a non-finite clause (*unable to grow or repair themselves*) and two conjunctions (*unless, and*) all indicate causal relations. Recognizing that causation is here expressed in ways different from how you typically present it (i.e., using conjunctions) is an important step toward expanding your linguistic repertoires for making logical meanings.

Along the same vein, when reading a piece of literary work, you likely have come across various expressions that show a character is disappointed, such as *Mei-Mei was sad, Mei-Mei sobbed uncontrollably, Tears came to Mei-Mei's eyes,* and *Mei-Mei stormed into her room*, where Mei-Mei's feeling is conveyed directly through telling (via the adjective *sad*) or indirectly through showing (via a behavioral verb *sobbed*, a noun *tears*, or a doing verb *stormed*). Equipping yourself with different ways of saying essentially the same thing gives you choices that serve your needs and intentions, enabling you to demonstrate your own stylistic and rhetorical competence in academic writing.

Be Curious about New Words, Phrases, or Other Grammatical Structures

When you encounter an unfamiliar word/phrase or a novel grammatic structure during reading, you may want to look it up in a dictionary or Google it. For example, you may not be familiar with the word *intransigence* in this sentence— *International pressure is losing effectiveness as China grows in economic clout, but*

Beijing's intransigence will only damage its international standing. By Googling *intransigence* on your iPhone, you will learn that the word means *refusal to compromise or to abandon an often extreme position or attitude*. With knowledge of the word, you now have an additional synonym that you can use for expressions such as *refusal to compromise, bullheadedness, firmness, inflexibility, stubbornness,* or *obduracy*. You can then experiment with using the new word in your own writing.

Similarly, when reading this sentence from a newspaper—*South Korean scientists have produced what they describe as a "high-resolution map" of the novel coronavirus' RNA genome, in which its genetic information is stored, paving the way for a better understanding of its characteristics and life cycle and allowing the development of vaccines and more precise tests*—you will pause to take note of how the interruption construction *what they describe as* is used in the sentence to attribute source and eschew authorial responsibility (i.e., It is the South Korean scientists themselves, not the journalist writer or other experts, who proclaimed that the RNA genome map has "high-resolution"). You will also stop to marvel at the sentence structure, examining carefully how dense information is packed into one sentence through the use of a non-restrictive relative clause (*in which its genetic information is stored*) and two nonfinite clauses (*paving the way for...*, *allowing the development of ...*), as well as several long noun phrases (e.g., *a high-resolution map of the novel coronavirus' RNA genome, a better understanding of its characteristics and life cycle, the development of vaccines and more precise test*).

This kind of noticing can take place not only in your own professional reading, but also in other more casual reading activities. For example, I was reading an informational book (Gibbons, 1998) with my eight-year-old son one day, and we came across this sentence in the book: *Bald eagles are excellent hunters, gripping their prey with claws, also called talons, that are razor sharp and four inches long*. A linguist by training, I was immediately sensitized to the structure of the sentence, marveling at how the children's book author packed a load of ideational, interpersonal, and logical meanings into the sentence. Here, the logical link between *Bald eagles are excellent hunters* and *gripping their prey with claws* is one of exemplification, but the relationship is unmarked. Words like *excellent, grip,* and *razor* convey a positive evaluation of bald eagles' hunting prowess. In more everyday writing, the same information would have been expressed in four to five sentences (e.g., *Bald eagles are excellent hunters. For example, they grip their prey with claws. Their claws are called talons. These claws are razor sharp, and they are four inches long.*).

In yet another instance, one day I was reading a book (Arnold, 2003, p. 29) about Australia's aboriginal heartland, Uluṟu, in planning a vacation trip overseas. I came upon this excerpt (see Text 11-1), taking note of how the author used a zig-zagging pattern of thematic progression to facilitate her presentation of information. Specifically, the subject of the second sentence (*arkose*) picks up the last word of the first sentence. The beginning of the third sentence (*when the iron in arkose...*) picks up something from the end of the second sentence (*traces of iron oxides*). The last sentence begins with *this*, which refers to *a rusty red* at the end of the third sentence.

Text 11-1

> Uluru is composed of a coarse-grained rock called arkose. Arkose is a mixture of small particles of sand, quartz, and feldspar, along with traces of iron oxides, clay, and small pieces of other rocks. When iron in the arkose is exposed to oxygen during the weathering process, it turns a rusty red. This gives Uluru its distinctive hue.

While you do not need to pause to look up (or reflect on) every unfamiliar word/ phrase and analyze every intriguing grammatical structure you see in print every time you read (as learning content or, in the case of leisure reading, entertainment should justifiably remain your primary objective), it is a good idea to do so regularly, particularly when the linguistic pattern seems central to text understanding, occurs with regularity, fascinates you, or could be useful in other contexts. If practised over a long period of time, this habit will help increase your linguistic resourcefulness, affording you greater versatility in making meaning.

Compare How Texts Are Similarly or Differently Structured within and across Genres

Texts belonging to the same genre but written by different authors or for different audiences may be structured somewhat differently. Texts also differ by genre in terms of their structures and language choices. During reading, you may want to pay some attention to how authors structure their messages, develop a line of reasoning, quote and reference others' work, infuse points of view, integrate visuals, facilitate transitions between sentences and between paragraphs, and use punctuations in more or less effective ways. You can also compare your ways of using language to the ways experts use language in crafting texts of the same genre, pondering over how different vocabulary and grammatical choices impact the meaning, style, flow, focus, and effectiveness of text.

For example, when you encounter this sentence in your reading—*Scattered across the desert are a few permanent water holes where underground water comes to the surface*—you may wonder about the author's choice of the unusual syntactic structure, referred to in Chapter 2 as thematic prominence. Had the sentence been worded in the traditional subject-verb sequence (e.g., *A few permanent water holes where underground water comes to the surface are scattered across the desert*), it will sound rather cumbersome because the subject is too long. It violates the end-focus principle of the English language, which states that new or the most important information in a sentence is normally placed at the end of the sentence. Moreover, it may interrupt the flow between this sentence and the adjacent (preceding/ensuing) sentences. Developing such linguistic sensitivity allows you to make language choices that best suit your needs and intentions, enabling you to write in more purposeful, effective, and powerful ways.

Play with New Language Patterns

When you encounter a new language pattern at the word, phrase, sentence, or discourse level, you may want to play with it by trying to use it in your own writing. Imitation is one of the most important ways of improving writing. Even accomplished writers examine how other writers fashion a story, a poem, or an essay and then try it on their own as a way of learning. It is important to note here that imitating is not plagiarizing in that the former focuses on structure, style, and craft, whereas the latter primarily concerns content. Imitation eventually evolves into emulation when what is imitated meshes with your style/structure and thus becomes your own.

Noted British writing researcher Debra Myhill encourages "creative imitation" (Myhill, Jones, Watson, & Lines, 2013), which allows you to imitate artful sentences, practise and manipulate new grammatical structures, and embed them in your own writing. It is fine if you do not use the new language pattern perfectly during the first try; you will learn from the experience and become better the next time you use it. Tools such as Google (http://scholar.google.com) can help you learn more about the nuances, as well as the frequency of occurrence, of different usages related to a target word, phrase, or grammatical structure. By imitating the language choices expert writers use, you will be less fearful of failure and more willing to try out new patterns, manipulate novel structures, recontextualize familiar grammatical resources, and experiment with creative ways of combining language resources. In short, trying out new language patterns with an awareness of their meaning-making potential and contexts of use facilitates linguistic internalization and eventual mastery. Ultimately, this habit will equip you with additional lexical and grammatical choices that you can adapt to convey the sort of meanings you intend. This helps expand your language repertoires, giving you flexibility, freedom, and power in meaning making.

Persevering through the Writing Process

Writing is a recursive process that involves planning, outlining, drafting, revising, polishing, and submitting/publishing (see Figure 11.1). The recursive nature of this process is aptly captured in the following quote by noted American writing researcher Constance Weaver (2010, p. 190):

> ...the writing process is recursive rather than linear: we draft, but stop to brainstorm ideas or even to edit; we write a snippet that doesn't fit here, but might go somewhere else later; we backtrack to revise and edit...before moving forward to draft more of the piece. Of course the actual process of writing is still more chaotic than that and, in fact, I suspect that chaos theory might offer the best explanation of this predictably unpredictable process.

Writing does not start with the moment when you are ready to type in front of a computer. It starts much earlier. A considerable amount of planning—such as reading, thinking, note-taking, talking, scribbling, brainstorming, and looping—is needed before the actual task of composing. To produce a quality piece of academic writing, you must have rich and clear ideas about what you want to write and how you want to write it. This requires that you generate an outline based on the ideas you have gleaned or developed during the planning stage. The outline can take the form of a bulleted list or a graphic organizer of some kind. Once a somewhat detailed outline takes shape, you can begin drafting by turning bulleted points or boxes in the outline into sentences and paragraphs and putting quotes in appropriate places. At this point, you do not need to worry about the flow or the mechanics of writing (e.g., spelling, punctuation, grammatical conventions). The important thing to do here is to unload all ideas related to each section of the outline onto the screen/paper. During the drafting process, you may find that you need to go back to refine the outline or read a bit more, which is a perfectly normal thing to do.

Once ideas and notes are developed into their respective sections and paragraphs, you have accomplished perhaps the most significant task of writing—a complete first draft. The next step is to revise it. Multiple rounds of revision are often needed to perfect the piece. Initially, you can attend to genre appropriateness, content adequacy and accuracy, idea realignment across sections, focus and clarity of message, logical development of argument, and relevance of evidence. In subsequent revisions, you can polish your paper by focusing on paragraph transitions, sentence connections, language and punctuation choices, integration of sources, use of citations and quotations, ownership (your voice vs. others' voice), and potential bias (multiple perspectives vs. single view). Of course, you may also find it necessary to do additional reading or conduct further research during these rounds of revision to update certain information or to beef up a particular segment of the paper. Sometimes, revisions result in a change of focus for the manuscript, which may in turn require restructuring, addition, or deletion of paragraphs, sections, quotes, or other materials (e.g., figures, tables).

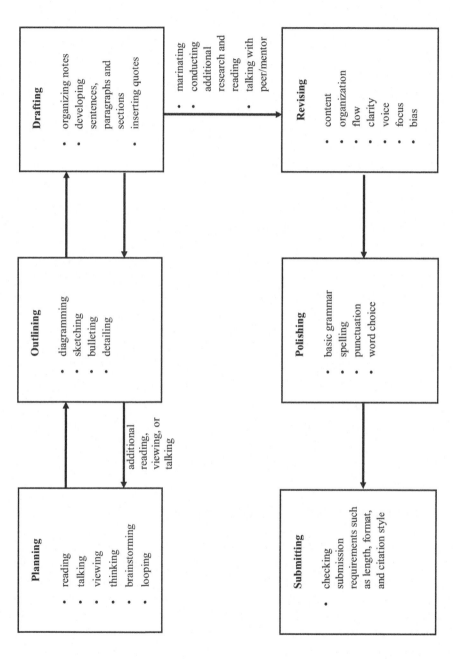

Figure 11.1 The Recursive Nature of the Writing Process

When you have a decent draft completed, you may want to get away from it and let the piece rest, or marinate, for a while without working on it. This "wait time" can vary from a couple of days to a few weeks, depending on the deadline you are facing. After having worked hard on the same manuscript for an extended period of time, you are probably exhausted or brain dead, and cannot seem to make further improvements on the manuscript no matter how many times you have reread it. This means that it is time to step away from it to take a break or to take on a different task. During this time away, you may have read some more articles/books and gained fresh ideas. You may also have talked with peers or mentors, who give you a different perspective or critical insights. The new information/insight and the additional energy harvested during the "wait time" will enable you to work afresh, leading to more substantive improvement in the quality of your writing.

One caveat during the revisions is to make sure that you save and date each draft of major revision. This can be done by starting a new document every time you anticipate significant changes to an earlier draft. In the process of revisions, you will often find it necessary to reinsert what you deleted during a previous round of revision. If you revise on a draft without retaining a copy of it, you will not be able to recover what you have deleted during the revision. This is why it is vitally important to save and date your drafts in separate files. With each major revision, you are adding, deleting, transforming, and moving sentences, paragraphs, or even sections. Having drafts of revision saved in separate files protects against the risk of losing what you once composed and enables you to avoid the unnecessary hassles of having to reconstruct what you have deleted.

Once you are satisfied with your revision, you need to double check the style, format, length, and mechanics to be sure the paper meets the submission requirements before turning it in to the course instructor or sending it to a publication outlet.

Attending to Key Elements of Academic Writing

When developing a manuscript, you should consider several key dimensions of academic writing that have a significant impact on your language choices and the quality and accessibility of the product you create. These dimensions are audience, purpose, organization, style, clarity, flow, and appearance (Gillett, Hammond, & Martala, 2009; Graff & Birkenstein, 2018; Swales & Feak, 2018). They shape the unfolding of meaning and at the same time construct your writerly self. Each of these dimensions is briefly discussed below.

Audience

Knowing who you are writing for will determine the degree of depth and technicality needed and the amount of details to be included, as well as the style of your writing. If you are writing for a specialized audience in your field for the purpose of demonstrating your scholarly competence, it is expected that you would be more rigorous in word choices to ensure that concepts are accurately and precisely presented and that you show deference to experts in your field. It is also expected that you would cover the topic in some depth. In some cases, logical links can be left implicit because your expert audience will have the necessary background knowledge to fill knowledge gaps or semantic leaps in your writing. The style of your writing will also fall further along the right side of the continuum depicted in Figure 2.2 (see Chapter 2)—that is, more abstract, dense, and metaphoric.

On the other hand, if you are writing for an audience outside your area of specialization or for a more practice-based audience in your field, you would cover the topic in less depth, make language choices that are less technical, use more signaling devices (e.g., *for example, thus, however*) to make the semantic links and logical relationships more explicit, provide more concrete examples or more detailed explanations, and take on a discursive style that is more easily accessible by disciplinary outsiders. In Text 11-2 (Henslin, 2007, p. 318), *for example* and *however* make the logical-semantic relationships among the first three sentences transparent to the reader who may not be familiar with the topic. However, the logical-semantic link between the last two sentences may not be clear to the same reader due to the absence of a signaling device (e.g., *that is*). Here, the last sentence elaborates on "*the conclusion*" presented in the preceding sentence. For disciplinary insiders who are familiar with the topic, the text likely presents little challenge for comprehension, even if all inter-sentential linking devices are removed. In brief, what you write and how you write will depend on who you are writing for—that is, your intended audience.

Text 11-2

Each of us carries around in our heads a favorable self-image in which we are essentially just, fair, humane, and understanding. For example, we could not imagine inflicting pain on others without much provocation or hurting people who had done nothing to us, who in fact were even liked by us. However, there is a growing body of social psychological research which underscores the conclusion derived from this prison study. Many people, perhaps the majority, can be made to do almost anything when put into psychologically compelling situations—regardless of their morals, ethics, values, attitudes, beliefs, or personal convictions.

Purpose

The purpose of writing determines which genre you write. As we discussed in previous chapters, each academic genre has a distinct purpose, and this purpose is realized through deployment of a particular set of rhetorical moves and a particular constellation of vocabulary and grammatical choices. For example, if your purpose is to explain a phenomenon, then you are likely to select from the linguistic resources that are effective for constructing an explanation genre. These resources include a variety of linguistic devices (e.g., verbs, nouns, prepositions, conjunctions, nonfinite clauses) to construct causal relations, as well as passive voice, nominalizations, and doing verbs. From an organizational standpoint, you are expected to identify the phenomenon to be explained and then discuss, in a sequential order, factors that contribute to and/or consequences that result from the phenomenon. You would refrain from using words or phrases that show explicit bias or emotion.

On the other hand, if your purpose is to argue for/against a specific point of view, you would provide a context that introduces the issue or problem to be addressed, state your thesis in relation to the issue/problem, make arguments with supporting evidence, and conclude the essay with reinforcement of the thesis. In terms of language choices, you are likely to use adjectives and verbs that convey value and judgment, words and phrases for comparison and contrast, frequent use of passive voice to help structure text, different types of verbs (doing, saying, sensing, relating), and mainly present tense. By some contrast, if you are writing a reading response, you would likely use adjectives that explicitly convey personal feelings and emotions, the past tense to indicate that the task of reading has been completed, and the first personal pronoun to show personal involvement.

Organization

Academic writing is not a matter of piling up information or observations. In other words, it is not knowledge telling. Rather, academic writing is about building a sustained argument. This is essentially a process of transforming what you know into a logical, coherent piece of work that makes sense to the reader. As such, academic writing is clearly organized around ideas and arguments. These ideas and arguments are divided into sections, with each section consisting of one or more paragraphs. Each section or paragraph has a major or minor theme. You should not try to jumble two or more ideas into one long paragraph, as this will make your writing confusing and difficult for the reader to follow. It is important that you mark and position the levels of headings for your sections/paragraphs correctly (level 1 heading vs. level 2 heading vs. level 3 heading) so that readers are not confused about the hierarchical organization of your ideas/content. Publication manuals such as the APA have specific guidelines for how to indicate different levels of headings in a text. Additionally, each academic genre has a discipline-legitimated, predictable organizational structure, but also allows for some degree of variation and creativity to account for differences in authorial preferences and the contexts of communication. Some of these patterns are discussed in the preceding chapters of this book.

Style

Academic writing can vary along the dimensions of formality, abstraction, density, objectivity, compactness, authoritativeness, and rigor. The stylistic variation, as depicted in Figure 2.2 (see Chapter 2), depends on audience, topic, genre, discipline, and context. Generally, articles written for a more specialized audience and on technical subjects tend to be more formal, abstract, dense, compact, and rigorous. Articles written for a less specialized audience and on more commonsense topics tend to be less formal, abstract, dense, and rigorous. Personal writing (e.g., stories, reading response) also tends to be less formal, dense, abstract, compact, and rigorous than factual writing (e.g., technical report) and analytical writing (e.g., explanation, argumentation). For example, the style of a book on academic writing can be more or less formal depending on its target audience (e.g., scholars who study academic writing vs undergraduate students learning to write for academic purposes).

Flow

As discussed in Chapter 4, crafting a paper that flows facilitates presentation of information and development of argument. It also helps the reader better comprehend and understand the messages in the text. Flow can be established through the use of connectors (e.g., *however, thus, and, while*), references (e.g., *it, this, they*), repetition (*immigration—immigrate—immigrating*), synonyms (e.g., *the novel coronavirus—the pandemic—the disease—Covid-19*), and a zig-zagging informational structure that enables the compacting of previously presented information for further discussion. In general, writing for disciplinary outsiders requires more signposting than for disciplinary insiders. On the other hand, overuse of connectors can make a text sound contrived and create the opposite effect.

In a text that flows, rather than starting a new thought, each sentence or paragraph grows out of or extends the thought of the previous sentence or paragraph. As Graff and Birkenstein (2018, p. 103) observed, the best and most cohesive compositions

> establish a sense of momentum and direction by making explicit connections among their different parts, so that what is said in one sentence (or paragraph) both sets up what is to come and is clearly informed by what has already been said.

This way of discoursing facilitates the development of ideas and argument and contributes to a tightly-knit texture.

Clarity

How a text is organized and whether it flows impacts the clarity of writing. How sentences are worded and how punctuations are used also contribute to clarity or its lack. You will want to avoid using sentences that are awkwardly worded because these sentences may disrupt reading fluency and inhibit comprehension. The following sentences generated by native and non-native speakers of English at the (under)graduate level are all awkwardly worded and lack clarity.

- 1a. Bilingual education is a kind of newly arisen education mode and has caught attention of more people.
- 2a. For instance, researchers used an engaging and developmentally appropriate robotics curriculum with six lessons on engineering design, understanding robots, sequencing instructions, sensors, looping and branching and suggested that kindergarten children could reach the expected level of achievement on understanding programming concepts with proper guide and assistance.
- 3a. Spending too much time and too much money on college and finding a job which is not money making enough to pay for your student loans can be overwhelming.
- 4a. In addition, Bond maintains that student loan debt results in huge economic impact because of people's delay in car and house purchase, and even influences their marriage and baby birth.
- 5a. It is a tough choice for many American students that whether be burdened with the debt or not for college.
- 6a. The constant 'moving of the bar' in school grading has made it difficult for researchers to determine if it has authentically improved education or superficially or some combination of both.

- 7a. Krashen posits that comprehensible input is the prerequisite of language acquisition; that is to say, students acquire language when they receive input—in the form of listening or reading—which is slightly beyond their current level, which means that listening and reading meaningful content is far more efficient than grammar drilling to help students learn a foreign language.
- 8a. Seeing from the table, it seems that parents' attitudes toward the "television" decision are quite polarized. There are 43% of parents strict with what their children should watch, whereas there are also 42% of children are allowed to decide what they want to watch freely.
- 9a. To summarize, the National Music Standards assert that every student should be able to sing, play, improvise, compose, read, listen to, evaluate, understand relationships in, and understand historical references in music.
- 10a. The data reflects economy status of a country had a great influence on rankings for publication.

Sentence #1a uses expressions that sound rather cumbersome (e.g., *a kind of newly arisen education mode, caught attention of more people*). Sentence #2a is too long because it combines two ideas (i.e., *used, suggested*) that should have been presented in two separate sentences. Sentence #3a violates the processability, or end-focus, principle of English, which says that English generally prefers to put heavy, new information after the main verb of a sentence to make the sentence more comprehensible. It also uses awkward expressions, such as *not money making enough to pay for your [...]*, which is likely influenced by the student's first language (Chinese). In sentence #4a, student loan debt both *results in* and *even influences*. However, the two verbs that follow the subject *student loan debt* are too far apart, making it difficult for the reader to track down the subject of *influences*. Sentence #5a uses a syntactic structure that is grammatically unacceptable. In sentence #6a, the expression *has authentically improved education or superficially or some combination of both* sounds rather confusing because the two *or*'s are in close proximity to one another even though they belong to different semantic chunks. Sentence #7a is an example of a long, convoluted sentence that jumbles the message and diffuses the focus. Sentence #8a has a dangling structure, meaning the subject of "seeing" is unidentified. It also misplaces the adverb (*freely*), which should have come right before the verb (*decide*) it modifies. Sentence #9a uses a verb with negative connotation (*assert*) to summarize what the National Music Standards says and has unnecessary repetition (*understand...in*). Sentence #10a employs a verb (*reflects*) that is normally followed by a phrase rather than a clause.

Sentences like these are indicative of deeper issues with language proficiency, which will take time to develop and is best facilitated through wide reading and linguistic awareness, as discussed earlier in this chapter. Sentences #1a to #10a can be reworded below for greater fluency and clarity:

- 1b. Bilingual education is a new educational phenomenon that is gaining popularity.
- 2b. For instance, researchers used an engaging and developmentally appropriate robotics curriculum with six lessons on topics such as engineering design, understanding robots, sequencing instructions, sensors, looping, and branching. They suggested that kindergarten children could reach the expected level of achievement on understanding programming concepts with proper guidance and assistance.
- 3b. It can be overwhelming when you find out that the huge amount of time and money you spent on your college education does not guarantee a well-paying job that would enable you to pay back your student loans.
- 4b. In addition, Bond maintains that student loan debt results in a huge economic impact because people with debt tend to delay car and house purchase. She further notes that the debt also influences people's marriage and reproduction.
- 5b. Many American students face the tough choice of being burdened with college debt or not going to college altogether.
- 6b. The constant 'moving of the bar' in school grading has made it difficult for researchers to determine the relative success of the accountability system in improving students' education.
- 7b. Krashen posits that comprehensible input is the prerequisite of language acquisition. That is to say, students acquire language when they receive input—in the form of listening or reading—that is slightly beyond their current level. This means that listening to and reading mildly challenging but meaningful content is far more effective than grammar drills in helping students learn a foreign language.
- 8b. As can be seen from the table, parents' attitudes toward the "television" decision seem quite polarized, with 43% of parents deciding what their children should watch and 42% of parents allowing their children to freely choose what they want to watch.
- 9b. To summarize, the National Music Standards states that every student should be able to sing, play, improvise, compose, read, listen to, and evaluate music, as well as understand relationships and historical references in music.
- 10b. The data suggest that the economy status of a country has a great influence on rankings for publication.

Clarity is also affected by the use of punctuation. Punctuation may seem like a small aspect of writing and is, in fact, often neglected in writing. Writing that is properly punctuated helps indicate pauses and emphasis in the text. As such, punctuation matters; it makes your text not only clearer but also more logical and readable. When sentences are not properly punctuated, they may cause confusion to the reader, as can be seen in this sentence from a letter to parents written by an elementary school principal—*The preferred method is digital submission but if you can't then drop off at parent pickup is a last resort*—where the insertion of a semicolon right before *but* and a comma right before *then* would have made the meaning clearer and the sentence easier to read and process.

Three types of punctuation marks, often taken for granted by writers, are discussed below: comma (,), colon (:), and semicolon (;). Their use or non-use has consequences for the clarity of writing. To enhance clarity, comma should be used to

- separate adverb, prepositional phrase, adverbial phrase, conjunctive phrase, and subordinate clause (e.g., adverbial clause, non-finite clause) from the main clause
  - *Finally, in the late afternoon, we met our crew members at the camp site.*
  - *In secondary schooling, students are expected to engage with increasingly specialized knowledge of academic disciplines.*
  - *Compare, for example, the two texts in Table 1.*
  - *Content is made prototypically of language, however.*
  - *This is particularly true in middle and high schools, where the texts students read become more complex and specialized.*
  - *Teachers can refer to the framework presented in Table 2, using the metalanguage provided by SFL.*
- connect two independent sentences
  - *Different arrangements of words result in different meanings, and these meanings have to be interpreted in context.*
- introduce an appositive phrase or some other non-defining phrases (e.g., interruption construction) into the sentence
  - *Langer (2011), a literacy scholar, reminded us that reading needs be taught in content areas.*
  - *This pedagogy, with its focus on language, has the potential to improve students' writing proficiency.*
- separate words, groups, or clauses in a series
  - *They develop a framework for unit planning that involves developing guiding questions, selecting challenging texts for analysis, conducting intensive work with vocabulary, and using functional grammar analysis strategies.*
  - *These texts are meant to be read silently, slowly, and closely.*

Colon is used to add extra information after a clause. It can be used to introduce a list, as in *Our data analysis proceeded in three phases: (1) content analysis, (2) linguistic analysis, and (3) statistical analysis.* It can also be used to introduce an explanation or an elaboration, as in *Dinosaur eggs come in all shapes and sizes: round like a softball, oval like a football, large like an ostrich egg, and tiny like a hummingbird egg.* Sometimes, colon is used before a quotation when the quotation is independent of the structure of the main clause, as in this sentence below:

> Smith (2020, p. 53) reported the following results: "The experimental vaccine produced neutralizing antibodies in the blood at levels well above those found in people who recovered from COVID-19."

Semicolon should be used to separate items or chunks in lists, especially when the items or chunks are long and already have commas in them. Consider this example: *The authors characterized British soldiers as drunken and profane, but nervous; Bostonians as angry, violent, and unhinged; and the clash between the colonists and the soldiers as inevitable.* Here, the use of comma in place of semicolon would have confused the reader, as there are already commas in some chunks of the sentence (e.g., *Bostonians as angry, violent, and unhinged*). On the other hand, turning the long sentence into several independent sentences would have made the text sound more fragmented, which is uncharacteristic of academic writing. Semicolon can also be used to separate two sentences that could have been written as independent clauses but are very closely related in meaning, as can be seen in this example—*Readers do not process a text word by word; rather, they do so in meaningful chunks.*

Sometimes, parenthesis ( ) or dash (—) is used to separate peripheral information from the main information in the sentence. As discussed elsewhere in the book (e.g., Chapter 4), if the peripheral information is presented separately as an independent clause, it may become just as important as the information presented in the main clause of the sentence. This can potentially result in a lack of focus in writing. In the sentence below, *18 hours in 6 weeks* is considered peripheral information and hence placed in parenthesis. Had the same information been presented in a separate sentence, as in *The course lasted 18 hours in 6 weeks*, then it becomes just as important as the next sentence, which states the aim of the course.

> Love (2010) described a short but intense training course (18 hours in 6 weeks) titled Language and Teaching in a two-year Master of Teaching program at the University of Melbourne, Australia. The course aims at preparing middle and high school teachers with no prior linguistic knowledge.

In Text 11-3a, dash is used to explain *the derived sense of disciplinary literacy*, and a preposition (*or*) is used to explain *the fundamental sense of disciplinary literacy.* If separate sentences are used to explain these two concepts, Text 11-3b results.

Text 11-3a

The development of what science educators Norris and Phillips (2003) referred to as the derived sense of disciplinary literacy—knowledge about the content of a discipline, including its key concepts, core ideas, and unifying themes—is highly dependent on the fundamental sense of disciplinary literacy, or the ability to read and write in the discipline. This suggests that reading and writing are central to disciplinary learning.

Text 11-3b

The development of what science educators Norris and Phillips (2003) referred to as the derived sense of disciplinary literacy is highly dependent on the fundamental sense of disciplinary literacy. The derived sense of disciplinary literacy means knowledge about the content of a discipline, including its key concepts, core ideas, and unifying themes. The fundamental sense of disciplinary literacy refers to the ability to read and write in the discipline. This suggests reading and writing are central to disciplinary learning.

In Text 11-3b, which is a reformulation of Text 11-3a, the two definitions become foregrounded because they are now presented in sentences equal in status to the main clause of the first sentence in Text 11-3a, which states that the development of the derived sense of disciplinary literacy is highly dependent on the fundamental sense of disciplinary literacy. This reformulation also disrupts the flow of information, as the last sentence is supposed to pick up the main idea presented in the first sentence, rather than the definitions provided in the second or third sentence of Text 11-3b.

Another way to enhance the clarity of your writing is to avoid presenting a long list of extended items in a sentence, especially when some of these items contain commas. Instead, you may want to use bullets or numbers to separate the items in the list. Text 11-4a below packs three long items into one sentence, resulting in an exceedingly long and confusing sentence that is likely to frustrate readers.

Text 11-4a

Frequently, discussion about language and grammar in teacher education is perceived to be a discourse of "deficit", as if such discussion is exclusively about "proper" English and remediation of grammatical errors, relevant only to those with the responsibility of teaching English language learners, as if students who are native speakers of English were already proficient with language and required no further support in developing advanced literacy, or too technical to be useful to practicing teachers.

When the three items in the sentence are broken up with semicolons (instead of commas) and numbered or bulleted, as seen in Text 11-4b and Text 11-4c, the structure of the sentence becomes much clearer, making it easier to read and comprehend.

Text 11-4b

Frequently, discussion about language and grammar in teacher education is perceived to be (a) a discourse of "deficit", as if such discussion is exclusively about "proper" English and remediation of grammatical errors; (b) relevant only to those with the responsibility of teaching English language learners, as if students who are native speakers of English were already proficient with language and required no further support in developing advanced literacy; or (c) too technical to be useful to practicing teachers.

Text 11-4c

Frequently, discussion about language and grammar in teacher education is perceived to be

- a discourse of "deficit", as if such discussion is exclusively about "proper" English and remediation of grammatical errors,
- relevant only to those with the responsibility of teaching English language learners, as if students who are native speakers of English were already proficient with language and required no further support in developing advanced literacy, or
- too technical to be useful to practicing teachers.

Appearance

Finally, having a paper that is clean (with visuals and prose well integrated), formatted according to requirements (e.g., font, size, citation style, margin, legibility), carefully proofread, and free of basic grammatical errors can enhance its appeal to the reader and receive more positive feedback. Many students and scholars, both native and non-native speakers of English, make basic grammatical errors such as misuse of articles (*a/an, the*) or homophones (e.g., *there, their; too, two; here, hear*), ambiguous references, misspellings, wrongly conjugated verbs, and lack of subject-verb agreement. These errors, due to sloppiness or lack of language proficiency, may not be noticed if they are kept to a minimum and when the flow, clarity, and focus of the paper are good. However, when the flow, clarity, and focus are not good, minor grammatical errors tend to be amplified and will catch the reader's attention.

Overcoming Cultural Barriers

For many students and aspiring scholars, writing for academic purposes in the English-speaking Western society can be a cultural struggle. Some of you are likely international students and scholars studying at a Western institution of higher learning or non-native English speakers studying or working in your home country. In either case, you may not be intimately familiar with or used to the Western ways of thinking and writing. This can present an additional barrier to your development of academic writing proficiency in English.

Let me share with you a little bit about my own struggle with writing for an academic audience in the Western hemisphere. As someone born and raised in China for the first 20 years of my life, I have not always felt at ease when writing for academic purposes in English. It was a struggle in the sense that every time I started the composing process, I felt the need to assume, albeit uncomfortably at first, a new identity, one that is diametrically opposed to my authentic self. My Chinese upbringing has positioned me to see writing as a piece of artwork for public appreciation and as such, it is expected to strictly observe discursive etiquettes (e.g., adhering to grammatical and rhetorical conventions), political correctness (e.g., sending positive messages about the family, the society, and the authority), and cultural virtues (e.g., demonstrating humility, self-control, and politeness). It has also instilled in me a Chinese way of thinking and writing, one that requires me to follow the logic of "circular" or "spiral" thought processes (cf., Yang & Cahill, 2008). Like my peers in China, I was taught that an index of sound scholarship is the extent to which one can recite, manipulate, and quote incisive, artful lines from classic work or the work of influential modern scholars. I was often reminded to reference renowned scholars (even when ideas are sometimes my own) in order to make my language look elegant and my arguments look credible. I was convinced that my words will never be as important as those of established scholars. I was cautioned not to put forth my arguments in a straightforward or blunt fashion (e.g., never say things like *my point is…* and *I argue that…*), but that I should labor to build up a linguistic context where the reader can infer (rather than being explicitly told) what my thoughts and arguments are. I had a tendency to place the responsibility for clarity and understanding on the reader rather than my writerly self.

In essence, my Chinese upbringing has taught me that my voice does not really matter in scholarly work, that it is the words of authority figures that matter, and that I should let the words speak for themselves without showing emotions and subjectivities. Having, by now, spent over two decades in the American academe, I have come to realize that writing for academic purposes in English necessitates the adoption of an American self, one that is authentic, confident, assertive, and not afraid to foreground my own views and voice. I have learned that my old Chinese approach of self-depreciation is not consistent with the Western ideals of individualism and authenticity. I have learned that my voice does count and is valued in research and writing. I have learned that personal vignettes, or storytelling, can be relevant, significant, and powerful in scholarly work. I have learned that my Chinese logic of "beating around bushes" has to give way to a more "linear" Western approach—one that values openness, directness, succinctness, and originality. Over the years, I have become more attuned to the nuances and complexities involved in writing for academic purposes in the English-speaking world. As I grow more accustomed to the new American identity and become more sensitive to the values and concerns of other discourse communities, I have found academic writing a much more exciting, liberating, enjoyable, and successful adventure.

Conclusion

Academic writing is different from other types of writing in purpose, structure, and style. It is an advanced literacy skill that takes time and effort to develop. To achieve proficiency in academic writing, you need, among other things, a keen understanding of the features that make writing academic, mastery of the linguistic resources that are functional and effective for instantiating these features, good writing habits that work for you, linguistic sensitivity, cultural awareness, capacity to read promiscuously and deeply, and a willingness to engage with different perspectives. This is indeed hard work, but you can do it.

Reflection/Application Activities

1 What do you think you do well and not so well in academic writing? What do you think are the factors that facilitate or hinder your writing development? What is your plan to overcome the writing barriers?
2 Can you recall an enjoyable or a traumatic writing experience in your life? What is it about this experience that makes it so memorable or transformative? What perspective do you have now on the experience?
3 Find a published article in your field and read it two times, the first time for content and the second time focusing on language choices. What language patterns do you notice that are novel, interesting, intriguing, unusual, or potentially useful?
4 Interview a prolific scholar you admire in your field and have him/her share tips and strategies that s/he thinks are particularly helpful for writing development. Be sure to share what you have learned with your peers in class.
5 Identify an article in your field or a piece of your previous writing and evaluate it by discussing its strengths and weaknesses in terms of the seven dimensions of academic writing discussed in this chapter—audience, purpose, organization, style, clarity, flow, and appearance.

References

Arnold, C. (2003). *Uluṟu: Australia's aboriginal heart*. New York: Houghton Mifflin.

Gibbons, G. (1998). *Soaring with the wind: The bald eagle*. New York: Morrow Junior Books.

Gillett, A., Hammond, A., & Martala, M. (2009). *Inside track: Successful academic writing*. London: Longman.

Graff, G., & Birkenstein, C. (2018). *They say I say: The moves that matter in academic writing* (4th ed.). New York: Norton.

Henslin, J. (2007). *Down to earth sociology: Introductory readings* (14th ed.). New York: Free Press.

Myhill, D., Jones, S., Watson, A., & Lines, H. (2013). Playful explicitness with grammar: A pedagogy for writing. *Literacy, 47*(2), 103–111.

Sharwood-Smith, M. (1981). Consciousness raising and the second language learner. *Applied Linguistics, 2*, 159–168.

Swales, J., & Feak, C. (2018). *Academic writing for graduate students: Essential skills and tasks* (3rd ed.). Ann Arbor: University of Michigan Press.

Weaver, C. (2010). Scaffolding grammar instruction for writers and writing. In T. Locke (Ed.), *Beyond the grammar wars* (pp. 185–205). London: Routledge.

Yang, L., & Cahill, D. (2008). The rhetorical organization of Chinese and American students' expository essays: A contrastive rhetoric study. *International Journal of English Studies, 8*(2), 113–132.

12

Writing for Scholarly Publication

Like writing, getting what you write published is also a challenging and sometimes frustrating process. In academic settings, students, especially those at the doctoral level, are expected to actively participate in research and contribute to publications in scholarly outlets (primarily academic journals). For scholars, especially new faculty members in research-intensive universities, the pressure to publish can be unrelenting. An understanding of what is typically involved in the publication process can help assuage some of the fears and worries you may have about writing for scholarly publication. This chapter describes the publication process, manuscript review criteria, and strategies for increasing success in getting published.

The Publication Process: From Submission to Print

Submission

Manuscripts submitted for publication typically go through a rigorous vetting process, as demonstrated in Figure 12.1. For an article to be considered for journal publication, it needs to be submitted to an appropriate outlet. For most academic journals, a manuscript is submitted through an online portal called editorial manager <editorial manager.com> or manuscript central <http://scholarone.com>. Typically, two versions of the manuscript are uploaded, one including a title page with all author details (full names and details of the corresponding author and all co-authors) and the other without author details. The file without author details is used for blind review, meaning reviewers would not know who wrote the manuscript they are reviewing. In addition to these two main document files, tables and figures, if used, are uploaded as separate files. Sometimes, supplemental materials such as original data or author biographical notes are also uploaded as separate files. It is important to note that submitting a manuscript to more than one journal (or publication outlet) at the same time is considered unethical and potentially illegal.

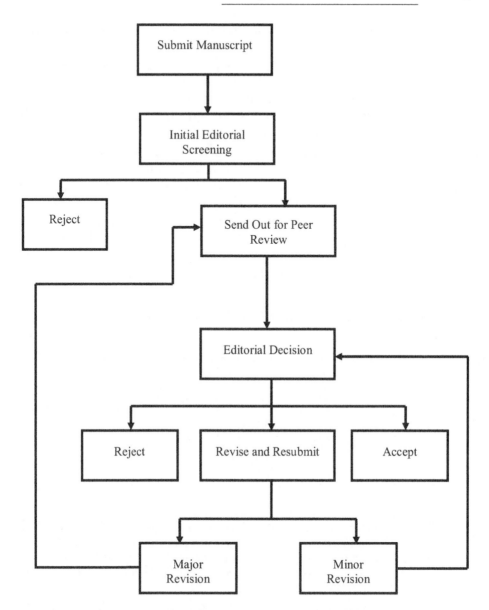

Figure 12.1 Manuscript Review and Publication Process

Review

Once the manuscript is submitted, you will receive an acknowledgment from the editorial staff. At this time, your manuscript will have a tracking number that you can use when corresponding with the editorial office. You will be able to track the status of your manuscript through the submission portal. Each manuscript submitted is assigned a tracking editor, who oversees the review process of your manuscript. The tracking editor can be the editor him/herself (in the case of sole editorship) or a member of the editorial team (in the case of co-editorship). The tracking editor or the entire editorial team will conduct an initial screening of the manuscript to determine its suitability for the journal in terms of topic, rigor, depth, length, author identity, format, tone, and writing fluency. (Sometimes, the online submission system automatically prevents you from submitting a manuscript that does not conform to specific submission guidelines.) Manuscripts that substantially exceed the length limit, are not formatted according to journal specifications, do not mask author identity, deal with topics outside the ambit of the journal, use grossly simplistic or clearly inappropriate methodology, lack basic writing fluency, are clearly not of publication quality, or are written in a tone inappropriate for the primary audience of the journal are returned for revision without further review. A letter informing you of the results of initial screening can read like Text 12-1 or Text 12-2 below.

Text 12-1

Dear Author(s),

It is a pleasure to inform you that your manuscript titled "xxx" (manuscript # xxx) submitted to [journal name] has passed initial screening and is now awaiting reviewer invitation.

Your sincerely,

Editor

Text 12-2

Dear Author(s):

We have completed our review of your manuscript "[manuscript title]". Prior to sending a manuscript out for peer review, we review it internally to determine fit for [journal name] and as to whether any significant challenges are noted that would make peer review inefficient. Unfortunately, based on our own review, we cannot accept your manuscript for publication in [journal name].

Your article addresses an important and timely issue. The challenge is that [xxx]. We suggest that you review the most recent issues of [journal name], which is free access online, because reading those articles can help you get a sense of the tone, detail, length, topic, and depth required for [journal name] articles.

We want to thank you for considering [journal name] as an outlet for your manuscript. If you have questions about this letter or the review process or if there are other ways in which we can be of service, please feel free to contact us.

Sincerely,

Editor

Manuscripts that pass initial screening are then sent out to two or more experts for review. In most cases, experts are selected based on the match between their expertise and the topic of your manuscript. Sometimes, however, experts whose expertise are not strictly aligned with the topic of your manuscript are also called upon to serve as reviewers. These experts are selected from the journal's reviewer pool; they can also be newly invited to serve as guest, or occasional, reviewers for your manuscript. Some journals require you to provide the names and contact information of two to three qualified reviewers for your manuscript, but may not use them. Experts who have a conflict of interest or are closely connected with you or your co-author(s) are generally excluded from reviewing your manuscript. Reviewers are typically given 4–12 weeks to review your manuscript.

Editorial Decisions

Once the reviews are returned, the tracking editor summarizes the reviews, highlighting positive and negative comments and key recommendations. The editorial team then weighs the reviews together and decides on the fate of the manuscript. Sometimes, editorial decisions are easy to render because there is a high degree of agreement among the reviewers. Other times, the reviewers can be quite different in their opinions about the significance and quality of the manuscript and thus in their recommendations regarding the disposition of the manuscript. Reviewers can also be quite different in terms of the amount and quality of feedback they provide, which makes the rendering of an editorial decision more challenging. In some of these cases, the editors may choose to send the manuscript out to one or more additional reviewer(s) for feedback before a final decision is rendered. In fact, it is not uncommon for an editorial decision to be rendered based on four or five reviews.

Four kinds of editorial decisions can be made. One is outright Rejection, meaning that the manuscript is rejected and the author is not invited to revise it for resubmission to the same journal. Manuscripts receiving this type of decision are often so seriously flawed conceptually or methodologically that it is practically impossible to revise them to meet the expectations of the journal. It could also be that the manuscript is a rehash of what is already widely understood or does not make new contributions in any way. A sample rejection letter reads:

Text 12-3

Dear Author(s),

The review process of your manuscript (# xx-xx-xxxx), titled "xxx", is now complete. Your manuscript has been assessed by two reviewers, whose comments are included below. Based on the reviews and our own close reading of the manuscript, we regret to inform that we are unable to accept the manuscript for publication in [journal name]. Therefore, an editorial decision of Reject has been rendered.

As you will see from the two reviewers, [...].

We know that letters of this kind are always disappointing. We wish you the best and trust that this experience will not discourage you from future submissions to the journal. Thank you again for your interest in [journal name].

Sincerely,

Co-Editors

The second, and perhaps the most common, decision is to reject but invite resubmission. This usually involves Major Revision, meaning that the editorial team sees merit and promise in the manuscript but requires the author to significantly revise the manuscript. Such revision can involve one or more of the following tasks: (a) adding or reworking the theoretical framework section; (b) expanding or refocusing the literature review; (c) delineating or refining research questions; (d) addressing substantive methodological issues such as reanalyzing data, using alternative analysis techniques, and providing additional details about sampling, data collection, and data analysis; (e) revamping the discussion section (e.g., interpreting findings in light of existing research literature and the study's context, discussing the study's limitations or implications); (f) reconceptualizing or beefing up the logic and substance of argument; (g) restructuring the manuscript in a major way; (h) significantly reducing manuscript length; and (i) improving language fluency. Most editors will summarize and distill reviewers' comments to highlight key issues to be addressed in the revision, but some editors simply tell authors to read the reviews and decide how to revise on their own. An editor that I know of recently composed, based on five reviews, a six-page (single space) de facto rejection letter detailing extensive issues to be addressed if the author decides to revise his/her manuscript for resubmission. Text 12-4 is a sample letter requesting major revisions.

Text 12-4

Dear Author(s),

I have now received and read the two external reviews of your submission, "[manuscript title]". One reviewer commented on the interesting nature of the study and the other on its compelling contribution to clarifying insights about [xxx]. However, overall, reviewers provide substantive arguments regarding the review of literature and discussion, rationale for the study, analytical processes undergirding the findings, data sources, and clarity, all of which point to the need for a major revision of this work.

I have summarized major areas for revision directly below, all of which should help you as you revise your paper. I encourage you to attend to all reviewers' comments and explain how you addressed them in a detailed revision letter.

Areas for Major Revision:
- Review of the literature and discussion: [xxx]
- Rationale for the study: [xxx]
- Analytical processes: [xxx]
- Data sources: [xxx]
- Clarity: [xxx]

I look forward to receiving your revised manuscript.

Kind regards,

Associate Editor

The third editorial decision is Conditional Accept. Manuscripts receiving this type of decision are substantively and stylistically ready, requiring only minor edits such as tweaking a few awkwardly worded sentences, reconfiguring tables or figures, moving a few small things around, trimming a few sentences here and there to reduce length, cleaning up references and citations, addressing formatting issues, beefing up a certain section, clarifying or elaborating on certain points, or adding/deleting certain details in various sections of the manuscript. The manuscript is generally accepted once these minor edits are approved by the editorial team. A sample letter requesting minor revision follows.

Text 12-5

Dear Author(s),

Manuscript # xxx entitled "xxx", which you submitted to [journal name], has been reviewed. The comments of the reviewers are included at the bottom of this letter.

Given the range of reviewers' comments and our own reading of your manuscript, our editorial decision is MINOR REVISION. Therefore, I invite you to respond to the reviewers' comments and revise your manuscript. Your revised manuscript is due within the next 30 days. Please note, the revision due date expires at the beginning of the stated day, not the end of the day.

When you revise, please pay particular attention to the following: [xxx]

You will be unable to make your revisions on the originally submitted version of the manuscript. Instead, revise your manuscript using a word processing program and save it on your computer. Please also highlight the changes to your manuscript within the document by using the track changes mode in MS Word or by using colored text.

Once the revised manuscript is prepared, you can upload it and submit it through your Author Center.

When submitting your revised manuscript, you will be able to respond to the comments made by the reviewers in the space provided. You can use this space to document any changes you make to the original manuscript. In order to expedite the processing of the revised manuscript, please be as specific as possible in your response to the reviewers.

Because we are trying to facilitate timely publication of manuscripts sub-mitted to [journal name], your revised manuscript should be uploaded as soon as possible. If it is not possible for you to submit your revision in a reasonable amount of time, we may have to consider your paper as a new submission.

Once again, thank you for submitting your manuscript to [journal name]. and I look forward to receiving your revision.

Sincerely,

Guest Editor

The fourth type of decision is "Accept", which involves few or no edits. The edits, if any, are usually very minor, involving formatting issues or small gram-matical errors, but not content. This type of decision rarely occurs, accounting for no more than 1% of all manuscript submissions.

Revision and Resubmission

You normally will have 4–12 weeks to respond to the reviews and the editorial decision, but can contact the editor to request an extension if additional time is needed. You may receive reminders about the revision deadline. Along with the revised manuscript, you are also required to submit a letter detailing the revisions you have made to the manuscript, how they address the reviewers' comments and the editor's suggestions, and where they can be found in the manuscript (see Text 12-6 for a sample response letter). You do not have to make all the changes requested by the reviewers or the editor, but you have to provide rationale for your action or inaction regarding a specific comment or recommendation. Should you have questions about specific comments by the reviewers or editors, you may communicate with the tracking editor, but such communication should be kept to a minimum. On the other hand, if you de-cide not to revise or want to send the manuscript somewhere else, you should inform the editor of your decision, although many authors do not. According to some estimates (e.g., *Henson, 2007*), 60–70% of the revised manuscripts are eventually published.

Text 12-6

Dear Editor:

Thank you so much for the very thoughtful and constructive feedback to our manuscript titled "xxx" (MS# xxxx). We have revised our paper based on the reviewers' comments and your suggestions. Major points of revision, highlighted in blue in the resubmission, are listed below:

[…]

As a result of these revisions, we believe that the quality of our manuscript is (greatly) enhanced. We thank you and the reviewers again for the very helpful comments. Please feel free to contact us if you have questions about our revision.

Respectfully,

Author

Once the revision is received by the editorial team, an acknowledgment of receipt is automatically generated through the submission portal and sent to the corresponding author. Significantly revised manuscripts are sent out for another round of full review. Mildly revised manuscripts are sometimes also sent out for another round of review, but more often the review for this type of manuscripts is conducted in house by the editorial team. The reviewers for this round can be the original reviewers plus one additional (new) reviewer. They can also be all new reviewers, depending on how many of the original reviewers are willing to review the revision. If the feedback from the second round of review justifies another round of major revision, a third round of review is conducted. And the cycle continues until the editor decides to terminate the review process because it has not resulted in significant improvement in manuscript quality. In some cases, authors simply give up by refusing to make further revisions because they deem the process too demanding or that further revision compromises the integrity or intent of the original work. In this case, the manuscript is withdrawn and pulled off the review process.

In the case your manuscript is withdrawn from further consideration, you can rethink the audience or outlet for your manuscript. For example, instead of targeting a research-based journal, you can rework the manuscript for a practice-based journal. You can also repurpose your manuscript by lifting the meat of the manuscript for use in another paper or breaking the manuscript into two or more smaller pieces, each addressing a narrower or less ambitious topic for submission to separate outlets. Sometimes, you may decide to leave your manuscript alone for a while and revisit the work later to see if it can be salvaged for some other purpose.

Print

Once the editorial team determines that the revision (after however many rounds of review) satisfactorily addresses the issues raised by the reviewers and editors, the decision of Accept is rendered. This means the manuscript enters the final phase of the editorial process. It is sent to the production team, which is separate from the editorial team and affiliated with the publisher. The production team will require you to sign a copyrights agreement, that is, consent for publication. After the signed consent form is received, the publisher then sends you a typeset draft for proofreading. At this stage, only minor changes (typically word-level edits) are allowed. More substantial changes are discouraged and may require editors' approval and even incur a change fee.

Once the galley proof is checked and submitted, your manuscript moves onto the next phase, which is print. Often, the article is published online first, and it is assigned a digital object identifier, or doi, which is a string of letters and symbols that can be used to permanently identify an article, document and link it on the web, and help the reader easily locate it from citation. Once a sufficient number of articles have been accepted, a journal issue is filled and ready for print (or to become an online volume). It can take anywhere from three months to a year for an issue to be filled.

Manuscript Review Criteria

Manuscripts are reviewed along a number of dimensions. Editors typically ask reviewers to consider the following four dimensions when evaluating a manuscript: significance to the field, methodological soundness, rigor of interpretation and argument, and quality of writing.

Significance to the Field

Reviewers address this domain by assessing whether the study reported in the manuscript is worth doing, whether it makes a new/significant contribution to the field, and whether it is relevant to the mission of the journal or its primary readership. They look to see if you clearly identify a problem and purpose, provide a context and build a logical case for the problem, and delineate the research questions associated with the problem. They determine whether (a) the conceptual framework guiding the study is explicit and justified; (b) the literature review is comprehensive, focused, up-to-date, and critical; (c) the approach to addressing the problem is appropriate, original, or innovative, and (d) the findings or conclusions contribute new insights, lead to reconceptualization of existing theory, raise new questions in relation to the problem addressed, or hold important implications for policy and/or practice.

Methodological Soundness

Reviewers address this domain by evaluating whether your study's methodology or research paradigm is clearly described and consistent with the theoretical orientation that informs the investigation. For a quantitative study, reviewers scrutinize the sampling and selection of participants, setting, materials, and intervention. They look to see if (a) potentially confounding variables or biases are adequately addressed, (b) test instruments are reliable and have been validated, (c) data quality control is rigorous, (d) the intervention is described in sufficient detail to allow for replication, and (e) statistical tests are appropriate.

For a qualitative study, reviewers similarly ask if data collection and analysis procedures are appropriate to the research questions and described in sufficient detail. In addition, they check to see if the study incorporates validation strategies (e.g., triangulation, multivocality, member checking) and researcher positionality (e.g., subjective values, biases, and inclinations) to ensure trustworthiness. They also consider if the author is transparent about methodological challenges and attends to ethics in qualitative research, such as doing no harm, avoiding deception, negotiating informed consent, ensuring privacy and confidentiality, showing care and respect, warding off victim blaming and unjust appropriation of findings, and safeguarding participants' interests (Tracy, 2010).

Rigor of Interpretation and Argumentation

Reviewers address this domain by evaluating whether (a) the claims made in the manuscript are insightful and proportionate to the evidence provided; (b) the amount of data presented is relevant, sufficient, thickly detailed, balanced, accurate, and supportive of the inferences made or the themes identified; (c) the findings are interpreted in light of both the study's context and the existing research literature; (d) the conclusions address the problem and research questions and are supported by the data; and (e) the limitations and implications of the study are adequately discussed.

Quality of Writing

Reviewers address this domain by examining the extent to which your writing is well-organized, clear, coherent, focused, fluent, engaging, and easily accessible. They determine if (a) key concepts are clearly identified and described, (b) tables and figures are aligned with the text, (c) results are aligned with the methods and research questions, (d) quotes, references, and visuals are smoothly and strategically integrated into the text, (e) transitions among sentences, among paragraphs, and among sections are smooth and transparent to the reader, (f) sentences are fluent and clear, (g) word choices are accurate and precise, and (h) the style of writing is engaging and appropriate.

These dimensions are weighted differently depending on the types of manuscripts submitted. Research-based manuscripts, which can range from 6000 to 12,000 words in length, are evaluated more heavily on conceptual originality and methodological rigor. For practice-based manuscripts or argumentative essays, which are typically 2500–5000 words long, the logic of argument, quality of evidence, and implications for policy/practice tend to be scrutinized more closely. Regardless of the manuscript type, each published manuscript is expected to make an original, valid, and significant contribution to an area of inquiry.

Tips for Getting Published

Given the ubiquitous pressure to publish in academic contexts, it is natural that you want to know what you can do to enhance your chances of getting published. Many tips have been offered on this topic (see, for example, Jalongo & Saracho, 2016; Wepner & Gambrell, 2010). In the rest of this chapter, I share some tips that resonate with me the most. These are the tips I have found particularly helpful to my own growth as a writer and scholar.

Write about Something That You Really Care and Know About

Passion drives motivation and fuels confidence. The more you care about a topic, the more motivated you are to delve into it and to keep on writing about it. The more passionate you are about the topic, the more likely you are to do it in depth and become an expert on it. You may want to refrain from picking up fads or other topics that you are not genuinely interested in because you are likely to be superficial about it and not enjoy the experience of researching and writing about it. Successful scholars typically build a research agenda around the topic(s) or issue(s) that they truly care about; they make plans and monitor their own professional growth in pursuing the research agenda. With a clear idea of what honestly interests you, you will be better able to build your career around something that is especially meaningful to you, maintain a focus for your work, find ways to increase efficiency and productivity, identify emerging interests and areas for further professional development, discover interesting connections among projects, and reflect on your growth as writer and scholar (Jalongo & Saracho, 2016).

So, it is important that you take time to explore your passion and find what speaks to your heart and what it is that matters to you the most. This does not mean, however, that you should not worry about topics that do not interest you. On the contrary, it is always a good idea to have some sense of what is out there, as well as what is hot and what is not hot in your field. This breadth of knowledge will help you develop depth in, and make connections with, the areas that you care about the most. In short, having the breadth and depth of knowledge about the topic that genuinely interests you enables you to write more deeply and convincingly. The truth is that you will find it exceptionally challenging to write intelligently and critically about things that you do not know well or truly care.

Know the Outlet You Are Targeting

To ensure the match between your submission and the journal you are targeting, it is imperative that you take time to familiarize yourself with the scope and mission of the journal, the scholarly interests of its editorial review board members, and its primary readership. Some journals are more international in scope and regularly publish contributions from around the world. Other journals are more committed to local concerns and may be reluctant to publish contributions from abroad unless explicit connections to the local contexts are made. Some journals have readership consisting primarily of researchers and scholars, whereas others have practitioners as their primary readers. Many journals claim to embrace a plurality of theoretical orientations, methodologies, and epistemologies, but may not necessarily be practising what they proclaim, due in part to editorial preferences and/or the limited pool of reviewers. This is why it is important that you take some time to peruse articles published under the reign of the current editor or recent issues of the journal to gain a sense of the types of articles that get published in the journal as well as the topic addressed and the approach taken in these articles. It is a good idea to send a query to the editor if you are concerned about the fit of your manuscript for the journal. Your query can include a brief summary of what your article is about (e.g., abstract). Most journal editors or their editorial staff are quite responsive to this kind of queries. This preparatory work may seem trivial but can save you precious time in the often lengthy review process.

When searching for an outlet for your work, you will want to guard against predatory journals and publishers that trick scholars, especially those from developing countries, into publishing with them. Predatory publishing is "an explosive academic publishing business model that involves charging publication fees to authors without checking articles for quality and legitimacy and without providing the other editorial and publishing services that legitimate academic journals provide" (Wikipedia). From time to time, you may receive a flattering, and sometimes poorly worded, email letter, such as the ones presented in Text 12-7 and Text 12-8, that invites you to submit a manuscript (based on a conference presentation you did or an article you previously published) to a journal and to also serve as an editorial board member or reviewer for the journal. Other such letters are more succinct, issuing invitations worded as follows: *We are in shortfall of a single article for successful release of Volume xx, Issue xx. Is it possible for you to support us with your opinion or mini review or any article for this issue by xxx [date]?* You can check out <beallslist.net> for a sample list of potential predatory journals and publishers. These journals are sometimes titled very broadly or ambitiously in order to attract authors from a wide range of disciplines and appear willing to publish anything regardless of quality. They are generally not well regarded or valued by scholars in academic communities, and it is probably wise not to waste your time, energy and resources in trying to publish your work in these outlets of questionable quality.

Text 12-7

Dear Professor,

We have learnt your paper "xxx" on Literacy Research Association (2019), and we are interested in it. Therefore, we invite you to submit this full paper if it is not published or other unpublished papers in psychology area to xxx [journal name]. The journal is a peer-reviewed, multidisciplinary periodical published by xxx [publisher name] since July, 2011. It welcomes the submission of original manuscripts reporting innovations or investigations in the Psychology area. Successful general submission manuscripts may report interdisciplinary efforts or be of a sufficiently broad nature to be of interest to those centered in related disciplines. Manuscripts reporting innovations or collaborations leading to enhancements in Psychology are of particular interest to the journal.

If you have the idea of making our journal as a vehicle for your research, you can submit the electronic version of your unpublished and full paper (in English and in WORD format) as attachment to this email address when you have finished it. We appreciate your support.

We also seek researchers who have deep research in and outstanding contributions to Psychology area to be our reviewers/editors. Good review board has insightful understanding in Psychology field, and can provide professional suggestions to authors. Anyone who is interested in our journals can send us CV. We are looking forward to your contribution!

Sincerely yours,

Editorial Office

xxx [journal name]

Text 12-8

Dear xxx,

The journal [xxx] (ISBN xxxx-xxxx) is currently running a Special Issue entitled "[xxx]". Dr. [xxx], Prof. Dr. [xxx] and Dr. [xxx] are serving as Guest Editors for this issue. We think you could make an excellent contribution based on your expertise and your following paper: xxx [title of paper]

The aim of this Special Issue is to gather empirical research from xxx [journal name], as well as new theoretical and methodological approaches and literature reviews that address emerging issues related to these technological, societal and environmental changes. For further reading, please follow the link to the Special Issue website at [xxx].

The submission deadline is 30 April 2021. You may send your manuscript now or up until the deadline. Submitted papers should not be under consideration for publication elsewhere. We also encourage authors to send a short abstract or tentative title to the Editorial office in advance [email).

[journal name] is fully open access. Open access (unlimited and free access by readers) increases publicity and promotes more frequent citations, as indicated by several studies. Open access is supported by the authors and their institutes. An Article Processing Charge (APC) of CHF 1000 currently applies to all accepted papers.

For further details on the submission process, please see the instructions for authors at the journal website [xxx].

We look forward to hearing from you.

Kind regards,

Assistant Editor

Find People of Like Interest to Collaborate With

Collaboration increases the joy of research and writing. You get to share the pleasures and agonies of writing and publishing with your collaborators. As a result, you are less likely to feel lonely or get frustrated with yourself when things did not go as well as you had hoped for. The knowledge, skills, experience, and habits of mind that your collaborators bring to the task can complement the skillset that you possess. Not only can collaboration help enhance the quality of the work you are doing, it can also improve your productivity.

Scholars sometimes build a collaborative "family tree" that consists of mentors, classmates, and other peers with like interests. One mathematician I studied (Fang & Chapman, 2020) confided that his alma mater provided him with opportunities for collaboration, as he worked with former classmates and others who were trained through an institutional legacy of former advisors. He described his collaboration with his mentor as one such relationship that stemmed from his alma mater, noting:

> For me, the reason that I collaborate with the professor in Taiwan is because he is very famous in our field...and then he's also from the same school that I came from. Which means his advisor is the advisor of my advisor. So they are from the same person. They were working in fields very close to each other. Then there is another collaborator in Canada who is also from the same school and his advisor is also the advisor of my advisor. The same family tree.

In collaboration, it is important to show respect for and be considerate to your collaborators. Sometimes collaboration works out perfectly. Other times, it ends up miserably due to different work habits, incompatible personalities, lack of deep commitment or substantive contribution, or conflicting interests. So, you will want to take time to observe people around you and find the right kind of collaborators who can help make the collaborative experience enjoyable and the collaborative relationship productive and enduring.

Be Patient and Persistent

As noted earlier, writing can be a long, solitary, and agonizing process from idea generation to polishing the finished product. Similarly, getting published from submission to print can also be a long and sometimes frustrating process, with multiple rounds of review and each round taking two to six or more months. Thus, it is important that you prepare thoroughly and work patiently when writing for publication. The vast majority of manuscripts do not get accepted in one try. Often, major to minor revisions are required. Sometimes, a manuscript that is rejected after several rounds of review may also go through several rounds of review with another journal(s). All of these take time and can take a toll on your patience and confidence.

While waiting for editorial decisions can be uneasy at times, you should not nag the editor. Instead, you can track the status of your manuscript online through the submission portal. If you have not heard from the editor in three months, you can send a query to the editorial staff requesting an update on the status of your submission. Sometimes, reviewers procrastinate. Other times, the editor has a hard time finding qualified or willing reviewers. Your query will remind the editor to get on top of your submission and keep the review process moving. You will want to be sure to adhere to the journal submission guidelines (e.g., length, format, masking author identity) so as to reduce unnecessary delays in manuscript processing.

It is a good idea to make a list of three to five possible journal outlets—both domestic and international—for your work. If your submission gets rejected by one journal, you can submit it to another option on your list. If the rejection outlet is not appropriate, you can send it to a potentially more suitable one. If, for example, your manuscript is rejected for a lack of significance, you can send it to a lower tier journal or revise it to foreground the significance and contribution of your work. If your manuscript is rejected for a lack of methodological rigor, you can revise it based on the recommendations from the reviewers/editor or repurpose it for a more practice-based outlet, where requirement for methodological rigor tends to be less stringent. In short, the wait time and revision time can be significant in the review process. It can truly test your patience and resilience.

Simulate Dialogues with Potential Reviewers

In writing for publications, it is helpful to have imagined dialogues with potential reviewers. This ensures that you acknowledge and respond to opposing views or alternative perspectives. As an author, you need to have a keen awareness of the values and concerns of members of other discourse communities. All reviewers come with their own perspectives and biases based on their prior experiences and training, and each has things that they feel strongly about. As a writer, you have to anticipate, as well as address, questions and issues that may be raised by people with different theoretical, methodological, or practical orientations.

For example, if you are trained as a linguist, you may have a tendency to speak in linguistics jargons. When writing for publications outside your field (e.g., education), you will need to recontextualize your linguistics discourse for other audience. You will need to be sure to define terms that linguists often take for granted and be careful to avoid terms that may evoke overreaction from reviewers. For instance, some scholars in education detest using terms such as *at risk*, *struggling*, or *poor* to describe learners who are not reading on grade level. So, instead of saying *poor readers*, you can refer to these students as *striving readers* or *learners who are not reading on grade level*.

Furthermore, you have to predict what reviewers are likely to say and then incorporate statements that acknowledge your sensitivity to their concerns.

For example, when writing a paper on the language demands of science reading, you need to know that reviewers who are into the reader response theory will likely question your focus on language/text and raise the valid point that meaning does not reside solely in the text but in the transaction between the reader and the text. You also need to know that reviewers who are into multimodal meaning making or new literacies will question your lack of attention to other communication systems (e.g., pictures, graphs, diagrams) that are also important in the design of meaning in today's science texts. Additionally, you need to know that reviewers who are into inquiry learning will challenge your privileging of text over hands-on experience in science learning. Although all of these points are not central to the thesis of your paper, you still have to acknowledge and address them briefly (one to two sentences to one to two paragraphs); otherwise, some reviewers might go off a tangent in their critique. By including statements that acknowledge your awareness of these potential concerns and your readiness to address them, you are showing reviewers that you are cognizant of the broader issues associated with science literacy and that you can justifiably focus on one aspect of the science learning/teaching enterprise for the purpose of the particular paper you are writing.

Use Feedback to Improve Writing

It is always a good idea to seek out your peers or other experts for feedback on your writing. As you begin the process of crafting a draft, you can talk with friends, peers, or mentors about your ideas. Sometimes, even casual conversations yield insights that can be valuable. You can also present your ideas or early drafts of your writing at seminars or conferences, where you are likely to receive feedback from an interested audience who is knowledgeable about the topic/issue you are exploring. Some feedbacks will be more relevant and useful than others at different points of your revision process. You will need to carefully consider the feedback in light of your focus and needs. A good attitude to have is to embrace the feedback that you find relevant but also be appreciative of the ones that may seem more tangential at a particular point of your writing/revising.

Feedback from journal reviewers is expected to be substantive and relevant, but that may not always be the case, as some reviewers are more knowledgeable, responsible, and/or considerate than others. For reviews that you find relevant and to the point, take time to address the issues raised in these reviews. Other reviews may be written in a less considerate or even demeaning manner. You do not need to take these negative comments personally, as that can deal a serious blow to your confidence and increase your frustration. Instead, you will want to use these criticisms to improve your writing, as they may also have a point. Because you may understandably be upset or irritated when you first receive negative or condescending reviews, it is a good idea to leave these reviews aside for a few days before getting back to respond to them. The respite allows time for your anger to cool down so that you can read the reviews more carefully and understand them more thoroughly. It will also ensure that you address reviewers' comments directly but also graciously and professionally without being defensive.

Conclusion

Writing for publication can be a mysterious process that intimidates novice writers and academic neophytes. Developing and honing academic writing skills is key to having a successful publication record. Additional knowledge, skills, and dispositions are needed to increase your chances of getting published. These include familiarity with the publication outlet, the publication process, and the manuscript evaluation criteria; capacity to collaborate with others of like interest and complementary expertise; willingness to seek and embrace feedback of all kinds; and a positive, unyielding attitude. The road toward publication may seem long and rough, but you will find that the journey becomes less bumpy the more you have traveled on it.

Reflection/Application Activities

1 Have you ever submitted your writing to an academic publication (or conference)? If so, share your experience with your peers. Is it a positive and/or negative experience? In what way?

2 What concerns you the most in your decision to submit or not to submit your writing for publication in an academic journal? Do you think what is discussed in this chapter helps you navigate the publication process?

3 Read and analyze sample reviews of a journal manuscript (or a conference proposal) to identify what the reviewers perceived to be the strengths and weaknesses of the manuscript. Are the critiques fair, thoughtful, substantive, considerate, and helpful? What agreements or disagreements do you see among the reviewers? What editorial decision would you have rendered if you were the editor? Discuss how the manuscript can be improved based on the reviewers' feedback.

4 Interview someone you know who has a successful track record in academic publishing (e.g., your advisor), asking him/her about tips for increasing success in scholarly publication. Be prepared to share what you learn with your peers in class.

5   Use the self-assessment instrument in Appendix B to evaluate a piece of your past or current writing. Identify your strengths and needs in academic writing based on the evaluation. How would you use what you have learned from this book to improve your academic writing and your chances of getting published?

References

Fang, Z., & Chapman, S. (2020). Disciplinary literacy in mathematics: One mathematician's reading practices. *Journal of Mathematical Behavior.* doi:10.1016/j.jmathb.2020.100799

Henson, K. T. (2007). Writing for publication: Steps to excellence. *Phi Delta Kappa,* 88, 781–786.

Jalongo, R., & Saracho, O. (2016). *Writing for publication: Transitions and tools that support scholars' success.* New York: Springer.

Tracy, S. J. (2010). Qualitative quality: Eight "big-tent" criteria for excellent qualitative research. *Qualitative Inquiry, 16*(10), 837–851.

Wepner, S., & Gambrell, L. (2010). *Beating the odds: Getting published in the field of literacy.* Newark, DE: International Reading Association.

Appendix A
Survey of Academic Writing Needs

Rate your understanding or ability related to each of the following items on a scale from 1 (not at all) to 4 (great).

	Not at All (1)	A Little (2)	Average (3)	Great (4)
Understand why academic writing is needed or important	1	2	3	4
Understand academic writing as a social and cultural practice	1	2	3	4
Understand key elements of academic writing	1	2	3	4
Understand how academic language is different from everyday language	1	2	3	4
Write a reading response	1	2	3	4
Write a book review	1	2	3	4
Write a literature review	1	2	3	4
Write an argumentative essay	1	2	3	4
Write an empirical research paper	1	2	3	4
Write a grant proposal	1	2	3	4
Make connections with others in the field	1	2	3	4
Paraphrase, summarize, synthesize, and evaluate sources	1	2	3	4

Quote, reference, and integrate sources	1	2	3	4
Integrate visuals with prose in text	1	2	3	4
Make claims or generalizations that are proportionate to available evidence or reasonable assumptions	1	2	3	4
Construct a clear, focused text that is also tightly knit	1	2	3	4
Describe a thing or a process clearly	1	2	3	4
Write a brief or an extended definition of a concept	1	2	3	4
Explain a phenomenon clearly	1	2	3	4
Classify and categorize things appropriately	1	2	3	4
Compare and contrast things clearly	1	2	3	4
Agree or disagree with others in a substantive but considerate way	1	2	3	4
Acknowledge and respond to opposing or alternative views in a way that bolsters your argument	1	2	3	4
Make recommendations in a measured and non-hortatory style	1	2	3	4
Express the same meaning in varied and interesting ways	1	2	3	4
Develop a logical, coherent argument	1	2	3	4
Write grammatically and fluently	1	2	3	4
Use punctuations appropriately	1	2	3	4
Read widely and deeply	1	2	3	4

Know where to find information sources in your field	1	2	3	4
Think analytically and critically about what you are reading	1	2	3	4
Have a repertoire of strategies for effectively comprehending and critically appraising text	1	2	3	4
Plan, organize, and revise writing	1	2	3	4
Form productive writing habits that work for you	1	2	3	4
Understand the writing process	1	2	3	4
Have patience and persistence in writing	1	2	3	4
Have linguistic awareness and sensitivity	1	2	3	4
Have passion for your field of study	1	2	3	4
Understand discursive norms and conventions in your discipline	1	2	3	4
Seek out opportunities for collaboration in writing	1	2	3	4
Seek advice and embrace feedback for writing	1	2	3	4
Know markers of manuscript quality	1	2	3	4
Understand journal publication process	1	2	3	4
Know strategies and tips for increasing success in academic publishing	1	2	3	4

Appendix B
Checklist for Self-Assessment of Academic Writing[1]

1   Do you choose the right genre given the task at hand?
2   Do you include the common rhetorical moves typical of that genre? Do you employ linguistic resources that are functional and effective for instantiating these moves?
3   Is the content you present complete, accurate, and logically sequenced?
4   Is the scholarly literature reviewed sufficiently broad, deep, and focused? Are sources critically appraised?
5   Is each main point or argument well supported by details, examples, or evidence? Is the strength of your claim proportionate to the evidence provided or reasonable assumptions?
6   Are the transitions smooth between paragraphs and between sections?
7   Are sentences within each paragraph logically connected?
8   Do you mix academic and colloquial styles appropriately?
9   Do you use accurate and precise language?
10 Do you use cautious and non-discriminatory language?
11 Do you represent what others say accurately and adequately?
12 Do you summarize others' work in a way that connects with your argument? Is the length of your summary proportionate to the relevance/importance of the work being summarized?
13 Do you acknowledge and respond to alternative or opposing viewpoints? If so, do you do it in a way that is considerate and at the same time supports your argument?
14 Is there a clear distinction between your ideas/voice and those of others?
15 Do you repeat your points in interestingly different ways?
16 Do you use quotes? If so, do you frame each quote successfully and integrate it smoothly into the text?
17 Do you avoid over-quoting or plagiarizing?
18 Do you acknowledge all the sources used?
19 Do you use visuals? If so, are they clear and well-integrated with the prose in the text?
20 Is your writing clear and accessible to your target audience?
21 Do you foreground the significance and contribution of your writing?
22 Do you avoid use of awkward or obscure words, phrases, or sentences?

23 Do you acknowledge those who have contributed to your research and writing in some meaningful way?
24 Do you adhere to conventions in grammar, punctuation, and spelling?
25 Do you follow the assignment guidelines (e.g., length, style, tone, format, appearance, depth, submission deadline)?

Comments:

Note

1 Appendix B can be downloaded, printed, and copied for personal use. You can access these downloads by visiting the book product page on our website: http://www.routledge.com/9780367653545. Then click on the tab that says "Support Materials" and select the files. They will begin downloading to your computer.

Index